Telling the Truth to Your Adopted or Foster Child

Making Sense of the Past

Betsy Keefer and Jayne E. Schooler
Illustrations by Jack G. and Kristi Anne Kammer

BERGIN & GARVEY
Westport, Connecticut • London

Library of Congress Cataloging-in-Publication Data

Keefer, Betsy, 1949–
    Telling the truth to your adopted or foster child : making sense of the past / Betsy
Keefer and Jayne E. Schooler ; illustrated by Jack G. and Kristi Anne Kammer.
        p.   cm.
    ISBN 0–89789–691–2 (alk. paper)
    1. Adoption—United States—Psychological aspects.   2. Adopted children—United
States—Psychology.   3. Foster children—United States—Psychology.   4.
Secrecy—Psychological aspects.   5. Communication in the family—United States.   6.
Disclosure of information—United States.   I. Schooler, Jayne E.   II. Title.
HV875.55.K45   2000
155.44'5—dc21   99–056451

British Library Cataloguing in Publication Data is available.

Library of Congress Catalog Card Number: 99–056451
ISBN: 0–89789–691–2

First published in 2000

Bergin & Garvey, 88 Post Road West, Westport, CT 06881
An imprint of Greenwood Publishing Group, Inc.
www.greenwood.com

Printed in the United States of America

The paper used in this book complies with the
Permanent Paper Standard issued by the National
Information Standards Organization (Z39.48–1984).

10 9 8 7 6 5 4 3 2 1

01-01 B+T 17.95

Telling the Truth
to Your
Adopted or Foster Child

Copyright Acknowledgments

The authors and publisher gratefully acknowledge permission for use of the following material:

Excerpts from *Exploring Adoptive Family Life* (1998). Courtesy of H. D. Kirk.

Excerpts from Randolph Severson, *To Bless Him Unaware: The Adopted Child Conceived by Rape* (1992). Courtesy of authors.

Excerpts from Judith Rycus and Ronald Hughes, *Field Guide to Child Welfare* (1998). Courtesy of authors.

Excerpts from Vera Fahlberg, *A Child's Journey Through Placement* (1991). Courtesy of author.

Beth Anthony, "A Place for Mike/Mike's Story." Reprinted with permission from Guideposts Magazine. Copyright © 1999 by Guideposts, Carmel, New York 10512.

Excerpts from PACT, *An Insider's Guide to Transracial Adoption.* Courtesy of PACT.

From Jayne Schooler: To Sharon Kaplan Roszia and Dr. LaVonne Stiffler, role models of excellence and insight to me both professionally and personally.

From Betsy Keefer: To Dr. Judith Rycus and Dr. Ronald Hughes, directors of the Institute for Human Services, who inspire many of us in the Ohio Child Welfare Training Program to continually strive to enhance the lives of children and families.

We hold you all in highest regard.

Contents

Preface

You shall know the truth and the truth shall make you free!

What would it be like if you were Laurie? Laurie, now seventeen, was adopted at age three. One afternoon at a family reunion, she sat dumbfounded as her cousin told her what really happened in her past: her birth father killed her birth mother, and he was in prison. The problem was that everyone in the family knew it except Laurie. Why wasn't she told the truth?

What would it be like if you were Sarah? Sarah, age eleven, often drew pictures of the house that she imagined her birth mother lived in. It was a large house, encircled with beautiful trees and flowers. One day she announced to her adoptive parents, "Someday, I am going to visit my birth mother in her big house." The problem with that picture was that Sarah's mother did live in a "big" house: she lived in a prison. She was convicted of drug possession and assault and would be incarcerated for a very long time. Why wasn't Sarah told the truth?

What would it be like if you were Jason? Jason, age eight, knew he was "given up" for adoption, but he didn't know why. The truth was, his birth mother loved him very much, but as a young teen she was unequipped to raise Jason to adulthood. Jason's adoptive parents knew the whole story, but they assumed that the less said, the better—for everyone. The only problem was that Jason was left believing there was something "wrong" with him, that he had been unlovable from birth. Why didn't his adoptive parents realize the complex feelings their son was battling?

From a historical perspective, adoption has loomed under the cloak of secrecy for decades. Adoption practitioners believed it would be best to create a new world for all those involved in the adoption circumstance. This world would be a place in which adoptees were told to forget the past, as though it did not exist; adoptive parents were told to create a new reality, given freedom to exist in total anonymity; and birth parents were shoved aside and told to erase the present events from their memories.

Many individuals who grew up as adopted or foster children during those decades felt that they were reared under the shadow of secrecy, silence, and shame. It proved difficult for them to build their identity and feel secure when key aspects of their past were unknown, unimaginable, and even frightening.

The adoptive or foster family, through their child, becomes connected to the social problems that resulted in the adoption plan: alcoholism, drug addiction, teenage pregnancy, child abuse and neglect, mental illness, and so on. Although some adoptions occur because the birth parents were simply not emotionally or financially able to care for their child, a much larger majority happen because of traumatic or difficult life circumstances.

Because of that connection to troublesome experiences, adoptive and foster parents have a crucial responsibility to communicate the circumstances of their child's past in a manner that will lead to understanding, resolution, and healing. Many parents feel they lack the knowledge and skill to deal with this unique parenting challenge.

The goal of *Telling the Truth to Your Adopted or Foster Child* is to equip parents with the knowledge and tools they will need for a lifetime as they communicate with their adopted or foster child about the complex, troubling, and often painful aspects of his fragmented past. *Telling the Truth to Your Adopted or Foster Child* is designed to meet the informational and practical needs of the following groups.

1. Adoptive parents of infants, adopted domestically and internationally.
2. Adoptive parents of special needs/older children.
3. Foster parents.
4. Adoption professionals who work with and educate adoptive or foster parents.
5. Mental health professionals who work with adopted or foster children.

6. School teachers and counselors who have adopted or foster children within their population (which is in every school, in every city, in every state in the United States).

Telling the Truth to Your Adopted or Foster Child can be used as a topic resource for foster and/or adoptive parent pre-adoption groups or post-adoption support groups.

Adopted persons who are now adults have taught us important things:

- that secret keeping is damaging and divisive.
- that deception creates family mistrust and shame.
- that hiding the truth destroys family intimacy and security.
- that open, honest, sensitive communication about adoption and the past builds the gateway to healthy individual adjustment and family life.

Acknowledgments

It takes a team to write a book. We were fortunate to receive a great deal of help and support in compiling the information contained in this book.

We would first like to thank our consultant, Traci Mullins, for her continual words of encouragement. We would like to thank our Greenwood editor, Lynn Taylor, for her most competent direction and belief in the importance of this project. We would also like to extend thanks to Corinne K. Matyas for her capable and professional editing through the rough draft stages of this manuscript.

Many individuals paved the way for this work by their leadership in the areas of child welfare and adoption. Authors and experts we wish to thank include Dr. Ronald C. Hughes and Dr. Judith S. Rycus (authors of *Field Guide to Child Welfare*), Sharon Kaplan Roszia (co-author of *The Open Adoption Experience*), Greg Keck (author of *Adopting the Hurt Child*), Vera Fahlberg (author of *A Child's Journey Through Placement*), and Beth Hall and Gail Steinberg (authors of *An Insider's Guide to Transracial Adoption*). Other experts whose work informed this manuscript include Dr. Denise Goodman, Dee Paddock, Susan Cox, Dan Houston, Beth Brindo, Cheryl Reber, Jane Nast, and Susan Peleg, and Dr. Randolph Severson.

We would like to call particular attention to the outstanding work of PACT Press (publisher of *An Insider's Guide to Transracial Adoption*) and the Parenthesis Post Adoption Program in pioneering many of the materials and concepts used in this book.

Several exceptional adoptive families shared their stories with us so that other families might benefit from their wisdom. Norma and Anne

Ginther, the Erickson family, the Taggart family, and Dan and Theresa Balsbaugh were especially helpful in lending their time and years of experience to inform a new generation of adoptive families.

When we needed some aspects of this project illustrated for us, good friends, Jack A. Kammer and his daughter, Kristi, offered their time and talents.

We also wish to thank our colleagues and curriculum writers in the Ohio Child Welfare Training Program. Their assistance greatly enhanced the quality of the information presented in this book.

Finally, we wish to thank our families for their support, encouragement, and perseverance as this project was completed.

CHAPTER ONE

The Power of Secrets on Family Relationships

> To keep a secret from someone is to block information or evidence from reaching that person and to do so intentionally. It is a purposeful act. To keep a secret is to make a value judgement, for whatever reason, that it is not that person's right to possess the secret. To keep a secret requires a complicated maze of family communication manipulated by concealment, disguises, camouflage, whispers, silence, or lies.[1]

Laurie, a tall, beautiful adolescent with a gregarious personality, dark curly hair, and a winsome smile, always celebrated her birthday at the family reunion. This year, now her fifteenth birthday, would be no different. The entire clan was there. However, right after the usual rite of birthday songs and presents, a casual conversation with a cousin forever changed Laurie's perception of who she was and how she came to be with her family.

Laurie had always known she was adopted. She knew the story inside and out. When she was barely two years old, Laurie came to her family as a foster child. She had been told that her mother died of natural causes and that her distraught father could not care for her, left her with a friend, and took off. They didn't even know his name.

That afternoon after the celebration had quieted down, she and her cousin went to the pool. Laurie sat dumbfounded as her cousin told her what her mother had just told her—the truth about Laurie's birth family. Her mother had not died of natural causes. Her father hadn't just disappeared. What really happened in her past? Both her parents had abused drugs and alcohol. Her mother died of a drug overdose. Her father was still alive, but imprisoned for a long time due to a murder conviction. They knew who he was and where he was. The problem was that everyone in the family knew it, everyone except Laurie.

After Laurie and her family returned home from the reunion, Laurie began to change. She distanced herself from her parents. She challenged their every word. Her parents called it "the rebellious stage." Laurie had always had a lot of friends, and her school performance had been excellent. Both began to deteriorate. She started cutting classes and running with the wrong crowd. When she was at home she was increasingly moody and sullen. Her angry outbursts frustrated her parents. Were her parents the problem? Was school the problem? Were her friends the problem? No, the damage was done by the keeping of a powerful secret. Why wasn't she told the truth?

Family secrets . . . haunting words that evoke unsettling memories, disturbing thoughts and uncomfortable feelings. A family secret . . . something that hides in almost every family cedar chest . . . information that is banished to a darkened attic, buried under dust and cobwebs, hoping to remain forever under lock and key. What types of things do family members keep from one another? Why do families keep secrets? What impact does secrecy have on family relationships? Why has secrecy shadowed adopted children and their families?

WHAT DO FAMILIES KEEP FROM EACH OTHER?

Most families have secret-keepers. Secret-keepers cloud positive husband and wife relationships, block healthy communication of a parent to a child, and impede supportive extended family connections.

Families keep secrets from one another around potentially embarrassing, shameful, humiliating, or painful events. A teenage love relationship, an untimely pregnancy, an adoption plan, financial mismanagement, serious mental or emotional illness, a criminal history, drug use—all fill the compartments of that darkened cedar chest.

When Robert was twenty-three years old, his father died suddenly. He had a tremendous relationship with the man he called his hero. His world shattered one afternoon as he and his mother took a walk through a neighborhood park. On that bright, sunny day clouds overshadowed the memories Robert nurtured of his father. On that day, his mother told him of a relationship that she had had earlier in life. At nineteen she had fallen in love with a man who loved her and left her. After his departure, she discovered she was pregnant with Robert. When Robert was eight months old, she met David, the man Robert knew as dad. He never formally adopted him.

"We intended to tell you all along, son," she related in a trembling voice. "I kept putting it off."

WHY DO WE KEEP SECRETS? SECRECY AS A TOOL

When Jennifer was seventeen years old, she experienced an unplanned pregnancy. Feeling overwhelmed and inadequate to parent, she made an adoption plan. That was twenty-one years ago. She has told no one of her secret, not even her husband and family. Why? Control. As long as she kept her secret, she alone would have absolute control over it.

In her book, *Family Secrets*, Harriet Webster notes that "secrecy is a tool we use to adapt what has happened to us (or our children). Through the conscious, deliberate concealment or disclosure of information, we take some control of our life and exercise a degree of power over those with whom we interact."[2] *We use the tool of secrecy to keep control.* Why else do we keep secrets?

Individuals and families keep secrets from one another to keep a blanket of secure protection over them. The less other family members know about a particular past circumstance or event, the less vulnerable that person is to hurt. The less others know, the less chance that the family member will be placed under the microscope and subjected to unhealthy commiseration, unconscious criticism, judgment, or blame.

One rainy afternoon, Carla, age fifteen, and her older adopted sister, Rachel, age seventeen, were cleaning out the attic. They stumbled onto a shoebox full of old newspaper clippings. The articles told the grisly details of Rachel's birth mother's death at the hands of her father. The articles related the aspects of a very messy trial and his subsequent imprisonment. Rachel sat stunned. She knew she was adopted, but always thought her mother died of cancer and her father just couldn't care for her. When confronted with the information, her mother said, "We just wanted you to be shielded from such a hurtful history." *We use the tool of secrecy to feel protected or to protect.* There are still more reasons families keep secrets from each other and from those outside the family who could provide love and support.

Joyce and Kelly had been close friends for nearly six years. They shared hurts, joys, hopes, and dreams. Yet, there was still something that Joyce had never shared. While they were finishing their usual Thursday afternoon lunch together, Joyce opened up.

"I need to tell you something that I have told no one since we moved here. I need to tell you that I am adopted."

Kelly responded, "Why didn't you ever tell me? There wasn't any reason to keep that from me."

"I just couldn't," Joyce said. "I have always been ashamed of the fact that I was adopted. I have always thought of myself as not worth much because someone got rid of me. I thought if you knew, you wouldn't want to be my friend anymore." *We use the tool of secrecy because of our sense of shame.* It is a shame that leaves us feeling defective and without power.

To keep control, to protect or be protected, to hide shame, all these are reasons why families keep secrets. Another reason people keep secrets is to protect their public persona—their image. If others knew about their adoption plan or their adoptive status, would life be different?

Masking one's secret of childlessness through an adoption by never talking about it, either inside or outside the family, used to be a routine mode of family communication. Living as if an adoption plan never happened used to be a familiar route taken through life by birth parents years ago. Not telling a child about his or her adoptive status also was a means of quietly handling a child's placement in the family as well as the image of the family itself. What does that type of secrecy do to a child who discovers the secret?

Parents are forceful people in the lives of their children, Ken Watson says. They occasionally, through the strength of their authority, press a child into silence (if the secret is found out) in order to protect their public image. A child who feels that mentioning adoption in any way outside the family is a threat to the family's image begins to wonder what is really important—appearances or reality. "Are reputation and image so sacred that they must be preserved at any cost?"[3]

Questions begin to fill the mind of this silent child. "If my parents choose to protect the image of the family and if I am a sacrifice that has to be made in the process, the child wonders, how can I be worth anything?"[4] *We use the tool of secrecy to guard our public image and reputation.* There is yet one more reason why families use the tool of secrecy.

Fourteen-year-old Michael joined his adoptive family at two years of age. Michael had been severely neglected, often left an entire day by himself. The condition in which he was eventually found by social workers was beyond deplorable. It was beyond disgusting. Both of Michael's adoptive parents feel that the less said about Michael's past the better. If it is not talked about, it will be forgotten. The entire family maintained the attitude that bad things belong buried in the past. *We use the tool of secrecy to forget about the past.*

WHAT'S PRIVATE? WHAT'S CONFIDENTIAL? WHAT'S A SECRET?

What about privacy? Aren't there things that should be kept quiet? Of course, says Michael Mask. But there is a difference. "What sets a family secret apart from a matter that is appropriately kept confidential within the family is the effect it has on the family." Is the issue discussed freely and openly within the family? Or if the issue is raised, does a look or a word squelch it?

Secrets damage the family. Secrets have power over family members because nobody talks about them and yet a few influential ones know about them. A little lie is told. A little bit of a coverup is relayed. A secret is born. It gains more power, Mask says, as it passes from one generation to another.

Confidentiality, however, does not damage the family. "Confidentiality," stresses Mask, "protects and strengthens the family."[5] It teaches families to deal with issues openly and honestly. Confidential matters allow for appropriate communication within healthy boundaries by those directly touched by the event or circumstances or with those who can act within the arena of support.

THE HIGH COST OF KEEPING SECRETS WITHIN THE FAMILY

Secrets are powerful things. Secrets within any family can distort reality, undermine trust, and destroy intimacy. Secrets create exclusion, destroy authenticity, produce fantasies, evoke fear, and kindle shame. Each one of these deserves further examination from the perspective of adoption.

Secrets Distort Reality

Lois Roberts, now in her early fifties, grew up as an only child, loved— almost worshipped—by her parents. Occasionally, her mother would say to her, "We couldn't have any children and then you came along." The phrase had no real meaning to Lois.

Following the sudden death of her mother and during the subsequent resident nursing home care needed by her father, a family secret emerged. As Lois visited with her father, each time she entered the room he would ask the same question, "Are you adopted?"

Puzzled, Lois contacted family members, who confirmed the truth. All the other relatives knew. Everyone knew but Lois.

"I have a lot of questions," Lois stated. "I feel a sense of abandonment. I feel like the whole world is on the inside of a glass and I am on the outside. My prevailing emotional feeling is that everybody marches along to a family rhythm and I don't know what mine is and now it is too late. I don't know what my reality is. I should have counted somewhere enough to be told the truth."[6]

"While some secrets can bring people together by giving them a sense of intimacy and sharing," says Betty Jean Lifton, "secrets can be destructive if they cause shame and guilt, prevent change, render one powerless or hamper one's sense of reality."[7]

Secrets Undermine Trust and Intimacy

When Tonia found out that her older brother was adopted, it impacted her relationship with her mother. "My mother and I had always been close. I felt I could tell her everything. When I was seventeen she told me the family secret that Rich had yet to find out. He was adopted. What keeping this family secret did to our relationship was subtle and gradual. I found myself sharing less and less with her, guarding what I did tell and always wondering in the back of my mind, what else she hasn't told me."

Secrets Create Exclusion and Division

Keeping a secret puts family members into exclusive clubs—those who know it and those who do not. Secrecy impacts on many arenas in the secret-keeper's life. To keep the secret, the secret-keeper must carefully guard all communication with others close to him. This defense mode often leads to distance, anxiety, and awkwardness in relationships with intimate others.[8] Where there is exclusion and division from one another based on secrecy, the probability of mutual caring, mutual understanding, and mutual honesty is seriously diminished.

Secrets Destroy Authenticity

In families where secrets are kept, another problem emerges: the creation of the family mask. What the family members seem to be on the outside to one another is not what is truly on the inside. In secret-keeping families, the sense of authenticity is lost.[9]

Living with secrets, Mask offers, means remaining entangled in a web of deception, even if the motive is pure and protective. Deception is so destructive that it breaks trust and breeds confusion. When the truth is kept secret, then corresponding emotions are denied or repressed, and defense mechanisms rise to take their place. When children are told, "Don't think, don't ask, don't see, don't feel," they lose their sense of what is real.[10]

Secrets Produce Fantasies

Lynn, age twelve, was quite imaginative. She often would sit and tell her friends stories about her birth mother. The stories always included the same basic facts. Her birth mother lived in a beautiful home in a city near the ocean. In fact, she could see the ocean from her house. Her home had a pool and was surrounded by beautiful gardens and trees. The problem with Lynn's story was it was nowhere near the truth. Lynn's mother had been involved in selling drugs and was in prison. She would be in prison until well into Lynn's twenties.

Because Lynn never knew the truth, she created one for herself. It was a "truth" that would only serve her for a season—until the "real" story comes crashing in.

Secrets Evoke Fear

"I grew up never knowing anything about my past. No one would ever answer my questions so I stopped asking them," Kim Kelly related. "Because of that, I also was never able to share an overwhelming fear I had with my parents. I grew up with the fear that some day I was going to wake up and nobody would be there. The house would be empty. They would have all disappeared. I just wonder . . . maybe that is what really happened to me in the very beginning."

When secrets are kept, there is a vacuum that must be filled. That vacuum is filled with a preoccupation with the secret. That preoccupation then leads to anxiety and fear. "Secrecy . . . creates a condition (a feeling) of chronic vulnerability," says Jim Gritter. "Fear alters our ability to gather and interpret information, decisions are often based on fantasy-enhanced speculation rather than the fact. Secrecy can accentuate the distressing feeling of being different from others."[11] And when one feels different and doesn't know why, fear is a constant companion.

Secrets Kindle Shame

Drew, age twelve, knew he was "given up" for adoption, but he didn't know why. The truth was, his birth mother loved him very much, but as a young teen she was unequipped to raise Drew to adulthood. Drew's adoptive parents knew the whole story, but they assumed that the less said, the better—for everyone. The only problem was that Drew was left believing there was something "wrong" with him, that he had been unlovable from birth. A feeling of shame haunted his thoughts and impacted his relationships. Drew wasn't alone.

"I could never talk about adoption in our house. It was like the family's secret word. If I brought it up, you would have thought I'd said a dirty word," commented Jackie. "I grew up thinking that because adoption was never talked about, it was a horrible secret. If there was something wrong with adoption, there must be something terribly wrong about me."

All types of families keep secrets for a number of reasons. The effect of secret keeping on family members can be harmful to healthy family growth, intimacy, and communication. It is important for foster, adoptive, and kinship families to understand the power of secrets as well as to understand the origins of secrecy in adoption.

THE ORIGIN OF SECRETS IN ADOPTION

From history's earliest days until the present, the practice of adoption has served a variety of functions, according to Ken Watson, internationally known adoption expert. It has spanned a continuum of needs, from "providing a royal family with an heir, to adding 'indentured' hands, to making a family financially self-sufficient, to emptying orphanages to save community dollars."[12]

In recent decades, adoption has served two additional functions: to meet the needs of couples whose dreams of a family were shattered by infertility, and to provide a solution for birth parents who found themselves facing an unintended and untimely pregnancy.

What emerged from the latter two functions of adoption during the middle decades of this century was an idealist picture, one which characterized a perfect solution to a societal problem. As Miriam Reitz and Ken Watson state:

Adoptive families and adoption agencies collaborated to present adoption as what it can never really be—a chance for birth parents to go on happily with their lives, for children to grow up in trouble-free families, and for adoptive parents to fulfill themselves and find immortality through children to whom they have sole claim by virtue of adoption.[13]

"Years ago," according to Sharon Kaplan Roszia, "myths were perpetuated through the adoption community. One myth taught those whose lives were touched by adoption that the most healthy attitude for all members of the triad was to make a clean break."[14] That break meant no looking back, no information passed on, a story left untold.

Ken Watson remarked that "the implications of the adoption on the subsequent development of the child or family [were] either viewed as inconsequential or denied altogether." These perceptions—"We are just like a biological family: adoption has no reference to the future, and things are best kept a secret"—further established a precedent on how children were told about their adoption and what they were told, if they were told at all.[15] Little thought was given to the impact the lack of information would have on an adopted child, including the child's relationship with the adoptive family and eventually birth parents if a reunion occurred.

Adoption practitioners of the day followed a prescribed course—create a new world. It would be a world in which adoptees were told to forget the past, as though it did not exist. Adoptive parents were told to create a new reality and given freedom to exist in total anonymity with no pressure for disclosure. Birth parents were insensitively shoved aside and told to erase the present events from their memories.

Those who advised secrecy in adoption practice had good intentions. It was assumed that if the anonymity of all individuals involved was protected, then the following goals would be met.

- The birthmother could more easily resolve her feelings about the placement.
- The birthmother would be protected from the label of "fallen woman."
- The child would be protected from the label of "illegitimate."
- The child would be more easily integrated into the family.
- The family could portray their structure as that of a biological family.
- And . . . no one would have to look back.[16]

However, for all the efforts made to serve "the best interest" of adopted children by denying the past and delegating it to the sacred halls of secrecy, those efforts have not served them well.

SECRECY HAS NOT SERVED THE ADOPTED PERSON

Many adoptees experienced the "disquieting loneliness" Alex Haley, the author of *Roots*, described.[17] Devastating feelings of abandonment, rejection, shame, and guilt grew out of a lack of knowledge about their heritage and why they were placed in an adoptive family. Adopted youngsters were plagued by questions about who their birth parents were, why they couldn't care for their children, and whether they would ever meet. Concerns about their genetic past or their medical history left them wondering if something devastating would surface later in life. The need for such knowledge frequently nudged adoptees into a consuming and never-ending search for the truth, sometimes impairing their ability to lead productive lives.

"Adoptees can feel frustrated at their inability to connect with their roots," says Marshall Schecter, a psychiatrist at the University of Pennsylvania School of Medicine. "Some have trouble forming an identity when they reach adolescence because they have been told little to nothing about their past. Others may develop fantasies—both positive and negative—about their birth family. Some adoptees spend a lifetime never finding answers to their questions. For others, this black hole which exists where their past should be becomes too much of an emotional burden for them to bear, leaving deep psychological scars."[18]

Adoption scholar David Brodzinsky of Rutgers University says, "For adoptees, part of them is hurt at having once been relinquished. That part remains vulnerable for the rest of their lives as they grieve at various predictable points for the unknown parents who gave them away" and for the code of silence and secrecy that prevented them from finding out.[19]

Jim Gritter feels that secrecy has created a deeper issue within the heart and mind of the adopted person. That greater issue is shame:

Secrecy is symptomatic of a much deeper issue—namely, shame. Adoption flounders as an institution because it is built on a foundation of shame. For decades, adoption has functioned essentially as a two-step program of disowning and owning. In that form, it is an almost perfect script for shame, for there is great shame in disowning and owning; and obviously, there is great shame in being disowned and owned. Shame is a matter of defect, powerlessness, and rejection—all familiar themes in adoption. . . . I believe shame is at the heart of adoption, as we have known it in our lifetime. It is the DNA of closed adoption.[20]

Secrecy has not served the adopted person well.

DOES SECRECY STILL EXIST IN ADOPTION?

In a study of 288 adoptive families completed in the early 1990s, it was discovered that fewer than 40 percent of the adoptive parents had given their adopted children all the information they had. More than 25 percent falsified or omitted information. The remaining families gave little or no information about the adoption, and in some cases never had told their child.[21]

In another study, 25 percent of adoptive parents stated that they had given their child full and truthful information about their birth parents and family history. Of those same families, only 10 percent of the adult adoptees verified that claim. Half of the adoptees said they pressed their parents for information, while only 20 percent of the parents reported the same fact. Finally, three times as many parents as adult adoptees said that as children, the adoptees had never voluntarily raised the subject.[22]

Yes, dealing with truthfulness in adoption is still an issue of great debate today.

QUESTIONS

1. Have you ever found out a "family secret" that directly affected you? How did you feel? How did you respond short-term? Over time?
2. What are five reasons we keep secrets? Can you think of any more?

3. In small groups, discuss each reason as it relates to adoption.

4. What is the difference between confidentiality and secret keeping as you understand it?

5. What are seven consequences of secret keeping in the family? Discuss each as it relates to healthy adoptive family living.

NOTES

1. Jayne Elizabeth Schooler, *Searching for a Past* (Colorado Springs: Pinon Press, 1995), 105–6.

2. Harriet Webster, *Family Secrets: How Telling and Not Telling Affects Our Children, Our Relationships and Our Lives* (Reading, Mass.: Addison-Wesley Publishing, 1991), 11.

3. Ibid., 202.

4. Ibid.

5. Michael Mask, Julie Mask, Jeanne Hensley, and Steven Craig, *Family Secrets* (Nashville: Thomas Nelson, 1995), 9–11.

6. Schooler, 105–6.

7. Betty Jean Lifton, *Journey of the Adopted Self: A Quest for Wholeness* (New York: Basic Books, 1993), 22.

8. M. Weinrob and B. C. Murphy. "The Birth Mother: A Feminist Perspective for the Helping Professional." *Woman and Therapy* 7, no. 1 (1988): 30.

9. Mask et al., 11.

10. Ibid., 12.

11. James Gritter, *The Spirit of Open Adoption* (Washington, D.C.: CWLA Press, 1998), 73.

12. Miriam Reitz and Kenneth W. Watson, *Adoption and the Family System* (New York: Guilford Press, 1993), 3.

13. Ibid., 4.

14. Quoted in Schooler, 41.

15. Ibid.

16. R. G. McRoy, H. D. Grotevant, and L. A. Zucher, *Openness in Adoption: New Practices, New Issues* (New York: Praeger, 1988), 14.

17. Adapted from "Openness in Adoption," from the National Adoption Clearinghouse, www.calib.com/naic.

18. David Brodzinsky and Marshall Schecter, *The Psychology of Adoption* (New York: Oxford University Press, 1990).

19. Adapted from "Openness in Adoption.

20. Gritter, 12.

21. Mary Watkins and Susan Fisher, *Talking with Young Children about Adoption* (New Haven, Conn.: Yale University Press, 1993), 217–18.

22. Ibid.

CHAPTER TWO

Truth or Consequences:
A Great Debate

Children are afraid of the dark. Adults are afraid of the light.

If I tell my child about his birth father, he will be hurt and angry. It is best that he doesn't know the truth.

If I tell the children the whole story regarding their parents, they will have a better understanding of why they are in foster care.

Jennifer, age fifteen, was adopted shortly after birth into a family with two birth children, both several years older than she. At the time of the adoption, the social workers told her parents that Jennifer's birth mother was a patient in a psychiatric hospital. The mother claimed to have been impregnated following a rape by an African American man, also a patient at the hospital. Because Jennifer did not appear to be biracial, her adoptive parents never told her the birth mother's story about her father. Their older children overheard their discussions and did learn some of the information shared by the social worker. When Jennifer began struggling with her identity, the parents asked a therapist if they had been right to withhold this information from Jennifer, citing as an excuse the mother's lack of credibility. After some exploratory discussion with Jennifer, the therapist discovered that the older siblings had told her years before that she was biracial. She had been struggling alone, with no parental support or guidance, with this information (or, potentially, misinformation) about her racial/ethnic heritage for many years. It was small wonder that she was experiencing a crisis of identity formation as a young adolescent.

The wrestling match between the pros and cons of telling children the truth about their birth family and birth circumstances plays out regularly in foster and adoptive families. *Should we tell? How much should we tell?*

Most adoptive and foster parents are loving and concerned. They want to protect their children from pain and unhappiness. When adoptive parents consider the impact of separation from the birth family on their child, or less-than-ideal circumstances surrounding that separation, they sometimes imagine that they will "protect" the child from pain or difficulty in adjustment by

• not telling the child at all about the adoption;

• not telling the "whole" truth by telling a "hole" (partial) truth; or

• avoiding conversation that might be upsetting to the child.

In reality, parents who attempt to "protect" their child in this manner are creating a scenario in which the child lacks trust in and attachment to the adoptive or foster family. When a child, adolescent, or young adult finds information that has been known to the adoptive parents but withheld, the adoptee wonders what other lies or half-truths have been perpetrated by the adoptive family. The outrage felt by someone who has not experienced honesty from the people committed to one's protection and welfare can be intense, leaving no room for trust or attachment. Parents must remember that, in today's world of adoption, many adopted persons are reunited with members of their birth families; when those reunions occur, adoptees have access to information "from the horse's mouth."

A foster or adopted child, lacking a life story that makes sense, is forced to make one up. The imagined history is often either extremely positive or extremely negative. When the fantasy history is very positive, the adopted child may yearn for the fantasy parent who will never punish, will always be patient, will be famous, rich, and beautiful, and will lavish attention, gifts, and love on the child. When the fantasy history is very negative, the child may feel like a "low-life" who does not deserve a loving, stable adoptive family. The child may strive to be like the negative image of his birth family, an image that can be far from reality.

Often, the adopted child's self-esteem is more damaged by silence or deceit than by reality. The silence or deceit can create shame in the adoptee, who believes the information is withheld or distorted because of the parent's desire to shield him from knowing that he is of "bad" seed.

When parents are not willing to talk openly about the situation that led to adoption or foster care, the child is forced to cope with over-whelming issues with little or no parental support. It is hard enough for adults to make sense of difficult circumstances. Children and adolescents, without help, are not able to integrate information about innumerable social ills: war and political unrest, cultural beliefs that make it impossible for some single birth mothers to raise their children; alcoholism and substance abuse; discrimination that sometimes accompanies minority group membership; mental illness; and mental retardation, to name only a few.

Parents who withhold or distort key information about a child's past may be, in effect, protecting *themselves* from a task they find difficult: talking about the birth family, adoption, and the circumstances that led up to the adoption.

The adoptive family's task is to integrate diversity and use it to form a permanent bridge to and from the wider world. In forming that permanent bridge, the adoptive family, through their child, becomes connected to the social problems that resulted in the adoption plan: alcoholism, drug addiction, teenage pregnancy, child abuse and neglect, mental illness, and so on.[1]

Because of that connection to a difficult past, adoptive parents have *a lifelong responsibility*—communicating the circumstances of their child's past in a manner that will lead to understanding, resolution, and healing. As parents assume the lifelong commitment of adoption, they should examine the debate surrounding adoption disclosure.

THE DEBATE OF ADOPTION SECRECY: MYTHS AND REALITIES

Adoptive or foster parents may be reluctant to share the knowledge that their child is adopted or that very difficult circumstances surround his separation from his birth family. Sometimes, well-meaning relatives or friends may even advise foster and adoptive parents that what a child doesn't know can't hurt him. The debate can rage on within the minds, and marriages, of adoptive parents. A number of myths might serve to fuel a lack of honesty.

Fear of Losing the Love and Loyalty of the Child

Myth: The child will not be tortured by divided loyalties to both birth and adoptive parents if he simply does not know he is adopted. Or, it is acceptable to distort the truth with stories of birth parents who "died in a car crash" as a way of trying to remove the birth parents from the child's thoughts and loyalties.

Reality: One of the paradoxes of parenthood is that when parents try to hold on to their children too tightly, they will only ensure the loss of those children. Those who try to keep their children too close to home when the children are old enough to emancipate, for example, may find that their young adult children decide to move hundreds of miles away. Or stepparents who try to compete for the love and attachment of their children may find that those children turn away from them. Adoptive parents must remember that the child's love of the birth family does not detract from love of the adoptive family. When adopted children have the support of secure adoptive parents to have feelings for their birth families, the children are free to attach to the adoptive family. They are not caught in a competitive, divisive tug-of-war. By giving them honesty and understanding, adoptive parents give their children permission to love and attach to the adoptive family.

Mindy, a nine-year-old child, was adopted at age three. She has vague memories about her birth mother. Mindy was adopted due to neglect resulting from her birth mother's chronic depression. Mother's Day used to be a troubling day for Mindy as she struggled to honor her adoptive mother without being disloyal to her birth mother. Mindy's adoptive mother recognized her daughter's dilemma and suggested that Mindy write her birth mother a card every Mother's Day telling her about her accomplishments and feelings, and including drawings and collages about her life. Mindy works very hard on the letters she makes for her birth mother every year, and they are kept in a special album for Mindy to review when she wants to feel close to her birth mother or proud of herself. The understanding and acceptance of the adoptive mother has given Mindy "permission" to love both mothers. Mindy no longer holds herself behind a wall of fear in her relationship with her adoptive mother—she is now free to love her because she understands that, to do so, she does not have to stop loving her birth mother.

Fear that the Child Will Have a Poor Self-Image

Myth: Children should not be told that their parents were addicted to drugs or alcohol, incarcerated, abusive, mentally ill, or mentally retarded, and so on. Children will feel bad about themselves because their family had serious problems. For this reason, it is acceptable to hide or distort information, or to omit significant facts.

Reality: When a child does not have parental support in learning about his history, he is forced to develop an image of himself and his family based solely on misinformation and imagination. What he imagines and is unable to discuss with supportive adults may be far worse than the real situation. Further, it may be the parents' judgments about the circumstances leading to adoption or foster care that could create poor self-esteem. Adoptive and foster parents can learn to present even very difficult information in nonjudgmental ways, giving the child support and love while he is learning about his life circumstances.

Willy, age twelve, was adopted at the age of three following years of neglect by his mentally retarded mother. His adoptive parents were reluctant to tell him that his parent was mentally retarded. Willy assumed that his mother neglected him because she did not care about him. Willy's parents shared his history with him when he expressed tremendous rage about his birth mother's lack of concern. Willy understood that his mother had cognitive problems that made it impossible for her to care for her son. With the help of the child welfare agency, the adoptive family was able to obtain information about the extended birth family. Willy finally could feel proud of his ethnic heritage, his birth grandfather's and aunt's artistic talents, and, most important, his birth mother's attempts to care for him in spite of her handicap.

Fear of Telling the Child Information at the Wrong Time, Before He or She Is Able to Understand the Circumstances

Myth: The child is, and will always be, "too young" to understand prostitution, rape, mental illness, criminal behavior, and so on.

Reality: The child is able to understand his life story in layers. What he is told at age three may be a simplified version of reality, with more information supplied when he is better able to understand. The child receives another layer of understanding as he matures, and so on until the child has all the information the parent has.

Amanda, age fifteen, understands today that she was adopted because both of her birth parents were alcoholic and unable to care for her. When Amanda was a preschooler, her adoptive parents explained to her that her birth parents could not take care of her because they were not healthy and were unable to meet the responsibilities of parenthood. As Amanda reached the school-age years, she understood that she was removed from her parents' care by child protective social workers because her parents did not care for her properly. As a middle school child, Amanda learned about the disease of alcoholism and the history of her parents' ongoing struggle with sobriety. As an adolescent, Amanda is learning that her grandparents were also alcoholic. She is being taught about the genetic predisposition to this disease, and her parents are helping her learn strategies to avoid a future of alcohol abuse for herself.

Fear of a Self-Fulfilling Prophecy; the Child May Try to Model Himself after the Birth Parent

Myth: If the child knows that the birth mother was promiscuous, she might behave in sexually provocative ways during her own adolescence.

Reality: It is normal for all adolescents to try on multiple identities and to experiment with independence by being very different from their parents. It is likely that adopted youth, then, will try on identities that are different from those of their adoptive parents. They may choose to be like the birth parents (or what they imagine the birth parents to be like) during this process of identity formation, particularly if they find this identity to be troubling to their parents! This behavior is normal and to be expected. Problems can become more serious when adoptive parents, fearful of behavior that appears similar to the dysfunctional behavior of the birth family, overreact to the child's experimentation.

Beau was adopted as an infant. His birth mother had been a promiscuous adolescent who surrendered him for adoption when she became a parent at the age of sixteen. Beau began dating seriously just before his sixteenth birthday, and his adoptive parents were concerned that he might try to recreate the scenario of his own birth. Adoption had not been an open topic within the household for many years; the parents had assumed that Beau knew everything they knew, and there was nothing else to talk about. With help from a skilled post-adoption social worker, the parents learned that Beau needed to continue to talk about his history and his birth parents as his development allowed him to understand and integrate the complexities of his background. Just knowing the facts isn't always enough. Following an increase in open communication in the family, the adoptive parents were surprised by Beau's confused attitudes and feelings toward his birth mother. When Beau had his adoptive parents' help and support in sorting out these feelings, he no longer felt that he had to transfer a need to be close to his birth mother to his adolescent girlfriend.

Fear that the Information Cannot Be Shared in a Positive Light; the Adoptive Parent Does Not Know How to Tell

Myth: My child will be scarred for life if I don't find the right words to tell him about his past.

Reality: Adoptive and foster parents can learn to discuss histories in an age-appropriate, nonjudgmental way. The help of skilled post-adoption specialists can also be used when parents feel overwhelmed by very difficult information. While secrets can almost always be lethal, open communication rarely is.

Ben is ten years old now, and his adopted parents believe he has a right to know about his two older birth brothers. They worried about telling him that he was born to an older birth mother, a divorced woman with two older children. They worried that he would feel rejected because the birth mother made an adoptive plan for Ben but kept the older children. The parents decided to take Ben back to the agency that handled the adoption to talk to a social worker about his history. His parents remained with him throughout the interview, during which Ben was able to ask questions about his past and his mother's reasons for seeking an adoptive family for him. Ben initially expressed anger and feelings of rejection. He became interested in his birth brothers, however, and asked his adoptive parents if he might write to or visit them sometime in the future. The parents were supportive of his feelings, and, with the help of the social worker, obtained a picture of the brothers from the birth mother for Ben's room. He displays it proudly on his dresser.

Because of these fears and myths, parents can be tempted to withhold or change information. The consequences of changing the truth, however, can be devastating to the child and the adoptive family.

NOT TELLING THE CHILD AT ALL

Few parents today attempt to withhold the fact of adoption from the child. However, some families have been counseled to adhere to the "ignorance is bliss" policy: what he doesn't know can't hurt him. This is comparable to a doctor withholding communication about a terminal disease with the belief that, if the patient doesn't *know* he is dying, he won't.

Many individuals can relate stories about their cousin or neighbor who was adopted and never told. Everyone else in the family or community seems to know about the adoption except the person to whom it is of most importance, the child himself. Rarely can this secret be successfully maintained. When children or adults discover they are adopted, they feel disconnected from the adoptive family (and, often, from the rest of humanity), an overwhelming rage at the parents' lack of honesty, and a tremendous sense of shame that this information was regarded as so negative that it had to be hidden.

"When I was twelve years old, my father took me to the basement and showed me a picture of a woman I did not know. He said to me, 'You have the right to know this is your birth mother. But whatever you do, don't tell your mother that I told you about your adoption—it would kill her!' My father never spoke to me again about my adoption."

The implicit message in this situation is that the youth's status as an adopted child is somehow shameful, secreted from society and the child himself. This young man was adrift throughout the remainder of his life, unable to ask questions about his heritage, his ethnicity, or his personal and family histories.

Often, adoptive parents ask about the ideal age at which to tell a child he or she is adopted. Many well-adjusted adopted adults tell us that they have always known that they were adopted and cannot remember a "telling moment." These adults grew up knowing that they were adopted in the same way they grew up knowing that they were male or female, Catholic or Jewish, tall or short. When parents search for the appropriate telling moment, they find that it never comes. The child has just been sick, is about to begin school, just lost a beloved pet, and so on. The longer parents wait, the more difficult it becomes to tell the child; the parents are embarrassed that they have not found a moment of honesty before. And so the waiting for a perfect telling moment continues, sometimes until the parents lose the opportunity to tell because another person, almost always less concerned about the child's feelings, shares the information with the adoptee. This will be explored in more depth in Chapter Five.

TELLING THE "HOLE TRUTH" INSTEAD OF THE "WHOLE TRUTH"

Many parents fall into the trap of withholding complete information, either permanently or "until my child is older and can understand." Key pieces of information are withheld, making it difficult for the child to fully integrate the circumstances surrounding his birth.

In this type of communication, the adoptive parent might relate partial information regarding the child's ethnicity, medical history, or placement history in foster care. However, the parent decides not to tell the child that he or she was born to a drug-addicted mother who was engaging in prostitution to support her habit.

These types of omissions are necessary when the child is too young to understand the social situations and circumstances surrounding his adoption. Omission or simplification of some facts may be necessary while the child is very young, but harmful when the omission continues beyond the child's ability to understand. In determining when the child is old enough to know full information, parents can make the most accurate judgments. However, parents should remember that they usually underestimate their child's sophistication. Betty Jean Lifton, an adult adopted person and author of numerous books about adoption, asserts that all children should have complete information about their birth family history by the time they reach adolescence. It is important that parents share this information *prior to, not during*, the child's difficult journey through identity formation and individuation (separation from the family), key developmental tasks of adolescence.

A post-adoption counselor explained to twelve-year-old Cory that he was surrendered for adoption because he was conceived when his mother was raped by an unknown assailant. Cory, surprisingly, expressed relief that his mother "was not a slut." The child understood that his mother signed the surrender, not to reject him, but to reject the circumstances surrounding his conception.

In subsequent chapters, readers will learn techniques of talking with children about difficult topics in an honest, nonjudgmental, and age-appropriate way.

AVOIDING CONVERSATION THAT MIGHT BE UPSETTING TO THE CHILD

Talking about the circumstances that surround adoption often leads children to ask challenging questions, cry, express concern about siblings or birth parents, or display behaviors that indicate they are sad, angry, or confused. It is tempting for adoptive parents to cope with these challenges through silence about adoption or birth histories. They decide, "If he doesn't think about it, he will be able to forget about it."

Adoptive parents need to understand that children think about their adoptions and their birth families *often*, sometimes continuously. Studies have repeatedly demonstrated the surprisingly large incidence of attentional problems within the population of adopted children. Some studies indicate that one-third of all adopted children have attention deficit disorder with or without hyperactivity.[2] It is unlikely that all of these children have neurological problems resulting from genetics or exposure to drugs, alcohol, or other stresses in utero. It is more likely that many of these children are so preoccupied with trying to make sense of the losses that have occurred in their lives (and with preventing future losses from occurring) that they have difficulty concentrating. By discouraging communication about the topic most on the child's mind, the parent surrenders an important opportunity to influence the child's self-esteem, to promote attachment to the adoptive family, and to promote healthy forms of communication the child will be able to carry into his adult life.

Adoptive parents might assume that their children never think about adoption because they never bring up the topic. When these children are encouraged to talk about adoption through support group meetings with other children or through counseling with skilled post-adoption therapists, they often reveal that they have been consumed by a topic that is never addressed directly in the family.

Jermaine, an eleven-year-old boy, asked if he thinks about his birth mother, responded, "I am thinking about her right now. I think about her every minute of the day." His parents were very surprised to learn of Jermaine's concern, as he had never asked a question about her.

Parents of eighteen-year-old Greg, hospitalized following a suicide attempt, were shocked to hear his girlfriend say, "Greg cries about his birth family all the time." The young man had been adopted shortly after birth and repeatedly assured his adoptive parents that he never thought about his adoption.

Some adoptive parents believe that they should respond honestly to questions asked by the child, but that they should not raise the issue of adoption themselves. Such a policy ensures that adoption will be little discussed in the family. Many children rarely raise the subject of adoption themselves. They believe that they are being disloyal to the adoptive parents if they continue to have feelings about the birth parents. When some children ask questions about adoption, they pick up cues that the topic is uncomfortable for the adoptive parent and should be avoided in the future.

VALUES/BELIEFS OF ADOPTION DISCLOSURE

Certainly, then, we should affirm the following values and beliefs in talking with children and adults about adoption.

- All persons have a right to know their personal history.
- All healthy relationships involve hard work, open, two-way communication, and mutual respect.
- Adoption is a way of creating a family; it is not better or worse than other ways. Adoption should be celebrated, not hidden.
- Knowing about adoption includes an awareness that children will have questions and feelings about their birth parents. These questions and feelings should be acknowledged and addressed with honesty and respect.
- Birth parents and adoptive parents both care about the same child. They are not in competition for the affections and loyalty of the child. Parents can care about more than one child, and children can care about more than one set of parents. Withholding information about adoption because of a desire to have all of the child's loyalty and affection has a paradoxical outcome: the erosion of the child's trust, loyalty, and attachment to the adoptive family.

QUESTIONS

1. What "fear" have you experienced in relation to telling your child the truth about his birth family?
2. Of those fears discussed in this chapter, which is most intense for you?
3. What is the "worst case scenario" if you share information you have been withholding from your child?
4. If you had a terminal illness, would you want to have that information withheld from you by the doctor?
5. What might be some consequences of withholding information from your child?

NOTES

1. Mary Watkins and Susan Fisher, *Talking with Young Children about Adoption* (New Haven, Conn.: Yale University Press, 1993), 217–18.

2. J. T. Nigg, J. M. Wanson, and S. P. Hinshaw, "Covert Visual Spatial Attention in Boys with ADHD: Lateral Effects, Mehylphenidate Response and Results for Parents." *Neuropsychologia* 35 (February 1997): 165–76; L. Hechtman, "Families of Children with Attention Deficit Hyperactivity Disorder: A Review," *Canadian Journal of Psychiatry* 41 (August 1996): 350–60.

CHAPTER THREE

Just the Facts, Ma'am: Why Do Children Need Them?

Isn't fiction better than fact if the truth is painful and disruptive? Isn't it better to protect our children from difficult truths that might overburden them, destroying self-image and confidence? Can't we wait until our children are adults to share their story with them?

While it can be very tempting for adoptive parents to "protect" children from painful realities, we must question our motives. Are we protecting the feelings of the children, or protecting ourselves from those realities? By refusing to talk about painful history, we can pretend these circumstances don't really matter. When we try to ignore realities, they can become even larger, threatening to overwhelm the child with fantasies, guesses, and assumptions (many of which are more hurtful than the truth).

Adult adopted persons have taught us the importance of communicating information about a child's adoption as he moves from one side of childhood to the other. Why are facts so important to an adopted individual as he grows up and sorts out his identity? There are a number of reasons.

- Uninformed adopted persons develop unrealistic fantasies about their histories.

- Many adopted persons with little or no information about their histories become confused about their identities and experience long periods of experimentation, at times self-destructive experimentation.

- All children are magical thinkers. Adopted or foster children might believe themselves to be the "cause" of their separation from the birth family, negatively impacting self esteem.

- Children separated from their families of origin may not feel "free" to attach to new families; they may believe that they are being loyal to their birth families if they refuse to attach to another family. Separated children may refuse to have positive feelings toward the birth family, feeling disloyal in that case to the adoptive family. Without positive regard for the family of origin, the child's self esteem suffers.

- Children who have experienced separation from earlier families may fear a reenactment of this separation, thus impacting their ability to trust and feel safe in their new families.

- Separated children may feel disconnected from their past and may feel that a piece of themselves is missing and incomplete.

- Separated children may lack trust in adults who should have protected and cared for them. They may feel that others are lying to them or withholding information. This lack of trust can lead to serious difficulties with control battles as the children enter adolescence.

- Children with little or no information about their histories may develop anxiety about their histories, dating relatives, developing serious health or mental health problems, being "genetically" unable to be good parents or even good people.

These potential outcomes of limited background information create compelling reasons to share histories with children who have been separated from their birth families. Let's examine each in more depth.

UNREALISTIC FANTASIES

Without knowing the truth about his adoption status and the circumstances surrounding the plan, a child can develop unrealistic fantasies involving birth parents, former foster parents, and his new adoptive family. Sometimes a child begins to develop fantasies about the "ideal" birth parents who look like movie stars, never nag about picking up wet towels, and never insist that all of the green beans are eaten. Another child may develop negative fantasies about birth parents who were drug addicts, abusive, violent, mentally ill "street people," and so on. It is not uncommon to see adopted children who vacillate between positive and negative fantasies, changing their beliefs about themselves and their histories almost weekly.

Cathy was only five years old when she joined her foster family. Her birth father had disappeared before she entered foster care, and her birth mother was in and out of jail. When Cathy was six, her mother was convicted of murder in connection with a drug-related robbery. Her mother would be in jail for many, many years. Cathy's foster parents adopted her.

Because Cathy was so young when the birth family blew apart, her adoptive parents never shared the truth with her. They always told her that her mother could not care for her.

One afternoon when Cathy was ten, she was coloring a beautiful picture of a house surrounded by flowers and trees. When her mother asked her about it, Cathy replied, "This is my birth mother's house. I will visit her there when I get bigger. I know this is where she lives."

Susan, Cathy's adoptive mom, knew that she had neglected some very important facts regarding Cathy's history. The youngster was searching for information about her past, but finding only fantasy.

When children are unable to discuss their life situations as they develop more understanding about adoption, they may begin to hope or worry that their birth parents will reenter their lives and "kidnap" them from the adoptive family. Fantasies often revolve around the fear of, or the hope for, reunification with the birth family. Children who consistently refuse to sleep with their windows shut may be hoping for such a reunification. Those who refuse to sleep with their windows open may fear such a kidnapping.

IDENTITY CONFUSION

Establishing one's identity is not something that happens only during a certain period in one's life. Adoption therapist Joyce Maguire Pavao notes that "identity issues are an ongoing process, they just don't start in adolescence. However, the teen years are certainly the major developmental zone for identity formation. Every young person is trying to figure out who he is not—and who he is. He is trying to play different roles, experiment with different looks and figure out who he is along the way."

Maguire Pavao observes that "for adoptees, especially when there is little to no information about where they came from, there is an awareness that they don't really have the genetic information to do that kind of sorting out of their identity. They are basing it on their family of intimacy—the adoptive family, but that's not necessarily where their abilities, interests and traits have come from." Settling one's identity is more difficult for an adopted teen. "For most children," according to Maguire Pavao, "the people around them are mirrors on which they measure themselves, until the adolescent years. At that point they look in the mirror and see themselves. They become more and more aware of how different they are. I think it is a complicated process for adoptees during the teen years. It is at this point that they begin to realize that they do not know another person in the world genetically related to them."[1]

For some, the struggle for identity brings about major behavioral changes. The children may struggle to be like their birth parents or, in the absence of concrete information, what they imagine their birth parents to be.

Michelle, adopted at birth, began to change her looks and behavior when she was sixteen years old. She dyed her hair such a jet-black color that she looked like a caricature of Morticia from *The Addams Family*. She wore black leather clothes, and she had shoes that looked like combat boots. Her friends presented a similarly "tough" image and were heavy drinkers. While growing up, the only information she had about her birth parents was that they were both twenty-three years old when she was born. She also knew that she was born in a hospital affiliated with the university, on the "poor" side of town. She envisioned her birth parents to be hard-drinking, poor, uneducated, and dysfunctional. This youth was very surprised to learn, with the help of post-adoption counseling, that her birth parents had been graduate students who had experienced an untimely pregnancy. She was amazed to find that they were even more middle-class and conventional than her adoptive parents!

Some older adopted youth may not even have sufficient information about their own ethnicity on which to build an identity.

Sally, age sixteen, had been adopted at two months into a loving family with two other adopted children. She lived in a rural community with a sizable Hispanic population. The Anglo adolescents at school occasionally hurled racial slurs at the Mexican American teens. Sally, a dark-haired, olive-skinned girl, began to wonder if she might be of Mexican American heritage. She announced to her shocked adoptive family that she no longer wished to be part of their family, and that she was going to find and live with her birth mother. Counseled to obtain more information about her past, the parents took Sally back to the placing agency to begin an informational search for her roots. When the social worker mentioned that Sally's birth parents were both of German ancestry, Sally immediately stopped her and insistently asked, "Are you sure?" When she had the information she needed to understand where she came from, Sally quickly abandoned her need to live with her birth family—she only needed information about them to learn more about who she was becoming.

MAGICAL THINKING

All young children believe themselves to be the center of the universe and therefore responsible for everything that happens in their world. Young children believe that, if one event happens after another, then the first event caused the second. Inappropriate assumptions about cause and effect, while holding oneself as the cause of virtually everything, are called magical thinking by developmental psychologists. Children who have entered the worlds of foster care and adoption often struggle with shame and guilt as they interpret their life circumstances to be their "fault." Even children who have never lived with their birth parents may believe that they were not attractive enough, or not the "right" gender, or that they cried too much to be loved and wanted by their birth parents.

Doretha was placed in a kinship adoption with her maternal aunt shortly after birth when her birth parents went through a bitter divorce. As Doretha grew into adulthood, she remained positive that her birth father would have remained in the family, negating the necessity of the adoptive placement, if only she had been a boy. Doretha had never been told that either of her birth parents had desired a boy. However, as a young child, she examined her family to explain her father's desertion, and could find only her own gender to be the reason for the family's breakdown. Even as she grew older, she clung to the notion that she, not her birth parents, was responsible for her family's collapse and her subsequent adoption. She struggled with depression and poor self-esteem throughout most of her life.

DIVIDED LOYALTIES

If communication about adoption is not part of the adoptive family life, a child can develop confusion and conflict when emotions about birth parents remain strong. When new feelings for the adoptive family emerge, the child may feel that he is not "allowed" to love and care about more than one family at the same time. The system of closed or confidential adoption, existing in our culture for the past thirty to forty years, reinforces the concept that a child will be able to love only one mother and father. Therefore, birth parents must be erased from the child's life in an attempt to erase them from his thinking. Adult adopted persons have taught us that this system of adoption practice does not have the desired result. If anything, the disconnected adopted person spends more time and energy struggling with allegiances and trying to decide who he belongs to, who he should be attached to. One youngster whose family did not discuss any adoption-related issues blurted out one day to his adoptive parents, "What do I do about you? I still love my birth mom and dad. What do I do about my feelings for you?" This family needed to share the facts regarding his adoption and *also assure the child that it is possible to love more than one set of parents.* A child who does not receive this critical reassurance may not feel free to attach to his adoptive family. Permission to know about, and care about, his birth family actually frees a child to know and care about his adoptive family. Children, and adoptive parents, must understand that humans do not have to stop loving one person to start loving another. Parents are allowed, and expected, to love more than one child. Children must be allowed, by themselves and others, to love more than one parent.

John, adopted domestically after chronic neglect by his depressed mother, could not bring himself to attach to his adoptive mother, even after eight years in the home. As a very young child, John had been responsible for nurturing his depressed parent. John firmly believed that he had deserted his birth mother, and that any positive feeling for his adoptive mother was a sign of further disloyalty. While John could connect with his adoptive father, he continued to hold himself emotionally distant from his mother, believing that this was the honorable thing for him to do. Mother's Day was a particularly difficult time for John, as he could not bring himself to give his adoptive mother gifts or cards. John had frequent behavior problems during the spring months preceding Mother's Day—his behavior was an indicator of his conflict and confusion. With intensive post-adoption counseling, John was able to understand that he did not have to stop loving his birth mother in order to feel love and attachment for his adoptive mother. As he entered young adulthood, John was finally able to become a full member of the adoptive family.

FEARS OF FUTURE ABANDONMENT

Adopted children have all experienced a separation from at least one family, their birth family. They may also have been moved numerous times from one foster home to another. Or their placement may have occurred suddenly, as often happens when children are removed due to turmoil—abuse or severe neglect—or due to international adoption. The children have been traumatized by abrupt moves and the disappearance from their lives of trusted caregivers. They learn to fear another such move and are reluctant to allow themselves the vulnerability of believing that this new family is indeed a "forever family." Children who are fearful of future abandonment may be unable to attend school without severe school phobia, to attend summer camps for several days away from home, or even to spend the night with grandparents or school friends. They may become terrified if Mom or Dad is a few minutes late picking them up from soccer practice. Discussions about a family move may become unmanageable to a child who believes that he will not accompany the rest of the family when they move.

Kim was a fourteen-year-old Korean child who had been adopted at age two and a half. She had made a wonderful adjustment in the adoptive home, but was continually concerned about remaining close to her adoptive mother. As Kim was preparing to enter high school, her family decided to purchase a new home in a neighborhood with better schools for Kim. The young teen became extremely agitated, insisted that she would not move, and remained tearfully locked in her bedroom for several days. The situation reached crisis proportions when Kim attempted to commit suicide to avoid the move, signaling the family she was experiencing extreme panic. In the counseling that followed this crisis, it became clear that Kim had been devastated as a toddler by her separations from her birth mother, foster mother, and culture. She continued to have intense anxiety throughout her childhood that a similar abandonment would occur in her new home. When the adoptive parents began to talk about a move, Kim was convinced that she would be left behind—the abandonment she feared throughout her childhood was finally becoming, in her mind, a reality.

A parallel concern appears evident in children who may believe that they were inappropriately kidnapped by the adoptive or foster family, by the social workers, or by police. They may see their birth parents as searching frantically to be reunited with the lost child. These fantasies can be reinforced by children's fables such as "Hansel and Gretel" and even by Fievel the Mouse in the movie *An American Tale* (singing "Somewhere, Out There" as he yearns for the birth family to find him).

In both scenarios—fear of abandonment or anger over "kidnapping"— the result is the same. Children who believe that they are not going to remain in the adoptive family will not attach. They worry about the pain of becoming close to a family who will be lost—forever.

FEELING DISCONNECTED

Having little or no information about one's past does create, for many, a deep and pervasive feeling of disconnectedness, of having a piece of themselves missing, of being incomplete. Many adoptees feel an extreme sense of sadness, pain, and confusion. There is a sense of unreality, of not being born properly—not being real or not being a part of society.[2] Another term for this sense of disconnectedness is *genealogical bewilderment*. Providing an adopted child with information about his birth family, the circumstances of the adoption, and any other pertinent information can do much to alleviate this sense of disconnectedness.

"I feel just like a doughnut—someone with a gigantic hole in the center." Many adopted youth can identify with this young man's analogy— his feeling of being incomplete because he has been disconnected from his own history. Another young adopted adult comments, "I have always felt like a victim of amnesia. I can't remember who I am."

LACK OF TRUST IN AUTHORITY FIGURES AND CONTROL ISSUES

Children and teens must feel that issues of importance to them are shared honestly in order to develop a sense of trust within their family. A study conducted in 1983 of adults who were adopted as older children revealed that much of their discontent came as a result of never being consulted about what was happening in their lives, being moved with little or no preparation, and, finally, never being asked about their feelings. All of those in the study felt an incredible lack of control, the consequences of which have followed them into adulthood.[3] One adult adopted person exclaimed that she felt as though her parents were ignoring "an elephant standing in the living room." She knew she was adopted, but the family never discussed the adoption or her birth family.

Children also must know that talking about those issues openly and freely is permitted in their adoptive home. This awareness, along with the opportunity to be a part of the major decisions made for them, will add to their much-needed sense of control. If children and youth believe that they have little or no control over their own life histories, they often try to seize control in the family through negative means: power struggles, lying, chronic behavioral problems, or sending the adoptive family into crisis by running away from home.

Laura, age seventeen, was adopted at age three. Her teenage birth mother had struggled with the decision to make an adoption plan for her child, and Laura remained in foster care until her birth mother felt ready to sign a permanent surrender. Laura knew very little about her birth mother or her struggle with this decision. She was a very angry teen who often lied to others, as she felt deceived herself. Laura felt most in control when she ran away—she knew that her adoptive parents would experience a crisis when she did so, and that gave Laura an incredible sense of power. Laura always ran to areas of town where she imagined her birth mother would be. In essence, Laura was controlling her adoptive family and "searching" for her birth mother at the same time.

FEARS AND UNANSWERED QUESTIONS ABOUT GENETICS AND MEDICAL HISTORY

Having little or no knowledge about one's genetic background and/or medical history can add to the sense of disconnectedness. One adoptee summed up the feeling like this:

Where did I get my red hair? What nationality am I? What kind of body am I growing into? What talents or special skills are in my family line? What hidden illness may show up in my life? All these questions follow me as I move into adulthood, and no one has an answer. I feel like I am walking around with gaps and holes in my life which I cannot fill without answers.

Older adopted children may worry about dating or marrying a sibling or cousin, or may worry about mental or physical illnesses that may develop as they mature.

ANNE'S STORY

Let's look at the history of one young woman, Anne Ginther of Columbus, Ohio. Her history demonstrates the multiple impacts of a "mystery history" on a child as she matures.

In 1972, Norma and Jeff Ginther were a young, white married couple with one birth son, almost age three. They were living in Colorado and had applied to adopt an infant girl of mixed racial heritage. One Monday, the agency called to tell the Ginthers a seven-month-old child was available for adoption. The social worker said that the birth mother was Caucasian, but she was unsure if the birth father was African American, Hispanic, or Native American. The Ginthers were told that they could see the baby on Thursday of that week, and that placement could occur (with no pre-placement visitation) on the same day if they "approved of the baby." If the Ginthers could not see the baby on Thursday, they would have to wait one month for placement while the social worker went on vacation. Today Norma remembers the adoption as a "drive-by placement." At the time, the young couple believed that birth history was unimportant; the child's future would be molded by the adoptive parents, and the impact of her genetic background would be negligible. Over the next twenty years, they learned that they had gravely underestimated the importance of Anne's history. When they tried to get the information years later, they were unable to locate the birth family and received almost no assistance from the placing agency.

Jeff and Norma were told, when they arrived at the agency on that exciting Thursday in 1972, that the baby's mother had been nineteen years old, had graduated from high school, and was originally from Kentucky or Tennessee. She had liked music and art and had been an average student. She came to Denver a short time before becoming pregnant. There were three possible birth fathers: one African American, one Hispanic, and one Native American. The mother tried to parent the baby for six weeks. When she could not manage, she called her family. They would not accept a "mixed" baby. The birth mother returned to her parents' home in another state, but left the baby with a neighbor. The neighbor cared for the baby for approximately two to three weeks but became concerned when she realized she had no authority to get medical care for the baby. When Anne became sick, the neighbor called the child protective services agency for assistance. The baby was placed in an emergency foster home and then, later, in a regular foster home. The mother never returned to Colorado, and a permanent surrender was arranged through interstate authorities. Foster parents, in the 1960s and 1970s, were not allowed to adopt.

After meeting Anne on Thursday morning, the Ginthers returned to the agency in the afternoon to pick her up. One of the social workers accidentally used Anne's whole name at the time of placement. Norma remembered the name and shared it with Anne years later. The adoptive parents were told the adoption story verbally, but they never received written information from the agency.

The adoptive family had so little information to share with Anne that they told her everything they knew about her history while she was still in preschool. By the time Anne was ten years old, her anger was building to unmanageable levels. She often became violent, destroyed things in her room, and suffered uncontrollable crying bouts. Due to Anne's explosive behavior, the adoptive parents took her to a professional counselor when she was ten years old. He advised that Anne needed more information about her history and the reasons surrounding her adoption. Anne told the therapist that she particularly wanted to know "who I look like." The Ginthers, now living in Ohio, wrote to the Colorado agency that arranged the adoption. The agency social workers wrote Anne a nice letter, reinforcing the limited information that had been shared at the time of placement. That letter was very helpful to Anne. She was struggling because she had no pictures of herself prior to her adoption, but the agency was unfortunately unable to help her find pictures of herself as a very young infant. The agency sent a separate letter to the adoptive parents, questioning their motives for wanting additional information, expressing concern (and judgment) that they wanted to "give her back." Nothing could have been farther from the truth.

At about this same time, Anne received a school assignment to draw a family tree. This assignment proved challenging for Anne. She commented that she would "lie" and use the adoptive family for her family tree. Clearly, she needed help in understanding that all family trees hold multiple families. Her most realistic or honest family tree would hold both birth and adoptive families, perhaps depicting the birth family in the roots, and the branches of the adoptive family in the "branches" of the tree.

Also at that time, the movie *Annie* appeared in local theaters. The movie depicted the plight of an orphan who longed for a family. The movie Annie could not consent to her adoption by the benevolent Daddy Warbucks until she was positive that there was no hope of reunification with her birth family. The real Anne became obsessed with this movie and owned four or five videotaped copies. She watched the film so often that she wore out the videotapes.

By the time Anne was eleven or twelve years old, she began tirades that included, "You are *not* my *real* mom!" Her adoptive mother found her sobbing one day, "How could someone who didn't even know me give me away?"

Anne, now twenty-seven years old and the mother of two children, remembers her longing to know more about her history. She always knew that she was adopted, and she feels that her adoptive parents were always very supportive of her need to have more information. However, Anne remembers believing firmly, when she was ten to thirteen years old, that her parents had information that they were concealing from her (lack of trust in authority figures). She was extremely angry about her inability to access this information, and she projected that anger in outbursts directed at her parents.

Anne had many fantasies about her birth parents. She was convinced for some time that they had been rich and famous. When she was particularly angry at her adoptive parents, she would fantasize that her birth parents would send a limousine to pick her up for a joyous reunion (unrealistic fantasies). Another fantasy held for some time was that her adoptive mother had an affair with a man of color, conceived her, and kept the baby. According to this latter fantasy, the adoption itself was a lie because Anne believed she was with her birth mother!

Control battles and power struggles were common during Anne's adolescence. Even though her parents were very sensitive to Anne's need for information, the constant control battles were wearing for everyone in the family (need for control).

One of Anne's most difficult challenges has been identity formation. She is not certain about her ethnicity, and her appearance really does not confirm any ancestry. She knows that she is a multiracial person, but does not know exactly what constitutes "multi." She could be African American, but also appears to have Native American or Hispanic ancestors. During her adolescence, she identified with several different ethnicities, and, as an adult, still has questions about her roots (identity confusion).

Anne shares, however, that her greatest struggles revolve around fears of future abandonment. She commented that she worried incessantly about losing significant people. She tried to push people away from her to avoid the pain of being rejected. In other words, she tried to "quit before she got fired." The adult Anne comments that she worries about losing those who are close to her, and she still overreacts to losses and separations. For example, when in the military, Anne found it too painful and panic-inducing to be far away from her parents. She was married and had a child at the time, but missed her parents so much she received an honorable discharge due to intense anxiety around separation from her parents.

CONCLUSION

When caring parents consider the discomfort of talking about adoption and the very real dangers of not talking about adoption issues, they must conclude that:

1. Parents need to talk openly and honestly with the child in an age-appropriate way about the adoption, the birth family, and the circumstances of the adoption; and

2. Parents need the tools and knowledge to talk about adoption effectively.

QUESTIONS

1. How would a child's "unrealistic fantasies" impact his relationship with his adoptive parents?

2. What are signs that an adolescent may be struggling with identity confusion as it relates to adoption?

3. What are signs that an adolescent may be struggling with loyalty issues as it relates to adoption?

4. What behaviors and feelings might a parent see if a child is struggling with fear of future abandonment?

5. What behaviors and feelings might a parent see if a child is struggling with control issues?

NOTES

1. Joyce Maguire Pavao quoted in Jayne Elizabeth Schooler, *Searching for a Past* (Colorado Springs: Pinon Press, 1995).

2. Jayne Schooler, *The Whole Life Adoption Book* (Colorado Springs: Pinon Press, 1993), 20, 29.

3. John Young Powell, "Adults Who Were Adopted as Older Children." Ph.D. dissertation, University of North Carolina, 1983.

CHAPTER FOUR

A Fact-Finding Mission: How to Gather What You Need to Know

Carlton had just stopped at home for lunch when the phone rang. It was the adoption agency. A birth mother had just made an adoption decision and had chosen them to be the family for her unborn child. Were they interested in discussing the prospective adoptive placement in further detail? Could they come to the agency this evening?

Carlton and LaVonne had waited over five years for this call. For them, life without a child and the intense emotional roller-coaster ride of infertility was almost over. "Yes, of course, we will be there," Carlton responded.

Sandy Ridden hung up the phone. She could hardly dial her husband's office number to tell him the news. The adoption social worker at their public agency had just called asking Sandy and David to come in the next day and discuss the possible adoptive placement of two children, a four-year-old boy and a one-year-old girl. Neither one of them could rest well that evening. The following day they would face a decision that would affect them and two very special youngsters for the rest of their lives.

Each and every day in this country, prospective adoptive parents receive such phone calls. That call creates a myriad of intense emotions—fear, excitement, curiosity, doubt. Questions and concerns engulf their hearts and minds as they begin to process this monumental endeavor. "What will the children look like? What is their history? Why are they available for adoption? Do they have any significant medical concerns? What is in their background that we should know? And, most important, is it appropriate to ask? Do we have a right to know?"

What these families will hear and the openness they will experience regarding their children's social and medical history have been influenced by decades of controversy on the duty to disclose. For over seventy years, the contention over the issue of complete honesty and openness challenged those in the social work profession. In the 1990s, many agencies have attempted to return full circle to complete and honest disclosure, but the road back has not been easy.

A HISTORICAL PERSPECTIVE: HOW WORKERS VIEWED ADOPTION BACKGROUND DISCLOSURE AND THE IMPACT ON FAMILIES TODAY

As the practice of adoption entered the twentieth century, significant issues confronted adoption social workers. One of the most important questions, however, centered on adoption background disclosure. Workers faced an ethically and emotionally inflamed question: How much information should the adoptive family be given about the birth family, the child's history, and potential physical, emotional, or psychological concerns?

The 1920s and 1930s

For workers in the 1920s and 1930s the question of full and accurate background disclosure was not an issue at all. Against the backdrop of extensive openness between birth family and adoptive family, disclosure was an obvious conclusion. Honesty, openness, and accuracy guided communication.

A worker's perspective on disclosure in adoption in the early part of the twentieth century would go something like this:

When children whether infants or older children came into care it was the duty of the agency to do a thorough case study. Families needed this information to make a decision as to whether to receive the child or not. The study required a thorough analysis of the child's family—the physical condition of the parents, their personal habits in regard to intemperance, gambling, begging or other objectionable practices. The agency studied the child itself. They studied the child's heredity to discover, if possible, whether it is likely to be a victim of feeblemindedness, insanity, epilepsy, or syphilis, or tuberculosis. They studied the child's mentality and in some cases additional study was required if the children were found erratic, emotionally upset, or nervously disordered.[1]

Agencies always believed that the adoptive family should have all the information in their possession in order to fully know the child. They felt that the prospective parents should be a[s] fully informed as possible as to the child's history. Not only is this history usually of great assistance ... in the intelligent bring[ing] up of the child, but in after life, when the child realizes that he is adopted, he should be allowed to know the facts concerning his forebears.[2]

In 1932, the Child Welfare League of America (CWLA) issued the following statement on adoption disclosure:

No child that is . . . diseased and no child of feeble-minded parents should be placed in any home for adoption until the adoptive parents know the full facts of the case. Children with special handicaps of a physical nature or related to personality or behavior, and those whose heredity suggests that difficult problems may arise, should be placed for adoption only when the adoptive parents thoroughly understand the child's needs and concerns.[3]

The Fifties Bring Change

By the early 1950s the number of adoptions rose dramatically, fueled by the postwar era—the baby boom. Early in the decade of the fifties confidentiality and, eventually, secrecy filtered into adoption practice. It was assumed that if anonymity of all individuals involved was protected, then the birth mother could more easily resolve her feelings about the placement, the child would be more easily integrated into the family, and the adoptive parents could present their children as being biologically their own.

Along with the evolution of secrecy in adoption practice came the practice of withholding information about a child's social and medical history from adoptive parents. Two issues, according to adoption researchers Freundlich and Peterson, were at the core of these policies. The first concern centered on the need to protect adopted children from the stigma associated with illegitimacy. The second force that drove the movement to withhold information grew out of a need to accommodate what social workers construed as a general reluctance on the part of adoptive families to discuss adoption with their children.[4]

In 1954, one social caseworker wrote in defense of this policy, "Because of the possibility of neurotic character traits in the adoptive parents, they and the child must be protected by keeping from them any knowledge about the child's background." There was a fear that adoptive parents "hostilely envious of those who can bear children would use this negative information as a weapon when angered by this child's misbehavior."[5] Other workers felt that if the parents and child knew anything about the birth parents it would be devastating to the child's self-esteem.[6]

Still more workers labeled prospective adoptive parents who demanded knowledge of the child's past as "very anxious, narcissistic, and unconsciously sadistic." Many adoption workers were convinced that not disclosing information "would ease adoptive parents' discomfort in discussing the issue, would relieve them of the burden of possessing information they were not 'mature' enough to absorb," and would "avoid stigmatizing the adopted child."[7]

For some agencies, nondisclosure of background information became a matter of agency practice. All social information about the birth family was cleared through a few selected adoption agency supervisors. Caseworkers insulated from that information, along with these supervisors, would certify the child's adoptability. The worker would only have to say, "I know this to be a fine baby because my investigating chief and consultants have so agreed and that is fine enough for me."[8]

Some workers adamantly disagreed about adoption disclosure. It was not so much a question of total disclosure or total withholding, but of how much and what type of family information should be disclosed. By the mid-fifties most agencies gave families only selected information and left out sordid or irrelevant details.

In January 1955, during a CWLA National Conference on Adoption, a general consensus grew that "agencies should select pertinent facts helpful to the adoptive parents and child and withhold facts that were prejudicial and stigmatizing." A new adoption standard practice was later issued which read: "Member Agencies of CWLA are instructed not to give adoptive parents information, which is not relevant to the child's development and would only arouse anxiety."[9]

The Seventies and the Eighties

Policies on adoption disclosure began to shift again in the seventies and eighties toward a greater degree of information sharing. This change came about for a number of reasons. First, the majority of the population of children needing adoption shifted from infant to special needs. Second, adoption professionals realized that parents were willing to adopt children with special needs and that the information did not discourage them. Finally, advocacy movements led to greater demands by all members of the triad.[10]

By 1988, the Child Welfare League further elaborated on their standards concerning disclosure of background information. Those standards, currently in effect, require a developmental history and family history, a medical examination, and psychological testing as needed.[11]

What About Today?

In spite of the legal developments that require full and open disclosure to adoptive parents, it still today has not become a uniform mode of practice for all adoption professionals. Some agencies fail to disclose fully to a family because of the fear that the child would be "unadoptable" if all were known. Agencies have failed to disclose because they have not been able to locate information (due to understaffing) or because they did not recognize the need to make the effort to obtain all pertinent information. In the case of international adoption, often the country of origin has not obtained a child's social history or accurately diagnosed a child's medical problems.

What does this mean for adoptive parents? They are unprepared emotionally, psychologically, and financially to care for a child whose history was whitewashed, ignored, or erased.

WHAT IS WRONGFUL ADOPTION?

Wrongful adoption is a term used to describe adoptions in which the adoptive parents were "wronged" in some way. Most often this means that the adoption agency failed to provide them with adequate or truthful information.[12] Omissions in pertinent information include:

- *Child's risk factors*: Potential for medical, developmental, behavioral, or mental health problems or other difficulties based on genetic or environmental risk factors.
- *Child's disabilities*: Existing delays or impairments in relation to physical, developmental, psychological, or psychiatric functioning.
- *Behavioral problems of the child*: Current difficulties or those previously observed.
- *Background of the birth family*: Particularly information concerning genetic risk factors, other risky behavior, or complications of pregnancy or delivery.
- *Medical or other health-related factors*: Current or previous conditions and symptoms; treatment received or anticipated.[13]

In legal terms, wrongful adoption is generally based on allegations of *fraud* or *negligence* in regard to sharing information by the placing agency.[14] Some examples of the types of errors that have been cited in lawsuits are discussed below.[15]

Intentional Nondisclosure/Deliberate Concealment

The social worker withholds *known* information regarding the child or birth family. For instance, adoptive parents are not told that a birth parent has schizophrenia, that the child tested positive at birth for cocaine exposure in utero, or that the child has sexually molested younger children in the past. (In some cases, the information may be revealed, but discounted, such as presenting it as "normal misbehavior" or the result of a biased reporter, such as a foster parent who "didn't like" the child.)

Intentional Misrepresentation

The social worker knowingly gives the family information that is not true, generally for the purpose of presenting the child in a more positive light than is accurate. For instance, the birth parents are described as healthy teens who are unable to care for a child, when in fact the birth mother is a long-term patient in a state psychiatric hospital, and the birth father is unknown.

Negligent Misrepresentation

"[A]n agency volunteers information about a child . . . but the information given is at least partially incorrect. An example is an agency that shares with a family that there is a history of Huntington's disease in a child's family, but relates incorrect information about the possibility that the child will get the disease."[16]

Negligent Nondisclosure

Similar to intentional nondisclosure in outcome, negligent nondisclosure is an act of omission. The agency provides partial information but omits significant portions. In one lawsuit a social worker told prospective adoptive parents that there may have been incest in an infant's background, and asked the family if they were concerned about this.[17] The family said no, apparently believing that the incest did not involve the child in question. The social worker did not specifically tell the family that the child was the product of an incestuous relationship between a brother and sister.

A CASE OF WRONGFUL ADOPTION

In early 1988, Jayne and Frank Gibbons went to Gentle Adoption Options, an adoption agency, expressing an interest in adopting a healthy Caucasian infant. The agency told the couple that there was a two-year waiting list for healthy Caucasian infants and suggested that they consider adopting an older, hard-to-place child. The agency further informed the couple that they would be fully informed of any history of physical or sexual abuse.

On the basis of this information, the Gibbonses submitted a dual application for a healthy Caucasian infant and a hard-to-adopt-due-to-age child. Each time they reviewed photolisting books containing brief descriptions of older children available for adoption, the Gibbonses again specifically noted that they wanted a child who was hard to adopt due to age and did not have a history of physical, sexual, mental, or emotional abuse.

In late August 1989, the agency contacted the couple and informed them that they had been chosen to adopt a five-year-old boy who met their criteria of no history of physical or sexual abuse. The Gibbonses were also told that the child was Caucasian, hyperactive, and behind in his schoolwork, was presently repeating kindergarten, had been in foster care for two years with one family, and had been verbally abused by his mother. The agency noted that the child's major problem was maternal neglect.

The Gibbonses first met the child and his caseworkers in October 1989, at which time Gentle Adoption Options provided information about the child's foster family and reassured them that he had no history of physical or sexual abuse. The Gibbonses also met with a caseworker at Northwood County Children and Youth, the agency that had custody of the child. They asked Northwood for a more detailed social and medical history and were assured that Northwood would give Gentle Adoption Options the requested information.

The child temporarily was placed for adoption with the Gibbonses in November 1989. Shortly thereafter, Gentle Adoption Options forwarded to the Gibbonses the child's birth records and the medical history of his natural mother. At that time the Gibbonses again requested a more detailed social and medical history of the child before completing the adoption.

The Gibbonses at that time specifically asked Gentle Adoption Options whether there was anything in the child's file that had not been disclosed to them. The agency assured the couple that they had been given everything that Northwood had provided them. The agency told the Gibbonses that Northwood had "promised additional information," but that there was a "communication problem" with Northwood. The Gibbonses asked Gentle Adoption Options to review all of the child's complete records to ensure that everything was revealed to them before they finalized the adoption. The agency agreed.

The adoption was finalized on October 21, 1990. Immediately thereafter, the child began having severe emotional difficulties, including violence and aggression toward younger children, an attempt to amputate the arm of a five-year-old, and an attempt to suffocate his younger cousin.

The child was admitted to the Philadelphia Child Guidance Center for evaluation. The Guidance Center advised the adoptive parents that there was little chance of any improvement in the child's violent behavior. The child was declared dependent on September 15, 1991, by the Family Division of the Philadelphia Court of Common Pleas, and the Department of Human Services placed him in their custody.

In September 1991 a caseworker from the Department of Human Services informed the Gibbonses for the first time that the adopted child had been severely abused both physically and sexually as a toddler. Records in the possession of Northwood revealed:

- that the adopted child had been in ten different foster placements before he was freed for adoption;
- that there was a long, serious history of abuse, both physical and sexual, of the adopted child by his biological parents;
- that the adopted child had an extensive history of aggressiveness and hostility toward other children.

Gentle Adoption Options had received this information from Northwood one month before the adoption was finalized and did not disclose it to the Gibbonses, although it was in their possession. The Gibbonses filed action in April 1992 in the Court of Common Pleas of Wilson County, asserting causes of action for wrongful adoption and negligent placement of adoptive child.[18]

How can adoptive parents avoid such an outcome?

SIX PRINCIPLES OF INFORMATION GATHERING

Principle One: Adoptive Parents Should Recognize Their Right to All Social and Medical History Regarding Their Child and The Benefit of Obtaining and Maintaining it.

Adoptive parents, often intimidated by the adoption process because of lack of experience, may be hesitant to ask questions about the child they are considering for adoption. They may feel that their questions are intrusive, unkind, or insensitive to the child. Some feel that the information is not that important because the child will be in a new family with a new start. Some say, "It is best I don't know anything, then I don't have to lie to my child about the truth." However, gathering and maintaining that information is important not only for them, but for the child in the future.

What are the benefits of having a complete and accurate background history?

- It provides an opportunity for early diagnosis, treatment, and intervention for developmental problems and conditions.
- It prevents the need for repetitive testing for the child.
- It provides an opportunity for the adoptee, as a child, and eventually as an adult, to develop an accurate sense of history about himself and a more fully integrated identity.[19]

Principle Two: Adoptive Parents Should Understand How to Read a Waiting Child's Description and Social Summary.

In pursuing an adoptive placement, many families spend time either looking through sources such as CAP (Children Awaiting Parents) photolisting books, their state photolisting books, or on the Internet. In reading a child's description the following information will generally be available to prospective parents:

- Child's first name, date of birth, state and possibly county of residence, an ID number, and the date the listing was added
- A brief social/medical history
- Where the child is currently living (i.e., foster or group home, residential treatment center)
- What type of adoptive family is needed (i.e., single parent, married couple, other children in the home, older or younger children, etc.)
- The agency contact person's name and phone number.[20]

In *Adopting and Advocating for the Special Needs Child*, Anne Babb and Rita Laws note that adoptive parents need to understand how to interpret information given on a photolisting or social summary. Because brevity rules each listing, certain phrases or comments are used as shortcuts. The following is a type of matching quiz for prospective adoptive parents who read the photolisting:

And This Means What? Interpreting the Photolisting[21]

Match the descriptions with the possible translations from the photolisting book.

A. All boy, very active, impulsive, needs lots of attention, acts out. ___

1. Depression, dysthymia

B. Needs structure and supervision; bossy and manipulative; has had several losses and is grieving; has had many moves. _____

2. Failure to thrive

C. Moody or sad. _____

3. Fetal alcohol or drug effect syndrome

D. Victim of neglect. _____

4. Attention deficit hyperactivity disorder (ADHD)

E. Delayed speech; is immature. ___

5. Emotional or behavioral problems; reactive attachment disorder, conduct disorder

F. Developmentally delayed. _____   6. Malnourishment, attachment
                                                  disorder

G. Toileting accidents, still being   7. Emotional problems,
    toilet trained. _____   developmental delays

H. Drug or alcohol exposure in the   8. Mild to moderate mental
    womb. _____   retardation

I. Trouble gaining weight. _____   9. Enuresis or encopresis, emotional
                                                    problems

Answers: A–4; B–5; C–1; D–6; E–7; F–8; G–9; H–3; I–2.

As parents read these shortcuts, it then becomes imperative to explore the meaning behind the words with caseworkers and professionals.

Principle Three: Adoptive Parents Should Prepare a List of Questions for the Information Sharing Meetings with their Child's Caseworker and Other Persons Involved in the Child's Life.

During the decision-making time prior to an adoption, families will have the opportunity to talk with their child's caseworker. In cases of older special needs adoption, parents should also ask for the opportunity to talk with other professionals who have been involved with the child, including former foster parents, therapists, child care providers, and schoolteachers. The following are "starter" lists (special needs and/or infant adoption) parents can use when asking questions about their child:

Special Needs Adoptions

1. How complete is the social/medical history on the birth family, including the extended family? What is missing? Is it possible to obtain more information?
2. Is there a history of drug or alcohol abuse?
3. Is there any history of mental illness?
4. Is there any history of other genetically related illnesses such as diabetes, heart disease, etc.?
5. What is known about this child's prenatal care and birth history?
6. What is known about this child's developmental history—physically, emotionally, cognitively, including language development?
7. What is the child's current health? Allergies? ADHD related problems?
8. Why was the child removed from his or her biological family? Physical abuse? If so, what kind, how often, and from whom? Sexual abuse? If so, what kind, how often, from whom?

9. What does he/she understand about the reasons for removal?

10. When was the last contact the child had with the biological family?

11. Are there any brothers and sisters? If so, what contact has this child had with these siblings? Is it expected that these contacts will continue, and to what degree? Who is responsible for seeing that it happens?

12. In what ways is the child manifesting behaviors related to his or her abuse, separation, or other trauma? Are other children "victimized" by the behavior? In what way?

13. How has this child functioned in foster care? How many moves has this child experienced in foster care, and why was he/she moved?

14. What methods of discipline does this child respond to most often?

15. How does this child relate to his/her peers in the neighborhood and school?

16. What level of openness, if any, is possible with birth family members?

17. What special skills/abilities/talents/interests did birth family members have?

Infant Adoption

1. How complete is the social/medical history on the birth family, including the extended family? What is missing? Is it possible to obtain more information?

2. What is known about the birth parents' developmental history—physically, emotionally, cognitively, including language development?

3. Is there a history of drug or alcohol abuse?

4. Is there any history of mental illness? Is there any history of other genetically related illnesses such as diabetes, heart disease, etc.?

5. What is known about this child's prenatal care and birth history?

6. Are there any brothers and sisters? If so, what contact, if any, is planned with these siblings? How often and to what degree will these contacts be expected to continue? Who is responsible for seeing that it happens?

7. What special skills/abilities/talents/interests did birth family members have?

> **Principle Four: Adoptive Parents Must Realize that Even When the Best Effort is Made to Gather Information, There are Limits on the Extent to Which Health and Other Background Information May Be Obtained.[22]**

Adoptive parents must realize that generally the sole source of information for domestic infant adoptions is the birth family. In many cases, this information may only come from the birth mother. Information may be incomplete or inaccurate (intentionally or unintentionally).

In international adoptions, generally the only source of information is the agency in the country of origin. Their capability to get full and complete background information from the birth family is very limited due to the circumstances of the relinquishment. Many times, children are left at orphanage doorsteps with no way to trace the birth family. Other times, children are brought to an orphanage for "temporary" care and the family disappears. Agency staff is then left with the task of putting together information from almost nothing.

When children move into adoption from the domestic foster care system, health and other background information may or may not be more readily available. Again, the primary source for that information is the birth family, and complete and accurate information may not be obtainable. A second hurdle in gathering information about a foster child is that often collection, maintenance, and communication are handled by various units of a public service agency before the information reaches the adoption worker. Improving the flow of information is a task that many agencies are tackling with determination.

Principle Five: Adoptive Parents Must Realize that they Also Have a Responsibility in Regard to Background Disclosure.

One of the responsibilities that adoptive parents must assume is the awareness and understanding that there are risks involved in adoption, just as in parenting a child born to them. Prospective adoptive parents should understand that by pursuing adoption, they will be assuming responsibilities for which there are no guarantees of specific results or outcomes. It is not possible, according to Freundlich and Peterson, to be given an assurance "that all existing information has been discovered nor is it possible to predict the future health status of a child."[23]

Principle Six: Adoptive Parents Should Pursue Diagnosis and Prognosis of a Mental or Medical Health Concern from Professionals in the Area in Question.

In an attempt to fully disclose information to adoptive parents, adoption professionals may say that they have a suspicion about a particular problem, or they may attempt to interpret information given on the social/ medical history form. To avoid misinformation and errors, prospective adoptive parents should consult with professionals in the appropriate field (medical, mental health, education, etc.) for help in understanding the facts and reports the adoption worker shares with them.

What If You Don't Know the Facts?

Many adoptive parents find that they have only skeletal information about their child's history. Because the agency may have terminated a formal relationship with the adoptive family at the time of finalization, the parents believe that what they see is what they get—and all they will ever get. However, attitudes and laws about the importance of full disclosure to adoptive families have changed dramatically over the last ten to fifteen years in the world of adoption practice.

Adoptive parents should not hesitate to recontact the agent of the adoption to request a meeting regarding the child's history. The child, depending on the age and circumstance, might be included in this meeting or invited to a future meeting with agency staff. The agency should share all nonidentifying information about the child's history.

Identifying information that cannot be shared generally includes the following:

• Name of the birth family
• Address of the birth family
• Social Security numbers of birth family members
• Birth dates of family members
• School information about birth family members
• Places of employment of birth family members

All other information (medical, social, ethnic, religious, psychological information/history) must be shared with the adoptive family. Many families who return to their placing agencies after eight to ten years find that workers disclose much more information than was the practice at the time of the adoption.

However, in some situations it is difficult or impossible for parents to obtain additional information from the placing agent. Sometimes agencies do not have the desired information. Families can ask the placing agency to recontact persons in the birth family who might be willing to share information to help the child better understand why the separation from the birth family occurred. If the birth parents are not accessible or cooperative, perhaps grandparents or other relatives can be contacted.

The agency can serve as an intermediary in gathering information if the adoptive family is uncomfortable with opening the adoption, or if a relationship between the child and birth family relatives is not in the best interests of the child. At times, extended birth family relatives are willing to share mementos or pictures with the child as well as significant information that they were not willing to impart at the time of the adoption.

Occasionally, agencies place children who were abandoned, and there is no access to information about the birth family. These situations are especially problematic for the adoptive family and for the child. A child who has been abandoned may believe, at least during adolescence, that the adoptive family has a complete history of the birth family and is withholding that information. If the child was in fact abandoned, the adoptive family should go with the child to the agency to hear that information from the social workers or attorneys who facilitated the adoption. Ways to share information about abandonment will be explored in a later chapter.

At times, families who have adopted internationally have very little information about the birth family, or they may be told that the child was abandoned. Those families adopting Korean children should be aware that "abandonment" is the way children are freed for adoption in that country. Birth mothers who wish to make an adoption plan for their child may leave the child at a police box and hide until they are sure that an appropriate authority has taken charge of the child's welfare. It is critical that international adoptive parents research and understand the social situation in the country at the time of the adoptive placement.

Some families have adopted privately through a physician or an attorney who may have retired or moved out of the area. Adoptive families can petition the probate or family courts that finalized their adoptions to determine whether the files can be opened for purposes of sharing more complete information.

SUMMARY

Gathering background information is an important task for foster and adoptive parents. It is crucial that they understand the importance of having the information. It is their right and that of their child to full and complete disclosure.

QUESTIONS

1. What barriers have you encountered in obtaining social/medical information from your child's agency?
2. What type of information do you feel is most valuable to you in making a decision to adopt a specific child?
3. What information is missing from your child's history? Why is it missing?
4. If you have missing information about your child, what are your options in obtaining that information?
5. What do you see as your responsibility regarding responding to background information?

NOTES

1. William H. Singerland, *Child-Placing in Families: A Manual for Students and Social Workers* (New York: Russell Sage Foundation, 1919).

2. Walter Carp, *Family Matters: Secrecy and Disclosure in the History of Adoption* (Cambridge, Mass.: Harvard University Press, 1998), 217–39.

3. Child Welfare League of America, *Standards of Adoption Practice* (Washington, D.C.: Child Welfare League of America, 1932).

4. Madelyn Freundlich and Lisa Peterson, *Wrongful Adoption: Law, Policy and Practice* (Washington, D.C.: Child Welfare League of America and The Evan B. Donaldson Adoption Institute, 1998), 2.

5. B. Kohstaat and A. M. Johnson, "Some Suggestions for Practice in Infant Adoptions," *Social Casework* 35 (1954): 91–99.

6. Carp as quoted in Freundlich and Peterson, 3.

7. Ibid.

8. Ibid.

9. Child Welfare League of America, *Standards of Adoption Practice* (Washington, D.C.: Child Welfare League of America, 1959).

10. Freundlich and Peterson, 4.

11. Ibid.

12. Anne Babb and Rita Laws, *Adopting and Advocating for the Special Needs Child* (Westport, Conn.: Bergin and Garvey, 1997), 34.

13. Jayne Schooler, Betsy Keefer, and Maureen Hefferan, *Gathering and Documenting Background Information: Preventing Wrongful Adoption* (Adoption assessor training curriculum) (Columbus, Ohio: Institute for Human Services and Ohio Child Welfare Training Program, 1999).

14. Freundlich and Peterson, 12.

15. G. Hochman and A. Huston, *Providing Background Information to Adoptive Parents* (Washington, D.C.: National Adoption Information Clearinghouse, 1994; updated 1998).

16. Ibid. (1994 ed.).

17. Freundlich and Peterson, 16.

18. Names of participants, agencies, and locations have been changed. Schooler, Keefer, and Hefferan. This case scenario was adapted from an actual legal case—*Baker, Robert, American Bar Association* (Fall Edition, 1995).

19. Freundlich and Peterson, 59–73.

20. Babb and Laws.

21. Adapted from Babb and Laws.

22. Freundlich and Peterson, 70.

23. Ibid.

CHAPTER FIVE

Adoption Through a Child's Eyes: Developmental Stages

As adopted children grow up, their understanding of adoption dynamics also matures. An incredible sense of loss and rejection may begin to shadow some adopted children during late childhood. This sense of loss and rejection can steal the excitement and joys of the teen years. This chapter explores the developmental stages children and teens experience and their perceptions of the adoption experience. When adoptive parents understand the sensitive nature of adoption through their child's eyes, they'll be better prepared to communicate effectively during each stage.

INFANCY—BIRTH TO AGE THREE

Child's Developmental Characteristics and Tasks Impacted by Adoption

According to Eric Erikson, the most significant developmental task of the infant and toddler is to develop trust. Attachment is built over time but begins optimally during infancy when consistent caregivers predictably meet the child's needs. After thousands of repetitions, the child learns that his needs will be met, and he becomes attached to those caregivers reliably meeting his needs.

Acquisition of language also occurs during infancy and toddlerhood. The child's understood language is far greater than the language he is able to articulate. How does this impact the adopted child?

Children under three years of age need to learn appropriate language related to adoption issues so that they may begin, as they mature, to understand the concepts underlying the words. Children need to begin using phrases like "birth mother," for example, instead of "real mother" because the connotations of words chosen are so important to the understanding of children as they mature.

Child's Perception of Adoption

Adoption is a very abstract concept. The idea involves a basic understanding of human sexuality, and such understanding is not found among infants and toddlers. Further, the notion of "letting go" of a beloved person or thing is much too sophisticated for a very young child. While children at this age are too young to understand the concepts of adoption, parents can begin foundational work to assist children in developing positive attitudes about adoption, their birth parents, and themselves during these early years.

Some parents may have adopted an infant or toddler who has experienced traumatic, abrupt losses, or a child who has experienced serious abuse or neglect. Instead of learning that the world is a safe, predictable place, these children have learned that they cannot rely on their caregivers to meet their needs.

While the children cannot verbalize their panic and distress, they communicate these feelings through behaviors. Clinging, night terrors, and other problematic behaviors signal that their comprehension of the parent/child relationship has been impaired. Infants and toddlers who have experienced institutionalization, maltreatment, or abrupt separations must essentially be "re-parented" until they can unlearn that the world is unreliable and dangerous. Such lessons are not easily or quickly taught, and adoptive parents may find that extreme patience and many years are required to assure these children that they will be safe, protected, and secure in their new homes.

Behaviors Related to Adoption During This Stage

A child who has experienced maltreatment or abrupt separations may cling to parents, cry inconsolably during brief separations, experience night terrors, or turn to self-nurturing or self-protection through obsession with food, rocking by oneself, or emotional withdrawal and isolation.

Strategies for Adoptive Parents

Talk about adoption comfortably from the time the child enters your home. If parents adopt a child who is preverbal (an infant or a child who does not yet speak English), they have a wonderful opportunity to practice talking about adoption and the birth family, building their skills and comfort level before the child is able to understand.

Children who are adopted during infancy should grow up knowing that they are adopted in the same way they grow up knowing that they are male or female. Parents who wait for the "right" moment often find reasons why they should postpone telling their child about adoption. Parents who talk comfortably about adoption from the time the child arrives ("Here are pictures of the day we brought you home from the agency [hospital; airport]. We were so excited when we adopted you!"). Adopted children at this developmental stage first understand in a limited way that they gained a family through adoption.

When talking about adoption with very young children, model correct adoption language. Parents should not tell children they were "given up" or "given away," as young children will almost certainly develop anxiety that this type of abandonment will recur. Birth parents should certainly not be called "real parents" or "natural parents"; after all, adoptive parents are not unreal or unnatural! More information about correct terminology to use when talking about adoption or the birth family will follow in Chapter Seven.

Gather as much information as possible about the child's history while the trail is still fresh. Adoptive parents should use these early years to gather as much information as possible about the child's history. Remember that the child may have important questions during early adolescence, but birth parents may, by that time, have different names, may have moved out of state, or may be involved in new relationships that do not allow for ongoing contact with the adoptive family or agency. The placing social worker may have retired or moved on to other employment. When the child has questions or asks for mementos or pictures from the birth family years after the adoptive placement, it can be difficult to meet those needs. Parents should *anticipate* the child's needs for information and concrete mementos from his history, and use early years of the child's life to gather the information as completely as possible.

PRESCHOOL—AGE THREE TO AGE SEVEN

Child's Developmental Characteristics and Tasks Impacted by Adoption

Preschool-age children are only capable of concrete thinking. Preschool children love to hear their "adoption story" and often ask to have it repeated as a favorite bedtime story. By the age of three or four, many adopted children can repeat the story verbatim as it was told to them.

Children between the ages of three and seven are developing independence from primary caregivers. They are moving out into the world, interacting with others as they participate in play dates with other children and go to preschool and on to elementary school. Most children spend several hours a day away from their families as they reach the end of this developmental period.

Young children are extremely self-absorbed and see themselves and their families as the center of the universe. They believe they have somehow caused everything that happens in their lives. For example, if a young child pulls the dog's tail, and the dog becomes sick the following day, the child may assume that he caused the dog to become sick by pulling his tail. The phenomenon of imagining one's behavior to cause unrelated events is known as magical thinking. The self-centered preschooler believes he magically causes all things that happen to him.

Child's Perception of Adoption

While children between three and seven have acquired language to talk about adoption, they are repeating words they really do not understand. For example, the concepts of growing "inside the birth mother's tummy" and living with another family are very abstract, and essentially unintelligible to the young child. Children under the age of seven rarely have the cognitive ability to understand the concepts behind the words in their adoption story. While they can parrot the words, the lightbulb of understanding has not yet clicked on.

Adopted children at this stage may have fears of separation from the adoptive family. Separation from parents can be extremely threatening to children who have already lost parents. The first day of school is a challenge for most children, but such "emancipation" from the family can inspire full-blown panic in a child who has already experienced permanent parental loss.

Children under the age of seven, as magical thinkers, often believe that they caused their birth parents to "abandon" them. Young children may believe they cried too much, were the "wrong" gender, were too ugly, or in some other way so offended their birth parents that these people left their lives permanently. In other words, children assume responsibility for the adult decisions and behaviors that led to adoption.

Behaviors Related to Adoption During This Stage

Adopted children ask a lot of questions about "being in Mommy's tummy" and about birth parents as they develop language and a limited understanding about their histories. They love to hear their adoption story and may repeat it to anyone who will listen. Children at this stage are quite ingenuous about sharing their histories, and they may tell playmates in the neighborhood or at school about their adoption. Children at this stage often play out their story with dolls or stuffed animals and may develop some highly creative ideas about how babies are made and how families are formed!

Children struggling with independence from the family may develop school phobias. They may become anxious when parents become sick or are away from home on business. As they become older, children may worry more and more about how the first family was lost, and wonder if this kind of loss will recur. If, as magical thinkers, they have assumed guilt for the original adoption because of an imagined flaw in themselves, they will wonder when the adoptive parents will discover this flaw and abandon them in the same way the birth parents did. Young children fearing such a calamity may struggle to be "perfect" in an attempt to keep the adoptive parents from discovering their faults. The adopted child at this developmental stage begins to understand in a limited way that he not only gained a family through adoption, but lost one in the process. Questions can begin in earnest toward the end of this stage.

Strategies for Adoptive Parents

Encourage questions and answer concretely and simply. Children under the age of seven will not have sufficient cognitive ability, knowledge of human sexuality, or understanding of adult problems such as drug addiction, poverty, or war to understand their entire story. Parents, better than anyone else, know the child's limited ability to understand the concepts being presented. Parents should answer the child's questions in an honest but simplistic way.

Listen for cues about misperceptions when the child is playing or talking with peers. Parents or older siblings may hear a young child playing out his adoption story, expressing beliefs that are quite inaccurate. When these situations occur, "replay" the scenario in an accurate way.

Ron, a six-year-old boy adopted from Korea, was playing at home with his best friend. His twelve-year-old brother heard Ron explain his history this way to his friend: "I was born to my parents and went to live with another woman in Korea for a year. Now I am back with my *real* parents." It was important to Ron to be with *real* parents, to be where he "should" be. He understood that another woman was involved in his history, but he misunderstood her role. Ron's older brother made a brief correction for Ron in front of his friend and shared the incident with the parents so that the story could be reexplained to Ron in private. It was important to Ron to hear about *real* parents, to understand that both his birth parents and his adoptive parents are real—that they have played different roles in his life. It was especially important for him to understand that he is, in fact, where he *should* be.

Don't assume that telling the adoption story every once in a while is adequate. The adoption story is often a favorite bedtime story, but parents should not assume that they can stop talking about adoption when the child seems to know the story. Remember that the child's perceptions about the circumstances of the adoption, the birth parents, and even himself will change as he matures and becomes more sophisticated in his thinking.

Tell the adoption story positively but realistically. Birth parents should not be painted in a totally positive or totally negative light. Both positive and negative aspects of the birth parents' situation are important in helping the child understand why a separation from the birth parents was necessary. In telling the adoption story, parents must be careful about using glowingly positive scenarios. If the explanation is "Your birth parents loved you so much, they placed you for adoption," the child may wonder if the adoptive parents will do the same! Further, many adult adopted persons have expressed their discomfort with the "chosen child" story: "We picked you to be our child—other parents had to settle for whatever they got." Adult adoptees have told us that they felt enormous pressure to be worthy of being chosen. They also worried that they might be "unchosen" if they did not measure up.

Reassure the children that they will not lose the adoptive family. A terrifying fear of young children, underlying most school phobias and night terrors, is separation from parents and family. This fear is graphically portrayed in many children's movies *(Bambi; An American Tale; Annie)* and stories ("Hansel and Gretel"). For adopted children, this common childhood fear has become a reality—they have been separated from at least one family. They must be reassured that their position in the adoptive family is permanent.

SCHOOL-AGE—AGE EIGHT TO AGE TWELVE

Child's Developmental Characteristics and Tasks Impacted by Adoption

By the time children reach the age of eight, their ability to think in abstract terms increases dramatically. At this point, children comprehend the meaning behind the words in their adoption story.

Children in the "middle childhood" years are striving to be successful and industrious in school, in sports, and with same-sex peers. It is important to preadolescents to be capable and to be similar to their friends.

Child's Perception of Adoption

Because children understand the concept of adoption for the first time around the age of seven or eight, they realize at that time that a significant loss has occurred in their lives. If they were adopted as infants, the children are now mature enough to understand the significance of this loss. Children have lost connections and a relationship with the birth family, knowledge of their own history and roots, and perhaps cultural understanding and continuity. Even if adoptions are open, children have still lost the lives they would have lived with their birth families. Because they become aware at this age of the significance of these losses, a grieving process begins, even though several years may have already lapsed since the separation.

Children at this age are very concerned about fairness. The game-playing of school-age children quickly displays their preoccupation with rules and fairness. Many children of this age worry about the fairness of adoption. They wonder if they are with the "right" family and fantasize about lives that might be spent with the birth family or with another adoptive family. Children at this stage may also worry that they are not being fair to the adoptive family if they have feelings or questions about the birth family. For this reason, they may be reluctant to ask questions about the adoption or about the birth family, particularly if they sense discomfort on the part of their parents.

Behaviors Related to Adoption During This Stage

The first stage of the grieving process, according to Elisabeth Kübler-Ross, is denial. Adopted children may stop asking questions about their birth parents or the adoption as part of this initial stage of grieving. A common behavior among eight- and nine-year-old adopted children is an insistence they were not adopted, even when the adoption may be a transracial placement.

Adopted children in preadolescence will probably stop asking about the adoption story. They may refuse to talk about adoption as a form of denial, or they may be concerned about showing disloyalty to the adoptive family, thereby violating the "rules" of adoptive family life. Even though children in this stage may not be talking about adoption, they are most likely thinking about it. The eight- to twelve-year-old begins to consider that he not only gained a family through adoption and lost one in the process, but was actually given away. He may wonder, but never discuss a potentially damaging thought. "People don't give away valuables; I must not be worth much."

Strategies for Adoptive Parents

When children are not talking about adoption, don't assume they aren't thinking about it. Adoptive parents sometimes interpret children's reluctance to discuss adoption as an indication that they know their story and no longer need to talk about it. There may even be some relief for the adoptive parents in the child's silence on this sensitive topic.

While the child should not be forced to discuss adoption-related issues, he should be aware that parents are open and comfortable with the subject when he is ready. Parents can periodically remark about the child's skills, looks, or interests, indicating that some of these positive attributes might have come from his birth family ("You have such beautiful eyelashes/great musical ability. I wonder if anyone in your birth family has eyelashes/talent in music like yours. Do you ever wonder about that?").

Learn to be alert for anniversary reactions. As with other grief reactions, the child may begin to experience anniversary reactions at the time of his birthday or his adoption. Instead of allowing the child to suffer in silence with these feelings, parents should anticipate the child's feeling and help him express it ("I always think about your birth mother when it's time for your birthday. Do you think about her too? Do you have any questions about her that I could answer?"). Because the child will rarely bring up the subject of adoption, parents should look for opportunities to let children know they are not threatened or angry about questions regarding birth family and history.

Let children know they can love two sets of parents. Because children at this stage are concerned about fairness and loyalty, they are likely to believe that they are disloyal to the adoptive family if they have feelings, or even questions, about the birth family. Children need to know it is expected that they can love both sets of parents. They do not have to choose. Explaining to the child that adults are allowed to love more than one child in a family can alleviate some of that struggle. When additional children join a family, parents do not have to stop loving the children who were already there in order to start loving the children who have just arrived. In the same way, children are able to love more than one set of parents. They do not have to stop having feelings about the birth family when they become part of the adoptive family.

Parents may have appropriately withheld some of the more troubling details of the child's history while the child was too young to comprehend the information. However, as the child approaches adolescence, adoptive parents must provide the details to help children make sense of their own histories. Because adolescents often do not believe what they are told by adults (especially by their parents), adoptive parents should try to share whatever information they have *before the child enters adolescence*. If more information is needed, parents should recontact the placing agent, and take the child to that agency to learn all of the non-identifying information in the case record. Parents should take the child with them to hear the information firsthand so that they are not later accused of distorting or withholding information. While some adoptive parents are tempted to omit information until the child reaches adulthood, they find, often too late, that the child *must* learn about his history in order to successfully navigate through the identity formation tasks of adolescence. These tasks cannot be accomplished in a vacuum. Strategies for disclosing especially troubling information will be shared in Chapter Seven.

EARLY ADOLESCENCE—AGE TWELVE TO AGE FIFTEEN

Child's Developmental Characteristics and Tasks Impacted by Adoption

The early adolescent is working on two important developmental tasks: identity formation and separation/individuation. Both tasks are challenging for all young people, and both are impacted by adoption.

Identity formation begins as a youth examines his own roots, questions his beginnings, and begins to experiment with identities different than those of his parents. We are often perplexed or amused, depending on our perspective, by young people who look very different from the larger culture—youth with long hair, no hair, purple spiked hair, and so on. The adopted youth may seek to try on identities different from those of his parents by emulating the identities of his birth parents. If his information about birth parents is limited, he may try on identities he *imagines* to be like those of his birth parents. He may seem to reject the values, customs, religion, and appearance of his adoptive family and adopt those codes of conduct or values he believes are held by his birth family.

All young people, some more forcefully than others, demand independence. Remember that the adopted youth has already lost at least one family. He may be particularly threatened by the need to assert his independence, or individuation. Paradoxically, adopted youth who are nervous about separation from the adoptive family may actually go overboard during early adolescence, angrily asserting their independence and ranting about wishing they had never been adopted—"You can't tell *me* what to do! You're *not* my *real* mother!!"

The adopted youth continues to work on resolution of his grief, begun with the realization of his loss during an earlier developmental stage. The second stage of grieving is anger. The adopted youth enters this stage of grieving at the same time he is rejecting the family's identity and support. While adolescence can be an angry period for all young people, it is even more exaggerated for the adopted person. Many parents find that the anger begins to build when the child is twelve years old (even earlier for some girls) and peaks when the child reaches thirteen or fourteen.

Child's Perception of Adoption

The early adolescent, capable now of sophisticated, abstract thought, is confused about the reasons the birth parents have abandoned him. The teen's understanding of adoption progresses at this age. The adopted teen has moved from gaining a family to losing a family, to being given away, to arrive at the conclusion: "I was rejected."

The teen may be angry about a lack of control in his adoption, and he may look for someone to blame for earlier separations and the lack of information about his history. Often, the adoptive parents are selected to be the scapegoats for the child's rage and confusion. If the history has not been discussed since the child was a preschooler, as happens in too many adoptive families, the child may have used fantasy to create a web of new information, implicating the adoptive parents as kidnappers responsible for the separation. The adopted youth may firmly believe that the adoptive parents know full information about the child's history but, in collaboration with social workers, have chosen to withhold the information or even actively lie about it.

Behaviors Related to Adoption During This Stage

The early adolescent is an angry, confused young person who often resists authority and seems to constantly seek control. He may seek control through lying, even telling lies that seem to give him no advantage. He may seek control over the family by creating chaos, a family crisis precipitated by his own angry outbursts.

An adopted youth struggling to separate and individuate will engage in "distancing behavior," behavior that pushes others away from him. Assertions that he hates the adoptive family and that they are not really his parents are excellent examples of distancing behavior.

Adopted youth may try on multiple identities, seeming to be a different person every few weeks. Their identity may fluctuate with their current fantasy of the birth family. Some adopted youth may seek to be like the birth family in some way, getting tattoos, dying their hair, or adopting a tough exterior.

Strategies for Adoptive Parents

This angry stage can be a real challenge for adoptive parents. Several strategies will enable parents to emerge successfully from a difficult three-year period.

Allow the child to exercise control whenever possible. Allowing the child to exercise control whenever possible and providing opportunities for the young person to make decisions permit some sense of control for young people. It may be necessary for parents to lose a few battles during this stage in order to win the war. For example, parents should examine, when engaged in a power struggle with their teen, if the issue at hand is really dangerous to the child or to others. Hair or clothing styles, for example, do not pose a threat to anyone. The child should be allowed freedom to make decisions that do not threaten him or others.

Try to keep from responding to the child's anger with more anger. If parents can understand that much of their child's anger is generated by his "rejection" by the birth parent, and not aimed at them, they might not over-respond to angry outbursts. When an angry teen asserts that he wants to leave the family, try to hear this as a question instead of a statement. He is not saying, "I am leaving!" He is asking, "Will you keep me, no matter what? Will you abandon me too?"

Be firm in limit-setting. Sometimes adoptive parents do not feel really entitled to be the parent of their child, and they treat their child as though he belongs to the neighbor. Remember that you are the only parent he has, and you must take responsibility for being very firm about limits that protect his safety. A good rule of thumb is to have only a few rules, but enforce those completely. Decide what is most important, and stick to it.

Establish consequences for broken rules prior to misbehavior. Parents should not try to respond to misbehavior by developing a consequence after the problem, when they are angry. Reasonable, logical consequences can only be developed by parents in reasonable, logical frames of mind. Once logical consequences have been established, parents should not make excuses for the child or "bend" on consequences when the child tests their authority. Teens learn from mistakes by experiencing consequences, positive and negative, for their behavior.

Keep your sense of humor. Remember that adolescence is chronic, but not terminal. Adoptive parents should network with other parents of teens, particularly *adoptive* parents of teens, so that they can share successes and learn from each other's experiences.

LATE ADOLESCENCE—AGE SIXTEEN TO AGE NINETEEN

Child's Developmental Characteristics and Tasks Impacted by Adoption

Late adolescents are preparing to leave the family. They will soon emancipate or live independently. Emancipation, like many life transitions, involves loss: loss of dependency and childhood, loss of life with the family, loss of the familiar and safe. Again, while emancipation presents a stressful challenge to most young adults, the losses associated with independence are even more threatening to the adopted young person.

Many adolescents begin to have their first experiences with romantic intimacy between the ages of sixteen and nineteen. While younger adolescents may have a "steady," relationships during early adolescence tend to be superficial and fleeting. The older adolescent is ready for a relationship with more depth and commitment. Older teens, threatened by the loss of intimacy they experience when emancipating from their family, often turn to a romantic involvement as a replacement for that lost intimacy. Romantic relationships during late adolescence, especially for youth needing assurance that they are lovable, can become extremely intense.

Many young people between the ages of sixteen and nineteen have their first experiences with sexuality. Adolescents are often faced with value conflicts related to religious, family, and cultural beliefs about morality as they approach their first sexual encounters. Adopted youth who perceive their birth parents as sexually irresponsible or promiscuous will have even greater challenges as they become involved in romantic relationships.

Child's Perception of Adoption

Again, adopted youth may be anxious about growing up and leaving home. Losing the adoptive family may be a reenactment of their earlier "abandonment" by the birth family. While connections to family remain after emancipation, the adopted youth probably experienced a permanent termination of his relationship to the birth family when the adoption occurred. In other words, the last time he lost a family, it was forever.

As adopted youth approach legal adulthood, they may have conflicts about beginning a search. They may fear a "second" rejection by the birth family, and they may worry that the adoptive family will see their interest in their birth family as disloyal or hurtful. Some adopted youth may feel pressure from peers, the media, or family to search (or not to search). Some adoptive parents, in an attempt to be helpful, may even initiate a search for the birth family. A search for birth family members needs to be in the control of the adopted person. If a reunion is thrust upon him before he is ready for this relationship, irrevocable damage can be done. It is critical that adoptive parents understand that adopted persons have already experienced tremendous loss of control in the original termination of parental rights. They need to maintain control over a reestablishment of a connection to the birth family. Only they can know if, and when, they are ready for such a relationship.

Adopted youth may be fearful of intimacy or may feel unlovable. This fear of close personal relationships may be expressed either through avoidance or through over-involvement in romantic relationships and sexuality before the individual is really mature enough to handle the consequences of that decision. If the youth is very enmeshed in a romantic entanglement that ends abruptly, as many adolescent relationships do, this may feel very much like another abandonment, leaving the teen devastated, and confirming his belief that he is unworthy of love.

As the youth continues the work of resolving his grief related to loss of his family, he enters the depression stage of grieving. Adoptive parents may experience tremendous relief, as their child is no longer so angry. However, parents should be alert for signs of serious depression, particularly around times of loss (graduation from high school, moving to college or the armed forces, breakups of significant relationships, loss of grandparents). The depressed youth will withdraw into his own world, and knowledgeable parents should be available for support and guidance as the older teen progresses toward resolution of his grief.

Behaviors Related to Adoption During This Stage

An older teen afraid of independence from the family may fail in school to delay emancipation. While this type of academic "backsliding" is not uncommon for high school seniors, it can be more serious for a young person who unconsciously tries to sabotage his own successful independence.

Separating from the adoptive family may be so threatening to the adopted youth that he "replaces" parents with intense romantic entanglements. When these relationships fail, the adopted teen is shattered. The older teen may overreact to such losses and strive irrationally to remain in relationships that are unhealthy or unproductive.

Older teens may be troubled and withdrawn as they consider their transition to adulthood. "Should I search for my birth family? Will they want to see me? How will my adoptive parents feel? Will they understand? Why can't my friends understand my need to know?"

Strategies for Adoptive Parents

Make it clear that the child may remain at home for a time following graduation. He may live at home and work, go to a commuter college, or board at a college near enough to allow for frequent visitation and parental support. The adopted youth must feel in control of the timing of his departure from the nest.

Be alert for overreactions when relationships with peers fail. Without hovering, parents of the older adolescent should be observant of the youth's struggle for independence, and they should be available for support and reassurance when needed.

OTHER TRIGGER TIMES FOR ADOPTION ISSUES

There are other predictable times, not related to child development, when adoption issues can become more difficult for children. Adoptive parents should be aware of their child's development and be alert as well to these potential triggers of emotional pain, grief, divided loyalties, or anxiety.

The Child's Birthday

The child's birthday may be the time of separation from the birth family, if the birth parent's parental rights were terminated shortly after birth. Even those children who experienced separation at much older ages, however, will wonder if their birth parents even remember the child's birthday. Sadness and anger, both part of a grief reaction, can begin building a month or so before the birthday and continue for a week or two following the birthday. Adoptive parents should be alert to see if this common pattern of triggered grief occurs annually. If so, direct communication about feelings of loss, powerlessness, and fear of being forgotten can ameliorate the child's grief.

Mother's Day

Mother's Day can be a time of divided loyalties for many adopted or foster children. Because Mother's Day occurs during the school year, many younger children make lacy, flowery cards for their mothers at school. An adopted or foster child may feel disloyal because nothing is made for the birth mother. It is not uncommon for adopted and foster children to have a stronger tie to the birth mother and little or no connection to, or memory of, the birth father. For these reasons, early May can be an extremely difficult time for adoptive and foster families. Recognition of the child's divided loyalties and acceptance of the child's feelings for the birth mother can be tremendously helpful. Some adoptive parents have encouraged children to make Mother's Day cards for their birth mothers to be kept in a special scrapbook. These can be saved and later given to the birth mother if a reunion occurs at some point in the child's future. Merely making such cards for the birth mother seems to help many adopted children express feelings and cope more effectively with this difficult time.

Placement or Separation Anniversaries

Obviously, we all experience grief reactions at the time of anniversaries of losses. We feel sadness, for example, on the anniversary of a miscarriage or the death of a parent. Adopted children experience many of these same anniversary reactions. It can be extremely helpful for adoptive parents to chart a Life Map (see Chapter Nine) for their children. They may be surprised to note that many children experienced moods at the same time of the year—in the fall, or at holiday time. During these seasons, parents will need to be especially alert and supportive to assist children in coping with grief.

Holidays

When anyone has experienced the loss of a significant person, holidays can become sad, difficult times when the loved one is particularly missed. Those children who remember holidays with birth or foster families may find it especially difficult to cope with the intense family atmosphere of the holidays. Adoptive parents should keep the intensity of holiday visits with extended family to a manageable level (easier said than done!) and try to keep their own expectations for close holiday memories manageable as well.

Any Experience of Loss (School Transitions; Loss of a Pet, Grandparent, Best Friend, etc.)

Any loss can trigger the grief experience. People who have suffered the loss of one significant person understand that they regrieve that loss when a second or third loss occurs. Many adopted children overreact to seemingly small losses. They are reexperiencing the pain of the initial separation (abandonment) from the birth family.

Perceived Loss of the Adoptive Parents Through Illness, Death, Divorce

Obviously, children who have lost parents will have anxiety about a recurrence of that traumatic experience. Because children so often believe that they caused the original loss of the birth family to occur, they believe that they are vulnerable to another such loss, loss of the adoptive family, simply because of their own unworthiness to have a family. If adoptive parents become ill, particularly if hospitalization is necessary, adopted or foster children might experience unmanageable panic. If loss of an adoptive parent actually occurs, through death or divorce, adopted children will likely have an even more severe reaction, with more self-blame, more anxiety, more anger than their nonadopted counterparts. Even when the "loss" of the parent is temporary and seems inconsequential to the adoptive parents (examples: parent out of town on business; child's first day of school; child goes to sleepover camp; parents leave for a getaway weekend without the children), adopted children and teens may respond with behavior that represents an extreme fear of abandonment. The intensity of this fear results from earlier separation experiences.

Moving

Moving the family is another form of loss, one that is particularly significant to a child who has lost family or families forever through moves. Many young children believe that they will be left behind when the family moves, and even teenagers can have an irrational fear of being abandoned at the time of a move. Allowing children to have as much control as possible during a move (selecting new bedroom colors, for example) can reduce the sense of powerlessness and fear they experience during moves.

Problematic or Insensitive School Assignments

Children often experience confusion or anger over school assignments related to family or adoption issues (see Chapter Fifteen). Many adoptive parents have "war" stories to tell about problematic assignments involving family trees, genetics studies, and so on that have created thorny problems for their children. Adoptive parents should be alert to assignments or experiences that can trigger pain for their children. Adoptive parents can give their children support or assistance to help them cope with both the assignment and the resulting feelings.

Films or Television Programs That Depict Adoption Insensitively

Sometimes children or teens watch a film or television show that triggers feelings of discomfort with adoption or issues related to the birth family (or birth country). When these programs engender emotional upheaval in children, adoptive parents may find an excellent opportunity to directly address the child's perceptions and engage the child in a dialogue about feelings. When programs or films are extremely negative, parents can talk with children about the mistaken ideas that some uninformed people have about adoption. The child may be helped to write a letter to the television station or theater to set the record straight.

Emancipation from the Adoptive Family

Most teenagers find emancipation from the family to be a challenging task. The adopted teen has already lost at least one family, perhaps forever. The prospect of separating from the adoptive family can be particularly challenging. Support and sensitivity from the adoptive parents, as well as "gentle" emancipation (not sending the child to the other side of the continent for college), can be helpful.

CONCLUSION

While adoption does not really change the way individuals experience normal human development, the typical developmental tasks are impacted by the fact of adoption. Adoptive parents will recognize the difficulty of differentiating which behaviors are related to normal child development and which are caused by adoption-related issues. Certainly, most toddlers are demanding and strive for control, and many adolescents experiment with different identities. However, when children have also experienced adoption and/or maltreatment, their journey through some of these developmental tasks becomes even more difficult. While their history does not *change* typical tasks, the behaviors associated with those tasks may become more extreme in nature. Many adoptive parents ask, "How do I know what is 'adoption' and what is 'normal development' "? The most accurate response is, "If your hair is turning gray, it's normal development. If it's falling out in clumps, it's adoption."

QUESTIONS

1. What is a child's perception of adoption at ages 3–7?
2. What is a child's perception of adoption at ages 8–12?
3. What is a child's perception of adoption at ages 13–15?
4. What is a child's perception of adoption at ages 16–19?
5. What is your child's age? What parenting strategies can you use in developing your child's understanding of adoption?

CHAPTER SIX

Through a Parent's Eyes: Core Issues, Coping Styles, and Communication

Mark is seventeen now. He used to ask a lot of questions about his birth family. I just told him that we are his family now and that is all that matters. He just doesn't bring it up anymore. I am glad he doesn't.

Kelly came into my room the other night and asked me why her birth mother got rid of her. We have always talked to her about adoption and the fact that she is our chosen child and that we really love her. I just always thought that would be enough for a ten-year-old.

Robert, who is fourteen now, has always had a lot of questions about his birth mother. We were given detailed information about her and have always answered his questions completely. I generally asked him about what he was feeling when he asked questions. He has always known that talking about adoption in this house is always welcomed.

Talking with children and teens about adoption and answering their questions doesn't appear on the surface to be a difficult problem for the family. Just answer their questions, one might be advised. However, for some adoptive parents, it is not that simple. Why?

CORE ISSUES FOR ADOPTIVE PARENTS

Much work and research have been done on the core issues of adoption as they relate to adopted persons. However, adoptees are not the only members of the adoption triad that confront concerns related to their adoption experiences. Adoptive parents do as well. How parents process these questions in their lives will have much to do with how they handle adoption as a family system and how they communicate about adoption to their child. Three important issues for adoptive parents are loss, shame, and rejection.

LOSS

> We became parents at thirty-eight years of age. Micah came home when he was three days old. We were ecstatic! However, we suddenly began to realize we didn't have a peer group as parents. The children of all our friends were teenagers. Who wanted to run around with a couple with a fussy infant? (Mark and Sheila, adoptive parents)

Adoption is the only relationship in life that creates loss for each person in the relationship. "Without loss, there would be no adoption. Loss is the hub of the wheel."[1] For many adoptive parents the initial issue of loss is created by infertility. Most young people think and dream of the day when they will become parents, never giving a thought to the possibility it may not occur. Parents entering adoption through this loss forfeit the dream of a biological child and the family as planned. Other losses occur as well, such as

• the loss of status as a biological parent
• the loss of providing grandparents with a biological child
• the loss of a biological connection to the future
• the loss of a parent peer group due to the age of the child

When parents adopt older children, loss is also a subtle part of the relationship for them as well. When parents adopt an older child, they lose the early years of development. They can't answer questions like "How much hair did I have when I was born? or "When did I walk?" or "What was my first word?" They have also lost the ability to protect their child from the early pain of abuse and neglect.

Understanding the dynamics loss can play in the parent-child relationship in adoption is an important task throughout the years. Consequences can occur when loss is not processed well. Robert Anderson, in

Second Choices, comments about loss. "Life consists of a series of losses, which by themselves do not cause psychopathology. One does better to confront a loss directly; ignoring it or wrapping it with platitudes may obviate the need for grief over a short term, but invites a problem with self-esteem over the long term."[2]

If adoptive parents fail to resolve loss in a healthy manner, it could have a domino effect on how they deal with adoption issues and their child. Failure to resolve loss could have the following effects:

- It could impair parents' ability to recognize pain associated with adoption issues and offer support through that pain.
- It could force parents into self-protection that will inhibit them from forming strong emotional attachments with the child.
- It could cause adoptive parents to project past fears and beliefs into present moments and relationships.

Unresolved loss can extend to every aspect of our lives: physical, emotional, relational, and spiritual.

Shame is another issue that impacts adoptive parents.

SHAME

> For years I struggled with the issue of infertility. My friends were having their second and third children, and I was left with empty arms. I began to believe that something was terribly wrong with me. I couldn't decide if it was because I just didn't deserve a child or it was something that I did to create this painful problem in our lives. (Terry and Teresa, adoptive parents)

"It is a very heavy feeling, this pervasive sense of shame. It is the ongoing premise that one is fundamentally bad, inadequate, defective, unworthy or not fully valid as a human being"[3] according to author Merle Fossum. The feeling of shame is not about what we did or did not do. It is about our very selves. It is about who we are. Shame tells us we are unworthy, horribly unworthy. "Shame is without parallel—a sickness of the soul."[4]

For some parents who embark on the journey into adoption because of infertility, the sense of shame is a dark shadow over their lives. Shame steals joy from their lives and their marriage. They ask, "What is so bad about us that we have been robbed of parenthood?" says Fossum. Loss and shame can impact adoptive parents as they communicate about adoption with their youngster.

REJECTION

Rejection is a third issue that can impact healthy adoptive family communication. Rejection is most often thought about when discussing emotional difficulties faced by adopted children and adults and is not often considered as an issue faced by adoptive parents. Nevertheless, rejection, often in a subtle form, can significantly impact the lives of adoptive parents. It has to do with validation of the parent-child relationship.

When family and friends fail to validate the role of the adoptive parent as the true parent, it feels like rejection. When family and friends fail to validate the child as a "true" member of the family, it feels like rejection to parents. A personal encounter by H. David Kirk, the father of three adopted children, and his family many years ago paints a clear picture of such a rejecting experience:

On my return from a Chicago conference, I found that our landlady wanted our little cottage for her own use. It was time to search for a house of our own. We settled on the plan for a tract house that was to be built by late summer, but by the end of August only the foundation was visible. Within a week we would have no roof over our heads, an emergency that called for fast action. Both mine and my wife's family lived in California, but only my in-laws had room to spare. So a year after arriving in Montreal, my family took off without me. I stayed behind to get on with my university studies and to try to speed up the builder. . . .

Weeks later everyone was anxious to end the enforced separation. Our house would soon be livable, and we made plans for Ruth and the children to return to Montreal. Just before they left, Ruth asked her mother about the crib, the old family heirloom, in which Debbie had slept while at the maternal grandparents' house. "Could we have the crib for Debbie at our new house?" After a moment's hesitation her mother said: "I'm afraid not." [It had been promised to their first grandchild, soon to be born to Ruth's younger sister.][5]

Tim and Traci Miller, adoptive parents of Justin, experienced a similar experience of rejection and lack of validation. Justin was adopted as a five-month-old from Guatemala. Three birth children later joined him. Traci shares the experience:

I was shopping at a grocery story near our home. Justin, who was three and one-half at the time, was standing up in the cart along with two-year-old Jeb and one-year-old Allison. The three children are quite a contrast as Justin is dark complected, the other two extremely fair. A woman came up to me and asked about the children.

"Are these your children?" she asked.

"Yes," I replied.

"I can tell that these two are your own, but where did you get him?" she said pointing at Justin.

I was dumbfounded by such a comment, and quickly said, "South America," and continued to move down the aisle. I desperately hoped that Justin had not overheard the conversation.

This type of subtle rejection and invalidation cuts to the heart of adoptive parents and children as well. Dee Paddock says of this experience, "People often ask adoptive parents, in front of their children, 'do you have any children of your own?' Over and over, our children breathe into their souls this toxic cultural dismissal of who they are in relation to us!"[6]

Issues of loss, rejection, and shame do influence how parents develop coping styles to deal with adoption issues. What are those styles of coping?

WHAT DO WE DO WITH THE ISSUES OF ADOPTION?

Is adoptive parenting just like raising a child born into the family? Yes, almost. Of course the day-to-day needs of any child—whether born into a family or entering the family through adoption—are the same. Each child needs the same care and nurturing to ensure healthy physical and emotional growth. It is almost the same. The differences that make adoptive parenting unique stem from the family's need to recognize the adoption-related issues and struggles. Families develop unhealthy or healthy coping styles to deal with those differences created by traditional or closed adoption.

REJECTION OF DIFFERENCES

With an impending move out of state, fourteen-year-old Judy was given the task of cleaning out and packing the contents of the family attic. On that cold, rainy February afternoon, Judy set about the task with less than minimal enthusiasm. She came across an unfamiliar box filled with all sorts of documents and memorabilia. What she found there set her adrift on a course of uncharted emotions and events:

Before I taped the box, I decided to just go through it for fun. I found a large envelope that read "Court papers." My first thought was that one of my parents had been in trouble and never told us. When I opened the envelope a certificate of adoption fell out. It was a court paper finalizing the adoption of Judith Marie Walker. Adoption! I couldn't believe what I read. I didn't even know what to think or what to do. I put that paper back in the box and finished my job.

I was very teary for the next week. My mother kept saying, "Judy, I know you are sad about our moving, but you will be fine." I finally couldn't hold it in any longer and started shouting at her. "You don't understand. I am not sad about leaving."

I began to tell her what I had found in the attic. The only thing she could say was "At least now you know the truth. We never wanted you to know."

"Why didn't you tell me?" I pleaded.

Mother quietly told me, "We thought of ourselves as your family, your only family. I planned never to let you know." Later that afternoon, she told me more of the family secrets—my older sister Katherine was adopted, one of my cousins was also, and they didn't know either. Everything in my world changed for me that day.

At the time of Judy's adoption and in the ensuing years, her parents faced a critical decision encountered by all adoptive families. They must ask and answer key questions." As we raise this adopted child, will we be truthful and open regarding the adoption, or will we pretend it never happened and that this child is ours by birth? Will we deal with this adoption by rejecting the differences adoption creates in our family?"

Sociologist and adoption expert H. David Kirk says that "some couples in reacting to their role handicap of adoptive parenthood (due to infertility) try to take the 'sting' out of adoption by simulating non-adoptive families as closely as possible."[7] In relating to their child, parents send the message loud and clear to forget about being adopted and everything that goes with it. Kirk calls this style of managing adoption communication *rejection of differences*.

Such a view only breeds negative consequences in the future for the adopted child and family. Kirk suggests that this rejection of differences pattern potentially blocks "the development of an accepting and trusting family atmosphere—an atmosphere conducive to open, honest exploration of adoption related issues."[8]

As an adult, Betsy recalls with incredible pain how her family dealt with the issue of adoption as she was growing up. A lack of communication left an aching emptiness in her life.

My parents lost their only birth child in a car accident when she was only five years old. Two years after her death, they adopted me as a newborn. I can remember only one conversation about adoption when I started school. If I ever brought it up as I was growing up, my mother would get terribly upset. She would say to me, "We just don't talk about those things, you are our little girl, now."

As I reached my teen years, I had many, many unanswered questions. But for everyone in my world, the adoption never happened.

David Brodzinsky, in exploring the pattern of denial or rejection of differences, comments:

It [is] simply not dealing [with] the issues that the child deals with.

- The child says, "I feel bad because my parents didn't want me."
- The parents say, "Don't think about that now, we love you."

It becomes a series of behaviors that create an atmosphere in which discussions about adoption just don't happen. Parents ignore the issues. When there is an opportunity to talk about it, they choose not to. They sidestep the issues and discourage the child from ever bringing it up.[9]

Why do parents adopt this approach? Brodzinsky feels that there are several underlying reasons.

- It is an attempt on the parents' part to minimize their sense of pain around loss

(or)

- It is an attempt to protect the child from feeling the pain of loss and rejection

(or)

- It is an attempt on the part of the parents to protect themselves from potential loss—not the physical loss of the child, but the loss of the child's love, trust and commitment to them.[10]

ACCEPTANCE OF DIFFERENCE

Acknowledging differences is in direct contrast to rejecting differences within adoption and creating a closed communication system in the family. Adoptive parents realize the importance of talking openly and freely about adoption. Children learn early that "in this house, it is okay to ask questions." Children learn that it is okay to explore their issues and feelings, not going through life as if those concerns didn't exist.

For one teen, Anna, growing up in a family that acknowledged the differences created by adoption meant developing a healthy identity and self-esteem.

I always knew I was adopted. My parents shared my adoption story with me from a very young age. One special thing that my adoptive parents asked for from the adoption agency was to get a picture of my birth mother and a letter from her. I will never forget the day that my mom took me to lunch and gave them to me. I was probably about eight. What she did for me on that day over nine years ago opened doors for me in terms of finding out what I needed to know about my birth family, my background and myself. As I continue to occasionally deal with adoption stuff, I walk through those doors she opened for me that afternoon.

What does the acknowledging style within a family do for the parent-child relationship?

• It creates an atmosphere of empathy and sensitivity in which feelings, thoughts, and struggles can not only be expressed, but recognized as valid.
• It builds a firm foundation of trust between parents and child.
• It fills in information gaps from the child's past.
• It corrects fears and fantasies that a child may have developed.
• It provides a firm footing for the development of identity.

One particular concern of adoptive parents who understand the importance of open communication about adoption is that they may be talking about it too much. Is it possible to approach this need somewhere in the middle between the rejection of difference style and acknowledgment of differences? David Brodzinsky suggests how: "Parents have to create a balance between talking about adoption and living daily life. One way to do this is to ask oneself, 'When was the last time we talked about adoption in this house?' If one doesn't remember, there is probably a need to address it in some way.[11]

INSISTENCE UPON DIFFERENCE

The "insistence upon difference style"—one that places the adopted child outside the emotional security of the family, is a management technique found in families in crisis. This pattern often leads family members to view adoption as the foundational reason for family chaos and disconnectedness. It also absolves everyone—except the adopted child—of responsibility for the problems.

A number of years ago, an angry adoptive parent contacted the adoption worker in her agency to bring her up to date on the family. Nancy, mother of Cassandra, age sixteen and adopted at birth, and Katherine, age fifteen, their birth child, was enraged.
    "Cassandra told us last week that she is pregnant. I told her that if she wanted to keep the baby, she would have to find another place to live. If she would place the baby for adoption, she could come back home. How could she have done this to us? Even Katherine, our own daughter, would have never done this to us!"

Families can move into an insistence upon differences style without real awareness. It is a subtle slide into family disharmony and blame.

Jonathan joined his adoptive family when he was a year old. He had been in two foster placements prior to coming to his family. In the early years, Jonathan experienced a warm, nurturing family environment. However, by the time he was eleven, Jonathan and his parents began to experience difficulties. Jonathan started getting in trouble at school, on the school bus, on the playground—just about anywhere he went he encountered problems.

At home, his parents argued a lot and occasionally his father didn't come home at night. Jonathan became the target for his family's problems. He no longer lived up to his parents' dream of a child, and they began to talk in terms of "this adopted child" when referring to him to other family members or friends. Jonathan and his adoptive status became the center of family discussion. The "adopted child" caused these family problems. Although the family never legally dissolved the adoption, Jonathan was seen as the problem, and his parents emotionally dissolved ties to him.

Families do not usually begin using the insistence upon differences style until conflict and crisis erupt. According to Brodzinksy, it is generally found in families of teenagers where there has been a long history of parent-child conflict. Parents begin subtly to move from seeing the problems as issues of normal family growth and development to viewing all family problems through the lens of adoption. That is when they step right into the pattern of insistence upon differences. Adoption then becomes the rationalization for explaining problems, and it becomes the only one.[12]

STEPS OF ADOPTIVE EMOTIONAL (OR LEGAL) DISSOLUTION

Researchers in the field of adoption have identified several steps in escalation that are commonly experienced by families in prolonged crisis with their adopted child.[13] Understanding these family dynamics can alert parents to early warning signs within their own relationships. Once those signs are recognized, the family can seek services and support to stabilize the relationship.

Step One: Honeymoon

Adoptive families typically experience pleasure and excitement at the onset of the adoption journey. Each member enters the relationship with high hopes and high expectations. This phase may last several months or, in some cases, many years if no major crisis has affected the family.

Step Two: Diminishing Pleasures

The atmosphere in the home begins to change. Adoptive parents begin to feel tensions in their interactions with the child. What used to be cute is now irritating and frustrating. The family remains hopeful that "this is just a phase." Often at this stage, adoptive parents do not share their concerns with anyone, thinking this will soon pass.

Child is the Problem

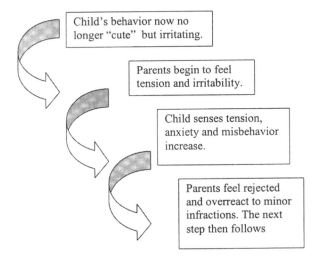

Child's behavior now no longer "cute" but irritating.

Parents begin to feel tension and irritability.

Child senses tension, anxiety and misbehavior increase.

Parents feel rejected and overreact to minor infractions. The next step then follows

Step Three: Child Is the Problem

The relationship with the child continues to deteriorate. Every negative thing the child does or says—from tantrums to misbehavior—becomes intolerable. The interactions continue to spiral downward. The child senses the tensions, which increases his anxiety, which increases his negative behavior. The parents perceive this as rejection of them by the child and overreact to even minor problems.

Step Four: Going Public

The problems within the family soon begin to impact the family's public life. The child's negative behaviors are no longer confined to the home, but are witnessed by family, friends, school, and so on. Frustration and embarrassment often lead the family to turn to others for sympathy with a long list of the child's problems. Supportive people offer advice which may line up with the family's view that the child is the problem, subconsciously feeding the family's need to distance themselves from the child.

Step Five: The Turning Point

The family continues to crumble. The child is involved in a "critical incident"—stealing, sexually acting out, truancy—which the parents have long expected. What happens in the heart of adoptive parents is that the child has "crossed the line," and there is no hope for a healthy relationship. The family usually continues to live together, but with impenetrable walls of hurt, anger, and rejection blocking future happiness. No one has any emotional energy to restore healthy family life. In most adoptive families the insistence upon differences style that controls the home does not lead to a formal dissolution of the legal relationship. It often, however, leads to unrelenting conflict and a barrier to any real relationships and intimacy. However, in some cases, an adoption dissolution is inevitable.

Step Six: The Deadline or Ultimatum

For some cases, the problems in the family culminate in a crisis. The adoptive parents establish a deadline by which the child must leave unless the problems are resolved or behavior drastically improves. Often, these demands are out of the range of what is reasonable—such as demanding that clothing never be left on the floor or that the child never become angry anymore or misbehave in any way.

Step Seven: The Final Crisis Ends the Adoptive Relationship

Jessica sat in the lobby of the girls' group home waiting for her caseworker. She was coming there to live. She had been adopted as a three-year-old, but now was back in foster care. "My parents told me if I came in late one more time, I would have to leave. I was late last night and here I sit today." In good times, Jessica remembers, "my parents introduced me as their daughter. When we had a problem or fight, I became their adopted daughter."

The day comes when whatever demand is made upon the child fails to be met. The final crisis erupts within the family. Even a minor incident can become the last straw. The family makes the decision to have the child permanently removed from the home, often demanding that the removal occur immediately. What is left is considerable pain on the part of everyone affected by the dissolution—an angry, confused, rejected child and angry, guilty, and grieving parents.

If the adoptive family recognize themselves on the downward spiraling steps toward adoption dissolution, it is imperative that they contact their adoption agency or support group for intervention and support. The following self-assessment is also a helpful guide to examining the adoptive family relationship and can aid adoptive parents in assessing their own style of coping with the differences that adoption creates.[14]

Since your child's legal adoption, how frequently have you:	**Never**	**Infrequently**	**Sometimes**	**Often**
1. Wondered whether the birth mother/father thinks about the child?				
2. Recalled that at one time the child legally belonged to someone else?				
3. Remembered the child's original name (either first or both)?				
4. Wondered whether your child's birth parent worries about the child he/she relinquished?				
5. Talked with someone about your child's birth parents?				
6. Wondered what your words about adoption mean to the child?				
7. Tried to imagine how your child feels about being adopted?				
8. Thought that your child might someday be curious about his/her background?				
9. Wished that you might understand adoption from the point of view of the child?				
10. Talked about adoption with your child?				
11. Celebrated the adoption day anniversary?				
12. Personally been asked by your child the reasons for his/her adoption?				
13. Answered your child's questions about his/her birth parents' history as honestly and completely as possible?				
14. Found yourself referring to your child as "your adopted child" to family and friends?				
15. Found yourself dreaming about how much easier parenting would be if you had a birth child instead of an adopted child?				

Since your child's legal adoption, how frequently have you:	Never	Infrequently	Sometimes	Often
16. Found yourself saying that this "adopted" child is the source of all family problems?				
17. Asked yourself if there is any way to end the relationship with the child?				

What Your Scores Indicate: Never = 1; Infrequently = 2; Sometimes = 3; Often = 4

Questions 1–5 deal with acknowledgment of differences. A low score means a coping style or a tendency to deny differences. A high score means a tendency to acknowledge differences. Low 5 ←——————→ High 20

Questions 6–10 deal with levels of empathy toward the child. A low score means a tendency to have little empathy toward the child. A high score means high levels of empathy toward the child. Low 5 ←——————→ High 20

Questions 11–13 deal with levels of communication. A low score means a tendency to communicate little about adoption. A high score indicates a high level of adoption communication. Low 3 ←——————→ High 12

Questions 14–17 deal with insistence upon differences. A low score means a tendency not to insist upon differences when the child is in crisis. A high score means a tendency to insist on differences. Low 4 ←——————→ High 16

CREATING THE ENVIRONMENT OF COMMUNICATION: HOW WE SAY WHAT WE SAY

Twelve-year-old Rachel sat staring out the family room window. Squirming around as if needing to say something, she finally blurted it out. "You guys, even if I did know my birth parents' name and where they live, I don't want to see them. I know they must be very happy without me."

Susan and Ken, caught completely off guard by this unexpected outburst, sat a moment without a response. Ken finally said, "Of course, Rachel, that is totally your call. You don't have to see them, but someday in the future, you might choose to do so." Ken used a rational response in addressing Rachel's dilemma.

Children learn very early in their adoptive life if it is safe for them to bring up the topic of adoption. The goal for adoptive parents is to establish conversation around adoption that is healthy, balanced, and meaningful for the child. In her insightful book, *Communicating with the Adopted Child*, Miriam Komar examines five types of responses that parents can use in discussing adoption issues with their child:[15]

- *Authoritarian* is a one-sided response. It is a style, according to Komar, that is designed not to teach or respond, but to silence.
- *Chosen Baby* is a reply that "emphasizes the notion that the adopted child is specially loved because he or she has been specially chosen by the parents. The intention is to support the child's sense of self esteem."[16]
- *Glorifying* is a response that is intended to glorify the birth parents and their background for the sake of the child.
- *Rational* is a reply based on fact. It is an explanation that seeks to give the adoptee a clear view of the realities of his life, a true sense of the other people in his past and their attitudes, and a view of his history.
- *Reflecting* is a response to the child that "mirrors the child's feelings contained in the questioning."[17] When a child asks an adoption-related question, most often there are feelings contained in the inquiry.

Revisiting Rachel's story gives a clear illustration of Komar's types of responses. Her parents could respond to Rachel's statement—"You guys, even if I did know my birth parents' name and where they live, I don't want to see them. I know they must be very happy without me"—in the following ways:

Authoritarian Response: "Don't worry about those things, Rachel. We are your parents now. If you just forget about it you will be better off."

Ramification of Answer: A child gets the message, "I don't dare bring up adoption around here."

Chosen Baby Response: "You know, Rachel, how much we love you. Just think about how beautiful this family is and all the love you have from your grandparents and us."

Ramification of Answer: A child's questions and feelings are never addressed. A youngster grows up feeling obligated to be the "grateful" adoptee and never ask the hard questions. Adult adoptees who grew up with the "chosen baby" explanation given to them in good faith by their adoptive parents have told us that they felt the burden of being worthy enough to meet the parents' expectations.

Glorifying Response: "We are very certain that everything is just fine with your birth parents now. I am sure that they know you are loved."

Ramification of Answer: It fails to give the child the true picture of reality and creates confusion and mistrust.

Rational Response: "Of course, Rachel, that is totally your call. You don't have to see them, but someday in the future, you might choose to do so."

Ramification of Answer: Answers the child's questions and validates his/her need to know about the past.

Reflecting Response: "Rachel, we know that sometimes children worry about their birth parents and have feelings and questions about them. I want you to know that it is okay to think about them and ask questions about them."

Ramification of Answer: Recognizes that along with needing facts, a child has varying degrees of feelings toward the adoption experience—feelings that it is safe
for the child to relate.

SUMMARY

Adoptive parents do have unique challenges before them to understand the subtle issues in adoption that impact them and their children.
Parents demonstrate growing understanding of those issues as they
adapt coping styles in talking with their children about adoption. It is
also critical for parents to be aware of what their own feelings and concerns as it correlates with their relationship with their child.

QUESTIONS

1. How has your life been impacted by the three core issues—loss, shame, rejection—discussed in this chapter?

2. What style of coping with adoption issues best describes you—denial, acknowledgment, insistence? Why?

3. How would you describe your most often used response in answering your
child's questions around adoption—authoritarian, chosen baby, glorifying, rational, reflecting?

4. Describe what dynamics might be found in an adoptive family who is in *"the
child is the problem,"* stage of emotional/legal dissolution.

5. Describe what dynamics might be found in an adoptive family who is in *"the
turning point"* stage of emotional/legal dissolution.

NOTES

1. Sharon Kaplan Roszia and Deborah Silverstein "The Seven Core Issues of
Adoption," workshop presented at the American Adoption Congress, April 1988.

2. Robert Anderson, *Second Choices: Growing Up Adopted* (Chesterfield, Mo.:
Badger Press, 1993).

3. Merle Fossum quoted in Lewis B. Smede, *Shame and Grace: Healing the
Shame We Don't Deserve* (San Francisco: Harper and Row, 1993), 4.

4. Gershen Kaufman, quoted in ibid, 7.

5. H. D. Kirk, *Looking Back, Looking Forward: An Adoptive Father's Sociological
Testament* (Indianapolis: Perspectives Press, 1995), 11–12.

6. D. Paddock, *Affirmations for Conscious Living as Adoptive Families.* (Highlands Ranch, Colo.: Families with a Difference, 1998), Web site: www.
adopting.org.

7. Quoted in David Brodzinsky and Marshall Schechter, *The Psychology of
Adoption* (New York: Oxford University Press, 1990), 19.

8. Ibid.

9. Brodzinsky quoted in Jayne Schooler *The Whole Life Adoption Book* (Colorado Springs: Pinon Press, 1993), 118.

10. Ibid.

11. Ibid.

12. Ibid.

13. S. Partridge, H. Hornby, and T. McDonald, *Learning from Adoption Disruption: Insights for Practice* (Portland: University of Southern Maine, 1986); Dr. Denise Goodman, "Here Today, Gone Tomorrow: An Investigation of the Factors that Impact Adoption Disruption," *Dissertation Abstracts International* 54, 4259A (University Microfilms No 94–11 949). The steps toward adoption dissolution were adapted with permission from Judith Rycus and Ronald Hughes, *Field Guide to Child Welfare, Vol. IV:-Post Placement Services to Adoptive Parents* (Washington, D.C.: CWLA Press; Columbus, Ohio: Institute for Human Services, 1998).

14. The assessment questionnaire is adapted from the work of Dr. H. David Kirk and Dr. Hal Grotevant. Available from On Demand Service, Authors Guild, New York, NY 10036.

15. Miriam Komar, *Communicating with the Adopted Child* (New York: Walker Publishing, 1991), 253–67.

16. Ibid.

17. Ibid.

CHAPTER SEVEN

The Ten Commandments of Telling: Principles to Consider

"Do I really have to tell the whole truth?" "How old should my child be when I do?" These are questions frequently asked by adoptive parents. This chapter will respond to those questions and share other "commandments of telling" that will aid parents in this vital task. While few rules are really written in stone, some principles, applied consistently, will enhance communication about adoption. These principles can also provide some welcome direction to adoptive parents besieged with well-intentioned advice from family and friends who really do not understand the complexities of adoptive parenting.

THE TEN COMMANDMENTS OF TELLING

1. Initiate Conversation About Adoption.

Parents often handle discussions about adoption in the same way they handle conversations about sex. They believe they should wait until the child asks questions and answer only the questions asked by the child. This strategy is not helpful in assuring that children understand their histories.

Children often believe that they are being disloyal to the adoptive family when they have feelings and questions about the birth family. As a result, they may avoid conversation about the adoption and the birth family even when they have burdensome questions or troubling feelings. Adoptive parents must look for opportunities to raise the issue for adoption, and *ask* the child for questions. In this way, the adoptive parents assure the child that his or her feelings are normal and expected, and that they, as parents, do not feel threatened or believe that the child is disloyal.

Elise had been adopted as an infant. Her parents had talked with her when she was three and four years old about her history, but they had not mentioned the adoption or her birth family since that time. Now, at age thirteen, Elise was dating a twenty-six-year-old man who was an alcoholic and physically abusive. She had a "gothic" appearance, wearing black leather, very heavy make-up, and a punk hair style. Elise was completely out of the control of her parents and was dangerously close to losing control of her own self. When her parents contacted a post adoption therapist, the counselor asked how they talked about Elise's adoption issues. The parents responded that they never discussed adoption within their family because Elise never raised the topic. They assumed her silence on the subject meant that she did not have any concerns or questions about her adoption. The therapist soon discovered, in talking with Elise, that she was consumed with fantasies, identity conflicts and confusion, and serious trust issues. Yet she did not feel comfortable in discussing her adoption because she feared her parents would be hurt if they knew she wondered about her birth family. Her struggle was displayed in behaviors and appearances because she felt blocked in addressing her questions directly and honestly.

There are a number of ways that parents can introduce the topic of adoption within the household and nurture the child's self-esteem at the same time:

1. When a program or movie with an adoption theme is on television or at the theater, watch the program or film with the child. Draw parallels and contrasts between the situation in the program and the child's own adoption. Use this conversation as a springboard to elicit additional questions.

2. Parents can also use key times of the year (often birthdays, Mother's Day, holidays, anniversaries of the placement) to discuss adoption issues. Example: "I always think about your birth mother on Mother's Day. I'm sure she is thinking about you today too. Would you like to make a card for her and keep it in a special scrapbook?"

3. Adoptive parents can comment on the child's positive characteristics and wonder aloud from whom the child inherited them. Examples: "You have such beautiful long eyelashes. I wonder who in your birth family has eyelashes like yours. Do you ever wonder that?" "You are so good at drawing (music, soccer, math)! Do you wonder if anyone in your birth family is as talented as you are?"

4. Finally, adoptive parents can comment on the child's accomplishments, including the birth parents in their own feelings of pride. Example: "What a great job! Your birth parents would be as proud of you today as we are!"

2. Use Positive Adoption Language.

When parents talk with their children, friends, and extended family members, they must model positive adoption terminology. Careless use of language may inadvertently connote negative ideas about the birth parents, the child's history, or adoption itself.

Here are some excellent examples of both positive and negative adoption terminology:[1]

Positive	Negative
Birth parents	Real parents
	Natural parents
Made an adoption plan	Gave up for adoption
	Put up for adoption
My child	Adopted child (when overused, it can become a label)
Birth child	Their own child
	Their real children
To choose parenting	Keeping
Waiting child	Hard-to-place child
Child with special needs	
Adopted person	Adoptee
Adopted adult or person	Adopted child (when speaking of an adult)

3. Never Lie to a Child About the Past or a Birth Family Member.

Lying about a child's birth parents or history generates serious trust fissures. When the truth is revealed in the future due to a search, a slip by either the adoptive parent or extended family, or an accidental discovery of adoption-related documents, a serious rift in the parent/child relationship occurs—a rift which is difficult to repair with an apology or explanation. What began as "protection" of the relationship with the adopted child can become a "termination" of trust and intimacy in that relationship.

Rachel was removed from her birth family as a toddler due to child neglect. She was placed with her adoptive family when she was four years old. The adoptive family, as Orthodox Jews, were very observant of conservative religious traditions. As Rachel grew up, she asked several times if her birth parents were also Jewish. The adoptive family had been told that Rachel's birth family was not Jewish, but they were concerned that Rachel, a strong-willed adolescent, would reject their family's religious and cultural practices if she knew this history. Therefore, they told her that they did not know her birth family's religious/cultural background and that her family might or might not have been Jewish. Not satisfied at age seventeen with this ambiguity about her birth family's culture, Rachel contacted her placement worker and asked if her birth family had been Jewish. The social worker, not realizing that the adoptive parents had not been honest with Rachel, shared with her that the birth family had been Protestant. Rachel was much more troubled by her parents' lack of honesty than she was about the information she received.

4. Allow a Child to Express Anger Toward a Birth Family Member Without Joining In.

Many adults remember that as children they became enraged when someone outside the family criticized any family member, even a family member who drove them absolutely crazy! Adoptive and foster parents find themselves in a similar position. They "share" the child with another family without being an "insider" in that family. While the child should be allowed to express both positive and negative feelings about birth family members, foster/adoptive parents cannot echo the negative sentiments. Many children who are caught up in multiple family systems (stepchildren, foster children, and adopted children) find themselves torn by divided loyalties. If members of any of those family systems berate other involved families, the child's conflict is greatly intensified.

Refusal to join the child's anger can be an easy concept to grasp but a difficult task to accomplish. After all, many foster and adoptive parents *are* angry at birth family members who harmed their children through substance abuse (during and after the pregnancy), physical and sexual abuse, neglect, abandonment, or emotional maltreatment. When the child expresses anger or outrage, it can be extremely difficult to restrain oneself from sharing that outrage. Maltreatment of a child should never be acceptable, but the adoptive parents cannot allow themselves the indulgence of speaking negatively of the perpetrators.

The following types of comments are acceptable and helpful to the child:

1. "I'm glad that we are able to keep you safe now."
2. "I can understand why you are so angry."
3. "That must have been an awfully hard time for you. Is there anything I can do to help you now?"

Comments like the following are unacceptable and potentially harmful to the child:

1. "If your mother had any sense in choosing boyfriends, you never would have been abused."

2. "I cannot imagine how anyone could abuse a child. They must have been awful people."

3. "They should lock up your parents and throw away the key. What they did to you was unforgivable."

5. Omissions Are Okay Until Age Twelve. After That, all Information Should Be Shared.

The complete history may be too complicated or too "adult" to share with a toddler or even a school-age child. For example, explaining prostitution to a child who does not understand human sexuality is not at all appropriate or advisable. It is sometimes in a child's best interests to learn about his history in increments appropriate to his developmental level. Chapter Eight discusses how to impart difficult information in developmental stages to a child.

Parents know their child's developmental level better than anyone. There are no rules about the right age for giving details to a child. This decision depends on the child's developmental level and understanding. Parents must assess each situation individually.

Almost all teenagers, unless developmentally delayed, have the cognitive skills and sophistication to know all of their histories. "In response to the question, 'What do you say to an adopted teenager?', the answer is everything. Adopted people deserve to hear all the facts, all the information that concerns their own lives, their own histories. In other words, an adopted person deserves to know his or her story. So if, for whatever reason, the full story has not yet been told during childhood, it should be told during adolescence."[2]

However, most teens believe very few of the things they hear from adults. It is part of the job description of the adolescent to challenge whatever messages come from adults, particularly from their own parents. Therefore, adoptive parents are advised to share information before their child enters the argumentative, stormy stage of adolescence. Paradoxically, children of eleven or twelve will understand and accept information that an older youth might not.

Holly van Gulden writes in "Talking with Children About Difficult Birth History":

The instinct of parents who plan to share difficult information is to wait until the child is older, perhaps in their teens. In my experience, this is not the optimum developmental time to share difficult information. Adolescents face two tasks which make processing and externalizing difficult information potentially problematic: individuation and separation. Teens are re-evaluating the question "Who am I?" based in part on their sense of their history to date. Teens are also preparing to leave the family nest . . . this is a critical and complex stage during which to offer new, different and negative information about the young person's heritage. Though they appear more vulnerable, younger children in middle childhood generally process negative information more easily—not without pain, confusion and some self-blame, but with less potential for internalizing self blame/shame for the actions/choices of others. Children ages 8–10 have more time to work and rework material and come to a positive sense of self before they begin to emotionally leave the family nest.[3]

6. If Information is Negative, Use a Third Party, Such as a Therapist, to Relate the Most Troublesome Details.

Because adoptive parents must be careful to avoid sharing extremely negative information about the birth family, they might choose to seek out a post-adoption specialist, a therapist who is sensitive to adoption issues, or an agency caseworker to give the child particularly negative information. There is an old saying about "killing the messenger" that applies here. In some cases, it is wise to avoid becoming the messenger!

Adoptive parents who decide to use a third party to share especially troubling information with their child must be careful to choose their helper wisely. Not all therapists are skilled in working with adoptive families, and some agency workers may even be insensitive to the needs of the child or the parents. Parents would be wise to interview the counselor prior to the meeting with the child to discuss parameters and engage in some form of "rehearsal" to avoid unpleasant surprises during the interview.

While parents may enlist the support of a professional in talking with their child about his or her history, they are not off the hook. It is critically important that parents are present for the interview for three reasons. First, they must provide emotional support to their child during a difficult interview. Second, they must be present to remember details that might be forgotten or misunderstood by the child. In fact, parents may want to audiotape the interview, with the permission of the child. The child will hear different information at different stages of maturity and may greatly value the ability to replay the interview as a young adult. Finally, parents must communicate to their child, throughout the interview and after, that they have heard "the worst" about his history, and they still love him unconditionally. Their presence sends a powerful message of love, support, and commitment to the child.

7. Don't Try To "Fix" the Pain of Adoption.

All parents naturally try to protect their children from pain. However, adoptive parents must recognize that their child must experience some pain in the normal resolution of adoption-related grief. The only way "out" is "through." Do not impose unrealistic expectations that parents can, by saying exactly the right thing, erase all of the pain and sadness caused by separation from the birth family.

When talking with anyone about a serious problem, particularly a loss, platitudes ("You'll have another child." "She was so old—it's better that she's no longer suffering.") are *not* helpful. Listening ears, soft shoulders, and understanding attitudes are *very* helpful. Sometimes in parental eagerness to take pain away from children, we instead take away the validity of their feelings. When in pain, children do not necessarily want explanations or reasoned thoughts about what has happened; they only want someone who understands and empathizes, "I know this hurts."

Beth Hall, founding Co-Director of PACT, an adoption alliance, writes that her daughter experienced a crisis when a storyteller at school talked about the importance of naming. The seven-year-old child told her mother, "I don't think my birth mother really loved me. She didn't give me a name. I wanted her to give me a name." Her mother responded, "I can't imagine how hard it must have been for you to realize that right in the midst of your class." The adoptive mother did her best to listen and support, "not to try to fix, not interpret," the child's grief.[4] The mother did not give reasons the birth mother might have avoided naming the child ("It might have been more difficult to sign the surrender if she had given you a name.") The adoptive mother also did not try to make her child's pain evaporate by ignoring it or redirecting attention from it ("But you are with our family now, and we did give you a name. So it doesn't matter that your birth mother did not give you a name.")

Often the best remedy for emotional pain is the support that comes from awareness that another understands and accepts our feelings.

8. Don't Impose Value Judgments on the Information.

Information about a child's history may seem very negative, even horrific, to adoptive parents or social workers, but may be interpreted quite differently by the child. As stated earlier, information about a child's history should never be changed, or given to an older child with significant omissions. Facts must be presented, however, without the overlay of values, without judgment.

The child's feelings for, or memories of, the birth family may alter his perceptions of events. And his *need* to have positive feelings for his birth family will definitely color his perceptions. If facts are presented in a negative, judgmental fashion, the child interprets this judgment as rejection by the adoptive family of his birth family, his origins, and, ultimately, himself. We do not have the right to judge birth parents; understanding comes from "witnessing" without judgment or censure. Children must develop the maturity to do the same, and this "understanding without judgment" must be modeled for them by the people most important to them: their parents.

This avoidance of judgment can actually be a relief for many adoptive parents. Sometimes, they worry for years about the right time and the right way to present information they perceive to be extremely negative. The child, when presented with the facts, may not see the information as negative at all.

Cameron was conceived as the result of a rape. He was placed as a six-month-old infant with Debbie and John. Cameron had never been told the circumstances surrounding his adoption, and he became obsessed as a preteen with curiosity about his story. His family wanted to protect him from learning, as his own awareness of sexuality was beginning to develop, that his birth father had been a rapist. Not wanting to lie, they simply told Cameron that his birth mother had been unable to raise him. Cameron interpreted this to mean that his birth mother had been a horrible person who had rejected him and found him so repulsive that she could not care for him. When told the actual circumstances surrounding his birth and adoption, Cameron expressed relief to learn that his mother was not a "slut." He understood that his mother had rejected the rape, not him. His imagination had created a far worse scenario than the actual one.

9. A Child Should Have Control of Telling His or Her Story Outside the Immediate Family.

Remember that the history belongs to the child, not to the adoptive parents. If friends or extended family members ask about sensitive information, simply tell them that the information belongs to the child. They can ask him about it when he is old enough to understand their questions. Parents should not decide with whom, when, and how intimate details of the child's life are shared.

Parents may want to assist the child in developing a short, simple version of his story that he feels comfortable sharing with neighbors, school friends and teachers, relatives, and other acquaintances. This "cover story" may be very similar to the information given your child when he was very young. Let the child know that one does not withhold information from acquaintances because it is shameful, but because one should not have to explain one's history in all its detail to anyone and everyone. Explain that some people don't have a lot of experience with adoption and might ask insensitive questions or make ridiculous remarks. At some point, a child will be very grateful to have developed and rehearsed a cover story that will short-circuit these questions.

Liz Clanton and her two children, Peter, age seven, and Katie, age five, both adopted from Korea, were sitting in a restaurant enjoying a few quiet moments together. A woman came up to them and commented to Liz about how beautiful her children were. The woman then directed her attention to Peter and asked, "Why did your mother get rid of you?"

Thankfully Liz knew that this day would come when her children would need to be prepared to answer uncomfortable questions . . . and prepared they were.

Peter, with respect, said to the inquiring woman, "We only talk about that at home." Peter was prepared.

There are two key points to remember when helping a child to develop a cover story:

1. *Discuss questions people might ask and the situations the child might encounter.* Such things might include introducing the child to a new neighborhood of friends, experiencing the first day at a new school or church, or, as in Peter and Katie's case, what questions curious people might ask at a mall or restaurant.
2. *Talk about what information should be shared.* It is not an easy task for children to sort out what should be told and what should be kept private. Children can be instructed to provide three basic responses to questions: their name, their origin, and the date they joined the family. It is important for a child to know that he or she is not obligated to tell everyone everything—that there are personal boundaries others must respect.

10. Remember That the Child Probably Knows More Than You Think He or She Does.

Sometimes adoptive parents tell others in the family about "troublesome" details of their child's history, and they believe they will tell the child—but later. No time ever seems like the right time because school is starting, the dog just ran away, the child just had a fight with his best friend. So parents never get around to telling the child, and someone else does. When information comes to the child from someone other than the parent, the child does not have the support of parents in integrating information into a positive self-identity. And, unfortunately, information is sometimes shared that is not entirely accurate because it has been passed through too many tellings.

Jordan, age sixteen, was placed as an infant with his loving adoptive family. He had two older sisters, both born into the family. Jordan had been born to a woman with significant mental health problems who reported that the father of the baby was African American. Social workers at the placing agency informed the adoptive parents that the baby might be biracial, but certainly did not appear to be a mixed-race child. The mother was described as "unreliable" as a source of information due to her mental instability. The adoptive parents were uncertain about what they should tell Jordan about his racial background. They talked about this dilemma to Jordan's two older sisters, but never spoke to Jordan about the issue. When Jordan and his parents attended a post-adoption support group for parents and adopted youth, the parents were advised to share exactly what the agency had told them: his birth mother, an unreliable source, reported that the birth father was African American. When they did so, Jordan commented, "Oh, I've known that for years. The girls told me all about it." While the parents had agonized over what information to share, their older children had done it for them—not nearly as well as the parents would have handled it. Though the adoptive parents believed that Jordan would eventually ask about his race/ethnicity, he never had. Jordan struggled with identity issues without the support and guidance his parents could have given him.

SUMMARY

Keeping lines of communication open is vital to adoptive family health. Observation of the ten commandments of truth telling can aid a family in assuring they are creating an emotionally healthy environment in which their child can develop a healthy sense of self and an experience of honest healthy family relationships.

QUESTIONS

1. Discuss ways that adoptive parents can initiate conversation about adoption.

2. Discuss the consequences of "lying with good intentions" to an adopted child about the past or a birth family member.

3. Why is it important to allow a child to express anger toward the birth family without joining in?

4. What does this statement mean to you personally—Don't try to "fix" the pain of adoption?

5. Do you find it hard to refrain from value judgments on the information about your child's history? What judgments are particularly hard for you to give up? Why?

NOTES

1. Adapted from the work of the Parenthesis Post Adoption Program, Columbus, Ohio, 1988.

2. Randolph Severson, "Talking to Your Adopted Adolescent about Adoption," in *A Collection of the Best Articles on Talking with Kids About Adoption: Best of PACT Press* (San Francisco: PACT Press, 1998), 33.

3. Holly van Gulden, "Talking with Children About Difficult Birth History," in *A Collection of the Best Articles on Talking with Kids About Adoption: Best of PACT Press* (San Francisco: PACT Press, 1998), 36–37.

4. Beth Hall, "Grief," in *A Collection of the Best Articles on Talking with Kids About Adoption: Best of PACT Press* (San Francisco: PACT Press, 1998), 20–22.

CHAPTER EIGHT

Sharing the Hard Stuff: The Adoptive Parent's Challenge

> If we aren't straight with our children about their past, they will pick up on it and fantasize something that may be much worse.
>
> Carol Williams, University of North Carolina

She approached the adoption speaker tentatively, waiting until the last person asked his question and the room cleared. She wanted no one to hear *her* question.

"Excuse me," she said to the speaker, "I need to ask you something. My son is seven years old, almost eight. He came to us through a public agency at the age of seven months. We were told that he is the product of an incestuous relationship between a brother and sister. He doesn't seem to have any major problems or difficulties. This is something we never have to tell him, right?"

This adoptive mom, like hundreds of adoptive parents, holds a secret to her child's past. She looks at the information from every angle, inside and out, upside down and right side up, hoping to find a way to avoid disclosing it. Yet the moment of disclosure is inevitable, unavoidable.

Imparting such information is difficult. The details seem far too painful. Yet, those distressing pieces—the missing pieces—are often the parts of a puzzle that bring understanding to a child and fill in the blanks in an otherwise jumbled perception of his past.

For many children, learning the difficult facts comes as a relief. Especially for older children, it affirms the emotional reality for which they have vague, fleeting memories of experiences and feelings.

"Children most often know the truth—they lived it," comments Greg Keck, an internationally recognized authority on attachment and bonding. "We need to validate their truth, document their truth, and where possible, show them the truth. Trauma is subjective. Therefore, we must present the facts as they *were*, and then it becomes the child's job to reframe it, repackage it and put it together in *their* understandable form."[1]

Keck said, "I think that in our efforts to protect hurt children, we often hurt them more. Somehow we want things to be nice or seem nice. I think that as a result of this, we want to reframe things so that they are comfortable enough for *us* to tolerate. In doing this, we often leave [children] incomplete, confused, and more unclear than they were."[2]

"We as parents often want to change our child's past reality. That is not our job," Keck pointed out.

When a child says, "I hate my birth mom," it is better for a parent to affirm this by saying, "I know," or "I bet you do." Instead, I have heard people say things like, "Oh, Bobby, they had so many problems of their own, they just couldn't take care of you. They drank. They used drugs." This response seems to explain and—even worse—excuse the behavior.

In working with kids, we want them to stop projecting blame and discontinue externalizing the causes of their problems and misbehavior. If someone thinks that they "hate" someone, the worst response we can give to them is some reason that they should not. When we do not validate their feelings and perceptions as accurate, we further complicate the healing process.[3]

Knowing that sharing the hard stuff is the right thing to do is one thing. Knowing just how to do it is another. Just how does a parent carry out this challenging task?

SHARING ABOUT ABANDONMENT

Josh's Story

Little is known about Josh's story. His adoptive parents have very little information about Josh, his birth family, or any other background. They do not even have his exact birthdate. Josh was found on a warm summer morning on the steps leading to the police station in his small Korean town. He looked just a few days old. A note was taped to his blanket. "I am young and alone. I cannot care for him." Someday his parents must attempt to tell Josh his story—without much knowledge or information to help.

For many thousands of children adopted internationally and some domestically, abandonment is the only word that describes their history. No name. No identifying information. Nothing. How does a family relate that information to a growing child?

Dee Paddock, a nationally respected therapist and adoptive parent, says that adoptive parents need to see sharing their child's story as a process in telling and understanding—not just relating the facts of the event. "Whatever happened in the child's life experience that led to adoptive placement for that child, from the very beginning and in every stage they need to hear the words, 'your birth parent couldn't parent you,' " says Paddock.[4] From that point on, parents can build the story developmentally.

When a child was abandoned at birth or early in life, Paddock suggests telling the story in the following increments:

Preschool Years: Your birth mother couldn't take care of you and wanted you to be safe. So she found a safe place to put you where safe adults would come and take care of you.

Early Elementary: We feel sad sometimes, and even mad sometimes, that we cannot give you any more information. Do you ever have any sad or mad feelings about not knowing anything? It is important that you understand that you are not responsible for the decision your parents made.

If a single mother: Being a single mother in Korea (or whatever country) may be extremely difficult. Single parents may have difficulty finding jobs and being able to provide for their child.

If a large family: Sometimes a family has too many children and is not able to provide for all of them. When the newest baby arrives, as you did, your parents felt they had no other choice but to take you to people who could care for you.

Middle School Years: Although we do not have information directly about your birth parents, we can explore all about your country and learn to understand why birth parents had to make such difficult decisions. When you think about your birth parents, what do you think about? Are you ever sad or angry that you don't know anything about them? What would you like us to do to help you? (Parents can begin to bring into the conversation the societal, economic, and cultural aspects of their child's country that would force birth parents to make such a decision.)

Preteen: Continue using educational resources to fill in a child's cultural and ethnic background. Continue to ask the questions mentioned above in greater depth. Consider locating a peer support group of other adopted preteens and teens that deals with open discussion regarding adoption issues.

Additional points for parents:

- Rough periods for children can create a period of real growth and understanding. Remember the maxim "No pain, no gain."
- One of the most helpful experiences for internationally adopted children has been the homeland tour—a return to their country of origin. "What we are learning from these trips back to the child's country," Paddock suggests, "is that some of these children spent far more time with their birth families than initially reported. As a result, some children do have vague memories of the birth family, and locating some of those families has been possible."
- Be careful not to say that the birth parent could not parent any children. On some trips, adoptive parents discovered that the birth family did have other children they were parenting.
- Many adolescents who have experienced the homeland tour make real strides in understanding the whys of their adoption experience. "They see real people who had to make real life decisions," Paddock comments. "After they return, they realize that they fit more into the culture of the country they grew up in, instead of the one in which they were born."[5]

SHARING ABOUT PROSTITUTION AND DRUGS

Chris and Kimberly's Story

Chaos, confusion, neglect, abuse are words that depict the early years of Chris and Kimberly. The children's birth mother, a single mom, was trapped by a life-threatening problem—drug abuse. A heroin and crack addict, their mother, Sharon, focused only on one thing—getting enough money for the next hit. Care of her toddlers fell to a distant second. On many occasions, various men paraded in and out of their small, cramped apartment because the only source of income that could support Sharon's habit was prostitution. Often the children were left alone when Sharon went out seeking customers. Other times, the children would be locked in the bathroom when their mother was "working." Neighbors, tiring of Sharon's lifestyle, reported the situation to the police and the local child services agency. The children were removed and placed in foster care. Because their mother failed to complete plans for their return, they were eventually adopted. Someday, their adoptive parents will have to tell them their life story.

   One of the important things to remember when talking with children who were old enough to have memories of previous families is that *they do have memories*. Parents often shy away from bringing up this difficult topic, but they must realize that such memories are there, even though the child may not have the words to describe their experiences. A child removed from his or her mother for child neglect related to involvement with drugs and prostitution might be told the following increments at the following times:

Preschool Years: Your first mother did not take care of you, and it is very important to be sure you are safe. She wasn't ready to be a mommy.

Early Elementary Years: Your mother had a lot of trouble making sure she could take care of herself. She did not have a "daddy" to help take care of you. She could not be responsible for a small child, so a social worker and a judge made sure you had a safe family who would take care of you forever.

Middle School Years: Your mother made some bad choices when she was a very young woman. She began to take drugs that were not good for her. She could not think well when she was taking the drugs. That caused her to make even more bad choices. That's why it was not safe for you to remain with her.

Preteen: Your mother could not support her drug addiction because she was not a reliable employee and could not keep a job. She had dropped out of school. Because she was addicted to drugs, she felt sick when she could not buy and use them. She was so desperate to get the drugs, she sold herself, through prostitution, to raise the money to get the drugs. While she was looking for customers, she left you alone in her apartment when you were only a baby. Neighbors were worried about you and called the police. They wanted to be sure you were safe.

Notice the way in which details are added as the child's cognitive abilities to understand the information develop. At no time does the parent relate something to the child that has to be contradicted later. More information is added as the child gains maturity.

SHARING ABOUT PHYSICAL ABUSE

Kenneth's Story

Kenneth came to the attention of child protective services workers after he entered Head Start at the age of three. With just one look at him, one could tell that he was an angry child. Even at three he struck out frequently at playmates—slapping, kicking, and biting them. His behavior mystified his teachers. They knew his mother. She was a very quiet woman who rarely said very much when she came to get him each day. He always seemed happy to see her.

On a rainy fall day, Kenneth was soaking wet when he arrived at school. The teacher always had extra clothes in the classroom. As she was helping this youngster change his clothes she was horrified by what she saw. Kenneth's back and legs were covered with varying shades of black and blue and green bruises. She could tell that some of the injuries were older. One seemed as recent as a day or two. She simply asked Kenneth who did this to him, and his reply was, "Daddy and Mommy." That simple question and response changed Kenneth's life forever. The local protection agency became involved with the family. Kenneth was placed in protective custody, and after eighteen months of attempting to work with his mother and father, efforts for reunification were discontinued. Kenneth became eligible for adoption. His foster parents adopted him. Someday Kenneth will have a lot of questions about the how's and why's of his life. His parents must be prepared to answer them.

Parents can aid their child in coming to some understanding about abuse as they move through their developmental stages.

Preschool Years: "Your mother and daddy did not take care of you the way that parents are supposed to. Mommies and daddies must keep children safe, and your parents did not do that."

Early Elementary Years: "You were not hurt because you are a bad child, even if someone told you that. You are not at fault for what your parents did. You were treated harshly because your parents were out of control in their lives." Adoptive parents can, at this age, begin to fill in some details about the birth parents, for example, drinking problems, family problems, or financial problems. If the children have memories of the abuse, parents can use joint storytelling and puppets to help them talk about their thoughts and feelings. (This technique is fully explained in Chapter Nine.)

Middle School Years: "Do you ever get angry at a friend at school or on the playground? Do you ever feel like hitting him? Many children feel that way. Your parents also got very angry. They never learned how to handle anger when they were growing up. So instead of handling anger in a good way, they took their anger out on you, even when they knew it was wrong. What do you think could make them so angry? Life circumstances were overwhelming to them, and they didn't know how to handle them. What could have been overwhelming for them?" Adoptive parents should fill in all the details they know about the parents' background at this point. (See Chapter Nine for tools to help children deal with their own anger and fears.)

Preteen: Continue to deal with all the child's memories, both positive and negative. Giving information (the rational style—see Chapter Six) and tapping into emotions (the reflecting style) are key in helping children move through the stages of their own anger and hurt. Information at this age includes such things as factors that contribute to intergenerational patterns of abuse, social/economic influences, and the psychological makeup of the family of origin. Children age twelve and beyond have developed abstract thinking and can begin to understand their birth family dynamics in these terms.

Additional points for parents:

Defusing the Time Bomb

Not dealing with the issue of abuse can create a "walking time bomb." Randolph Severson, an adoption counselor in Dallas, Texas, sees this in teens or adults who have not talked about their past:

Many come to me saying they feel like a time bomb ready to go off. This happens often in those who were under the age of six and [had few verbal skills] when the abuse or trauma occurred.

They have not seen their family of origin since that time and because of their young age, they do not have any context for relating to those persons outside the memory of the abuse.

Life is a continuum of human experience, and the abusive event was so overpowering it is the only memory from which they can develop a sense of identity from a historical context.

As these adults move through adolescence and attempt to develop self-image from their historical context, two issues present themselves. First, they don't have much memory to serve them and second, what memory they do have is often traumatic and even horrifying.

When I can, I work to get into the historical context of the person's memory. No one person abused a child twenty-four hours a day. I try to help this person recover any memory, however small it may be, that is positive.

I also use what I call "explaining therapy," that is, giving them as much information as possible, as a successful tool. Going back to an agency and getting as much information as is relevant to them is essential. Even if [it] is nothing more than information that can place this child into the social/economic, psychological and family problems that his parents faced it is helpful.[6]

Finding Out More

Agencies may have additional nonidentifying information about the child and the birth family's background that was not initially passed on to the adoptive family. It is worth the effort to contact the agency to update what information they have available.

SHARING ABOUT SEXUAL ABUSE

Dusty's Story

Dusty was three years old when her stepfather entered her life. Within a year after he came, life changed dramatically for her. John, her stepfather, began "grooming" Dusty for sexual activity. It started when she was four with fondling her genitals. By the time Dusty was in second grade, he would come into her bedroom late at night and force himself upon her. One afternoon when Dusty was in third grade, a teacher overheard her tell a friend at recess about the things her daddy made her do. Within hours, her life dramatically changed again—forever. The teacher notified the local child protective services agency. Her birth mother denied all of Dusty's allegations and essentially chose her husband over her daughter. Dusty entered foster care and was eventually adopted. Someday, her adoptive parents will have to tell her why.

Children often feel responsible for sexual abuse. Offenders often make the child feel responsible for what happened, both as a way of keeping their victims quiet and as a way of rationalizing their own destructive behavior. Perhaps the abuser told the child warm, wonderful things, like

"You are a special person to me and we could share some wonderful things together, but it will be our little secret."

Adoptive parents often have difficulty talking about sexual abuse. It is a subject that most parents would like to avoid. "Parents don't like to hear or say the words that their children use to describe what happened to them," says Greg Keck. "If the child has language, ask them to tell you what happened, without correcting their language or words. Their feelings are attached to their language. However, often parents change the words to much more pleasant ones—ones . . . they are more comfortable in using. If parents change how their children say what they say, they will not access their true feelings. They minimize their emotional and psychological reality."[7]

Many children who have been sexually abused ask such questions as "Why did they do it to me? Why did they do it at all?" Parents can make several important points while talking about sexual abuse with a child who has memories of the experience.

• Sexual abuse was never your fault, no matter what anyone said to you.
• (Name) was very selfish when he did that to you. (Name) was only thinking about himself first. He wanted to make himself feel good.
• (Name) touched you in ways that were wrong. (Name) is totally responsible for what he did.
• It took great courage on your part to disclose what (name) did to you. You did the right thing. I'm proud of you. You knew how to keep yourself safe.

WHEN YOUR SEXUALLY ABUSED CHILD WAS TOO YOUNG TO TALK

Cassie's Story

Cassie was four months old when she entered her foster home. It became apparent that her birth mother was unable to care for her. For over fourteen months, the agency worked to bring about reunification with her birth mother, but the efforts failed. Up to that point, Cassie's birth father had been out of the picture. Two weeks before the agency was to seek permanent custody of Cassie with plans for adoption, her birth father appeared. Cassie, now eighteen months old and having never met her father, began visitation with him. Within two months, the court ordered Cassie into the custody of her father.

The Weldons, Cassie's foster parents, were devastated by the court's decision. However, their devastation was even greater when in less than a year the agency called them and asked them if they would take Cassie back into their home. Her father had physically and sexually abused her. When Cassie returned to the Weldons' home at the age of three, she was a different child, now with a traumatized past that carried emotional scars hidden within her memory.

"In healthy adoptive families, the parents are the healers," says Paddock. It is their responsibility to create an environment in which discussion of this difficult subject can occur. What can parents say developmentally to bridge the gap for the nonverbal child who must someday understand his or her earlier life experience?[8]

Preschool Years: "Your first parents were not able to take care of you the way a child should be cared for. All children need safe mommies and/or daddies. Your birth parents were not able to keep you safe."

Early Elementary Years: Continue to reinforce the above story and begin discussion of sexuality. There are appropriate books for children that discuss this subject. (Suggestions are given at the end of this chapter.) Begin discussion about how the offending person made hurtful decisions and was not considering the child's feelings. Parents can begin asking questions like "Do you ever wonder about the time you spent with your birth parents?" The message needed early by the child from his parents, according to Paddock, is that "nothing is too scary or horrible to talk about. Nothing the child can say will cause the parent to send him back. Kids need to learn that no feelings will kill them, nor will any memory kill them either. Sharing it will help heal it."

Middle School Years and Beyond: As children prepare to enter adolescence, parents might consider counseling or a support group to help with resolution of early sexual abuse. Parents can contact the local child protective services agency to inquire about local resources for children who have been sexually abused. Parents should continue to respond to questions with openness, support, and reflective listening.

SHARING ABOUT MENTAL ILLNESS

Roy's Story

Roy was only three years old when he entered foster care, but already had more life experiences than many adults. Although Roy's mother loved him, she suffered with severe depression. She was totally detached from Roy's needs. Filthy and hungry, he often roamed around the apartment complex. Eventually neighbors reported the severe neglect, and Roy was removed. After eighteen months in foster care, it was evident that he could not return home safely. His foster parents ultimately adopted him. Someday his parents will need to share the truth about his past.

Preschool and older children who are placed for adoption because of a parent's mental illness may have memories of strange, even frightening behavior. Perhaps the child remembers his parent being severely depressed and dysfunctional. There were too many days to count, the child might say, when he came home from school only to realize that his parent never got out of bed. Perhaps the child can remember his parent's rapid mood swings, making it hard for him to know what to do. He can recount being locked in a room for doing something, when just the day before it was okay.

Although they may have lived in an upside-down, chaotic, dysfunctional, unpredictable home, these children love their birth parents and often ask with words or behavior, "Why couldn't I stay with them?" There are important concerns that parents can address in a developmental sequence.

Preschool Years: "Your first mommy (daddy) is not healthy and needs other people to help take care of her (him). She (he) has 'good' days when things feel fine, and 'bad' days when she (he) especially needs help from others. She (he) could not keep you safe. You need to be with a forever family that can take care of you every day and keep you safe. That's why you are with us."

Early Elementary Years: "Your birth mother (father) felt sad (or scared) much of the time. Because she (he) didn't feel safe, she (he) couldn't keep you safe. When you have a problem (can't understand your homework), you think about ways to solve it (get help from me, your older brother, your teacher). When your birth mom (dad) had problems she (he) got so upset and scared, she (he) couldn't figure out what to do. She (he) didn't do anything, and the problems just got worse (you know what happens if you never figure out your homework!). Your birth mom (dad) had trouble thinking clearly about what was happening and how to cope with problems. When thinking problems go on for a long time, we call it mental illness. There is medicine that can help your birth mom (dad) feel and think better. Sometimes talking to a doctor or social worker helps. We think that your birth mom (dad) is safe, but she (he) cannot take care of children. That's why you will always be with us."

Middle School Years and Beyond: "Your birth mother (father) has had mental health problems (depression or other diagnosis, if known) for a long time. The problems started long before you were born, and you did not cause your birth mom (dad) to be depressed or scared. She (he) doesn't choose to be unhappy, and she (he) cannot stop feeling this way. So your mom's (dad's) mental health problems are not your fault, and they are not your mom's (dad's) fault. Mental health problems happen to some people, and it is not anybody's 'fault.' Your birth mom (dad) has trouble with working and taking care of children. Sometimes, she (he) even has to go to a hospital to get help with medicine and to talk with the doctor. What kinds of things worry you about your birth mom (dad)? What questions do you have that I can answer for you?"

Additional points that parents can reinforce with their child

• Just because mom or dad couldn't make good decisions doesn't mean that he/she doesn't love you.

• It became very important that you could finish growing up in a stable home where it is safe.

• You did not cause this problem in your parent's life. He/she had it before you were born.

SHARING ABOUT SUBSTANCE ABUSE

Jimmy and Ashley's Story

Traumatic and harsh are two words that vividly describe the early life of Jimmy and Ashley, a brother and sister. Both children almost daily experienced unpredictable and often abusive treatment from their birth mother, a crack addict. The two children frequently slept all night in the family car, a trashed shell, alone and cold, while their mother attended to her drug addiction. A policeman walking by the car at 2:00 A.M. one morning heard the children's cries. The authorities removed the children from their birth mother. Over time it was obvious that she would not be able to parent the children, and an out-of-state family adopted them. Someday their parents will need to share the truth about their past.

Marty's Story

Marty, age six, was removed from her alcoholic mother after five years of neglect. Her mother would provide marginally acceptable care when sober, but would go on binges when she would drink cheap wine until she passed out on the couch. Her blackouts lasted for several hours, leaving Marty terrified and alone. When she could not rouse her mother, she feared her mother had died. No amount of crying or shaking could waken her mother. After the termination of parental rights and adoptive placement, Marty, an absolutely delightful child, was adjusting beautifully. Her adoptive family thought that her earlier difficulties were resolved until, one night, they served wine with dinner. Marty took one look at the wine bottle and became hysterical. She was absolutely inconsolable, associating wine with abandonment and lack of nurturing. Someday her parents will need to help Marty understand the ravages of alcoholism.

Even very young children who were placed for adoption may have vague memories of what life was like with someone who abused alcohol or drugs. Children need the opportunity during their developing years to voice their feelings about those memories of not having food to eat, or not having a clean bed to sleep in or clean clothes to wear. These children often have lingering fear of what it was like to live with someone who was chronically absent, leaving them alone or who was abusive or spaced out most of the time. (The suggestions that follow can be adapted to explain alcoholism.)

Preschool Years: "Your first mommy (daddy) took some medicine that wasn't good for her (him). She (he) did not get this medicine from the doctor, and it wasn't good for her (him). She (he) took the medicine because she (he) thought it would help her (him) feel good, but she (he) was wrong. When she (he) took the medicine, she (he) didn't feel good, and she (he) couldn't take care of you. You need a forever family that can keep you safe. That's why you are with us."

Early Elementary Years: "Your first mommy (daddy) made some bad choices before you were even born (when you were very little). She (he) listened to a bad person who said she would be happier if she took drugs. This bad person, a dealer, wanted to make money by selling drugs to people. Once people get started taking drugs, it is very hard for them to stop. They feel really bad whenever they try to stop. When your birth mom tried the drugs, she did feel better for a little while and thought the bad person, the dealer, was right! But the dealer did not tell her how bad she would feel when she stopped taking the drugs. And the dealer did not tell her she would not be able to take care of you, or any children, when she was using drugs because she would be too sleepy. Pretty soon, she was taking drugs every day because she felt sick when she didn't. She wanted the drugs so badly to stop feeling sick, sometimes she would even use money for groceries or rent to buy them. You need to be with a family that can always make sure you have a safe place and good food to eat. That's why you will always be with us."

Middle School Years and Beyond: "Your birth mom (dad) got hooked on drugs or alcohol because she (he) listened to the wrong people and made some bad choices. What do you remember about that time? How do you feel about it now? What questions do you still have?"

Additional points that parents can reinforce with their child:

- You did not cause your parent's drinking or drug problem.
- Your parent treated you as he/she did because drugs or alcohol controlled him/her.
- Just because mom or dad did not always treat you as a child should be treated doesn't mean that he/she doesn't love you.
- Your parents did not have control over their life and couldn't give you a safe, happy, and secure place to be.
- You need to grow up in a home where you can be safe from harm.

SHARING ABOUT LAWBREAKING

Kristy's Story

Kristy's life was never quiet. Home life was chaotic, loud, and unpredictable. There were always a lot of people—mean people—who came at all hours of the day and night. Her parents had a home business that provided money for the family. It wasn't a legal business, but a dangerous one. Her parents would steal cars, repaint them to sell on the black market, or tear them down and sell the parts. Late on a warm fall evening, Kristy's life changed forever. An undercover police officer came to their home to "buy" a car. After the transaction was completed, he arrested both of her parents. At age four and a half, Kristy entered foster care and was eventually placed adoptively. Someday her parents will need to explain to her the circumstances of her past.

Opening the door of communication regarding lawbreaking can begin early. For example, here is what parents can say to their children as they grow.

Preschool years: "Do you know how we have rules in our family? Some rules are so important that they are called laws. Everyone has to obey laws, even grown-ups. Can you think of any laws? When big people don't follow these especially important rules, called laws, they have to go away to a special time-out place to learn how to behave better. Your first mommy (daddy) is at a time-out place now because she (he) did not follow the important rules. You need to have a forever family to keep you safe. That's why you will be here with us until you grow up."

Early Elementary Years: "Your birth mom (dad) broke the law and had to see a judge. The law your birth mom (dad) broke was _____ (stealing cars from other people, selling drugs to other people, etc.). We are not sure why your birth mom (dad) decided to break the law, but we think it was because (she was taking drugs and needed money to buy more when she felt sick, or he was drinking and could not make a good decision about how to act, or he tried to solve his problems with fighting instead of talking, etc.). The judge decided that your birth mom (dad) had to think about the bad choice she (he) made, so the judge sent your birth mom (dad) to jail to think about it. She (he) will be there for _____years. You cannot wait that long for a family—you need a family to love you and keep you safe now! That's why you will be with us until you are grown up."

Middle School Years and Beyond: "Your birth mom (dad) probably wishes now that she had made a different decision when she was younger so that she didn't have to be separated from you. She loves you very much and is probably worried that you will be angry at her or, even worse, will forget her. How do you feel about your mom? What questions do you have about your birth family?"

SHARING ABOUT DIFFICULT CIRCUMSTANCES OF BIRTH: RAPE AND INCEST

Disclosing the circumstances of a child's birth if those circumstances involved rape or incest is not an easy task. Severson catches the intensity of the task for adoptive parents whose child was conceived as the result of incest or rape:

To actually have a child, a child of your heart and kindness, who sleeps warm and secure in the blanket after you kiss him goodnight, and to know that this child's life began in horror (fear, trauma or confusion as in the case of incest) and that you must tell him and watch his innocence be shattered, and know yourself to be an agent of that shattering, is a duty that no one would wish upon another.[9]

When to tell a child the story of his beginnings under these circumstances continues to be a question faced by adoption professionals whose task it is to guide and direct adoptive parents. Vera Fahlberg, whose experience in the field is widely respected, feels that the door of communication can be opened incrementally. "Waiting until the child is 18 or older and ready to leave home is *not a good time* for sharing this type of information," she asserts. "Many adopted individuals have a resurgence of feelings of abandonment as they approach moving away from home and family. It is important that the information about their origins . . . not be associated with the experience of parent separation and loss (even though this time the separation is developmentally appropriate)."

Fahlberg also suggests that the first step for parents when disclosing "hard stuff" is to discuss the information between themselves or with another trusted adult enough that they both develop acceptance of the facts and are able to talk about them without becoming emotionally overwhelmed. She continues:

Whenever people need to discuss difficult things it is probably best to "practice" before the actual event. Practicing with a tape recorder and then listening to oneself can help parents hear what the child will hear. Frequently, that helps adults modify how they will phrase the facts. Parents need to realize that although they are the custodians of the child's history during his/her early years, ultimately the history belongs to their adopted son or daughter.[10]

Specifically About Rape

The Early Years

The early avenue in, according to Fahlberg, is to have mention of the birth father in the lifebook. (See Chapter Nine for a full discussion on how to develop a lifebook.) The lifebook can simply reflect in those early years, in the case of rape, that no information was available about the birth father. Most children don't feel a sense of connection to a father they do not know until they are about eight to ten years old, Fahlberg points out. It is then that they develop a sense of genetic connectedness and usually want to know more about their birth father.

Susan Pelleg, an adoption therapist in Ohio, says that parents can progressively add an explanation, such as "Your mother didn't know your father well (or at all). The relationship was not a happy one. Your mother found herself in a situation that was not safe, but something good came of it, you were born."[11]

Middle School and Beyond

Severson advises that "as soon as your child asks or becomes aware—and only your love and instinct will hint at its emergence—that it 'takes two' to make a baby, he or she should be told that his birthmother and birthfather were not in love and perhaps did not know each other well, and that they did not "make love," but rather 'had sex' even though the birthmother didn't want to."[12]

Parents frequently ask the following questions about how to disclose sensitive information:

1. *Should I tell my child everything I know about the details of his conception?* Severson says, "No, no more than you would explain to any child every detail of his or her conception."

2. *When should I use the word rape?* Severson suggests that parents not "use the word itself until they feel the time is right when they are certain that [the child] understands the meaning, which usually occurs developmentally around late latency age." Severson cautions, however, that in an effort to defer a child's pain until the right time, that "right time never comes," and the child stumbles onto the truth from another source. What happens then is that the child is deprived of parental strength and support in coping with the harsh reality. The parents "have also added a new truth to his map of reality. Mom and dad cannot be wholly trusted."[13]

Specifically about Incest

The Early Years

The early avenue in again, according to Fahlberg, is the mention of the birth father in the lifebook. The lifebook can simply reflect in those early years, in the case of incest, that the birth father was a member of the birth mother's family. Another possibility, suggests Fahlberg, is for people to include a physical and ethnic history of the father in a way that leads to the logical assumption that the birth father and birth mother shared the same family. The important thing to remember about lifebooks during the early years is that they need to include information that is truthful yet simple, so that the information can be expanded as the child gets older. Information can be written in ways that make it easy for further questions to be developed as the child gets older.

The Middle School Years and Beyond

Severson's suggestions about the concept of the right time for explaining rape are appropriate here as well. Parents can begin to share with their child that their birth parents grew up in a family that did not know how to show love appropriately. "People didn't know how and to whom to express love. Because of that lack of understanding, you were born."

Vera Fahlberg offers these key points for parents of older children and teens to remember:

- Late latency and early teen years can be used for educating the child about the causes of rape or incest within a family. This can be done by visiting support groups or victim advocate groups, scheduling time with therapists skilled in the subject, or researching the topic in the library or on the Internet. It is important that children and teens learn that rape is about anger and control of others, and that incest is about extreme family dysfunction—it could be related to other forms of physical abuse, anger and control, lack of boundaries, and/or to the adult incapable of developing intimacy with other adults.

- Children and teens can be challenged to discover what they need to learn about life and about themselves that will enable them to function well in a family and society, and not make the same type of decisions that their birth parents made.

Whenever a child comes into this world as a result of rape or incest, that child is cherished and treasured by his creator. What ultimately does a parent tell a child about himself? Parents tell him the truth. That he was created in the image of God. That God knit him together in his mother's womb. That he, like every child, was fearfully and wonderfully made and that all the days of his life are ordained by God.[14]

SUMMARY

Sharing difficult realities with a child is a challenging task for adoptive parents. It takes courage and insight to impart potentially devastating facts sensitively but truthfully. The information in this chapter, as well as advice from other adoptive parents and professionals will help equip parents for the task ahead.

SUGGESTED BOOKS ON TALKING TO CHILDREN ABOUT SEXUALITY

Almost 12: The Story of Sex by Kenneth N. Taylor. Tyndale House Publishers, 1995.

Asking About Sex and Growing Up: A Question-And-Answer Book for Boys and Girls (any age) by Joanna Cole; Illustrated by Alan Tiegreen. William Morrow and Company, 1988.

How to Talk to Your Child About Sex: It's Best to Start Early, but It's Never Too Late-A Step-By-Step Guide for Every Age by Linda Eyre and Richard M. Eyre. Golden Book Publishing Company, 1999.

It's Perfectly Normal: Changing Bodies, Growing Up, Sex, and Sexual Health (ages 9–12) by Robie H. Harris, Illustrated by Michael Emberley. Candlewick Press, 1996.

Kids First Book About Sex by Joani Blank and Marcia Quackenbush. Down There Publishers, 1993.

QUESTIONS

1. For the small group activity and discussion for this chapter, spend the time asking each participant to practice writing their own child's story.

2. If some participants do not have a personal example, they can use the following example with which to practice.

Katie is now eight years old and has been in her adoptive home for six and one-half years. A lifebook was never prepared for her and her adoptive parents have returned to the agency for more information about Katie's past. They knew that her mother was dead and her father in jail because of the murder, but they did not have a lot of details. What they learned that day, they felt was important to pass on to her.

Katie came into foster care at fourteen months. She had witnessed the brutal stabbing of her birth mother by her birth father. After the stabbing, her father grabbed her and hid from police for two days. When she was eventually found at a friend's home, she was still wearing the bloodstained pajamas she had on the night of the horrific event. Her foster family eventually adopted her at two years of age. How would you write her story?

NOTES

1. Greg Keck, "Affirming the Hurt Adoptee's Reality," *Jewel among Jewell Adoption News*, Spring 1999.

2. Greg Keck, personal interview, May 12, 1999.

3. Ibid.

4. Dee Paddock, personal interview, May 29, 1999.

5. Ibid.

6. Jayne Schooler, *Searching for a Past* (Colorado Springs: Pinon Press, 1995), 91.

7. Greg Keck, personal interview, May 29, 1999.

8. Dee Paddock, personal interview, May 29, 1999.

9. Randolph Severson, *To Bless Him Unaware: The Adopted Child Conceived by Rape* (Dallas: House of Tomorrow, 1992), 4.

10. Vera Fahlberg. E-mail correspondence, July 15, 1999.

11. Sue Pelleg, phone interview, July 21, 1999.

12. Severson, 11–12.

13. Ibid. For a more complete treatment of the subject, contact House of Tomorrow, 4209 McKinney Ave., Dallas, TX 75205.

14. Adapted from Psalm 139, *The Life Application Bible* (Wheaton, Ill.: Tyndale House Publishers, 1991).

CHAPTER NINE

Tools of Communication Between Parents and Children

Children can not communicate about their feelings as adults can. Youngsters talk through dolls, puppets, drawings, and play.
                                                                Susan Pelleg

Using communication tools within the adoptive family can help both parents and children process the many issues that arise during the growing-up years. This chapter describes twelve interactive tools parents and children can use to explore important issues.

   Children who joined their adoptive families after living for a period of time with birth family members have memories. Adoptive parents have a special role, for they truly are the storehouses for those memories—the difficult ones as well as the pleasant ones. There are several tools and techniques that adoptive parents can use to store those fading memories and to aid their child in communicating his own feelings about his life experiences. The first six tools aid interactive communication from parent to child:

- The Lifebook/Life Story Box
- The Life Map
- The Eco Map
- The Family Tree
- The Family Collage
- Bibliotherapy/Videos

TOOL ONE: THE LIFEBOOK/LIFE STORY BOX

Why Children Need a Lifebook

The lifebook is useful for all adopted children, whether placed as infants or older children, and is helpful at all stages of child development. A lifebook records a child's family and placement history, according to Denise Goodman, a nationally recognized expert on adoption. It is a tool that gathers information about a child's growth and development, feelings, ideas, and hopes and dreams for the future. It is a vital resource in helping a child to understand the past and prepare for the future. Goodman gives seven reasons children need a lifebook:[1]

It Recreates a Child's Life History

This is important, as many of our children have had very confusing lives. They have been in and out of care and shuffled between family members. Each child's reaction to the separation from the birth family presents its own set of unique individual responses. These painful feelings weave a common thread throughout the lives of older adopted children. For children whose memories of former relationships smolder vaguely in their minds, themes frequently recur during the healing process. They need to have an accurate record of their past, because it will help them look forward to the future without fear.

It Gives a Child Information about His/Her Birth Family

Many foster and adopted children do not have a lot of information about their birth families, and they may not have any positive information at all. What did their parents look like? What talents did they have? What about their extended families? In fact, some kids have no information at all. Everyone has a "genetic road map," which is their parents. This "road map" helps in identity development. Individuals decide what traits they like and keep them. The traits they do not like, they reject. Youngsters who have no information make it up, and usually fantasies are negative. Some children only have negative information about their parents from which to construct their own identity. Children need both positive and negative details about their birth families.

It Gives Reasons for Placement

Frequently, children have the wrong idea about why they have been removed from their homes. Many times, they believe that it was their fault. This leads to feelings of guilt, and sometimes children will try to punish themselves. Therefore, children must have accurate and honest information about why they are in care.

It Provides Photos and a Pictorial History

Even when information is given in written form, kids generally want to know what their families look like. In addition, photographs also record family events such as holidays, birthdays, and special times. Children need pictures of themselves to trace the changes that have taken place.

It Records the Child's Feelings about His or Her Life

Too often, children are not given a chance to voice their feelings about their life and being in out-of-home care. The lifebook, in some ways, is a diary or log children can use to keep a record of their personal thoughts or feelings.

It Gives the Child Information about His or Her Development

How many people have baby books? If you are not the firstborn, you probably don't have one. How would you like a recording of all your important milestones—your first tooth, your first step, your first word—along with a record of all the other special things you've done? This is another important role that the lifebook plays.

It is a Useful Tool When Working With Children

As a way to organize information, the lifebook is a helpful tool for foster parents, adoptive parents, caseworkers, and therapists who must assist children struggling to cope with being away from their parents, siblings, and homes.

Developing an Age-Appropriate Lifebook

Lifebooks for Infants and Toddlers

Gathering information for the lifebook for an infant or toddler is far more important than one might assume. Children at these ages have no memory of their birth parents, foster parents, or other significant people who cared for them. They often have no pictures of themselves or any significant person to help fill in the gaps. Completing an infant's lifebook while in foster care, whether the child's outcome is reunification with the birth family or adoption, is a crucial activity.

What to Include	Where To Find It
Birth Information: Birth certificate, height, weight, time and date of birth, hospital (picture if possible from brochure or taken by family), names of doctors, special medical information or circumstances of birth, genogram, pictures of birth family, and cultural history	Bureau of Vital Statistics, case record and social/medical hospital, WIC clinic, hospital records, birth parents, extended family
Placement Information: Reasons for removal or placement. Include journal entry, chronological list for each move, good-bye letters from caregivers, names of other children child was close to, pictures of their caretakers, their birth and foster homes, bedroom, pets, etc.	Court records, intake worker, birth family, caseworker, previous caretakers
Medical Information: List of medical providers, immunization record, list of childhood diseases, injuries, allergies	Case record, health department, caretakers, pediatrician, WIC clinic
Developmental Information: Significant milestones of development	Previous caretakers, case record, medical history
Adoption Information: Date of finalization, adoption party pictures, any special mementos	Adoptive family and adoption caseworker

Lifebooks for School-Age Children

Children removed from their homes during the early school-age years may have memories of important people in their lives, but those memories are usually vague and fleeting. Those memories may also be attached to the trauma of abuse, neglect, and the experience of removal. The lifebook should be a tool that fills in the memory gaps for these children and also replaces the fantasies that have developed. In addition to the birth, developmental, and medical information recommended for infants and toddlers, the school-age child's lifebook should also include the following:

In Addition to the Information Already Cited, Include:	Where to Find It
Placement Information: Reasons for removal or placement. Include journal entry, chronological list for each move, good-bye letters from caregivers, names of other children child was close to, pictures of caretakers, their birth and foster homes, bedroom, pets, church activities, neighborhood friends, ball teams, scout troops	Court records, intake worker, birth family, caseworker, previous caretakers, school teachers, counselors, adult leaders, ministers

In Addition to the Information Already Cited, Include:	Where to Find It
letters, correspondence from birth family or other friends, names and addresses of separated siblings, mementos of special events	
Educational Information: List all daycare and schools attended with dates, names and addresses, and photos if possible, pictures of classmates, teachers, and other important adults, copies of report cards, samples of homework, special projects, pictures and mementos of special events, awards, achievements and certificates	School personnel, teachers, yearbooks, school and community newspapers, coaches, school records
Adoption Information: Tools used to prepare child for adoption (coloring books), date of finalization, adoption day pictures, etc.	Adoptive family, foster care and adoption caseworker

Lifebooks for Teens

Teens who have spent any amount of time in foster care and enter adoption or independent living have probably lost track of the important details of their lives. They probably do not have many mementos of their past, and may have little or no birth information, and few pictures, if any. They may not have a record of where they lived and the people with whom they lived, the schools they attended, or their achievements. Putting a lifebook together for a young teen requires investigative work and perseverance. However, it may be the youngster's only link from a confusing and disjointed past to a more stable future. The lifebook for the teen should include as much information from birth, medical, and developmental records as can be traced. It should also include the following:[2]

In Addition to the Information Already Cited, Include:	Where to Find It
Placement Information: Chronological listing of places where teen lived, with whom, reasons for moving, pictures of people and places that were important in the development of the teen	Previous caregivers, caseworkers, case record
Educational Information: List schools attended with dates, names and addresses, and photos, if possible; pictures of classmates, teachers and other important adults; copies of report cards; samples of homework; special projects; pictures and mementos of special events; awards, achievements, and certificates	School personnel, teachers, yearbooks, school and community newspapers, coaches, school records, band/music directors, drama teachers

In Addition to the Information Already Cited, Include:	Where to Find It
Independent Living Information: Information and mementos gleaned from teen groups and classes; pictures of other teens in independent living; pictures of group leaders; pictures of graduating from group and moving into the new apartment	Caseworkers, foster care and independent living caseworkers
Adoption Information: Tools used to prepare teen for adoption, date of finalization, adoption day pictures, any special mementos	Adoptive family and foster care and adoption caseworker

The Life Story Box

The life story box supplements the lifebook. It is a box or chest that will be the repository of all the child's mementos—everything from the first tooth, to sports or musical trophies, to report cards and teachers' special notes. The older the child gets, the more important these mementos—samples of homework, special projects, pictures and souvenirs of special events, awards, achievements and certificates—become.

TOOL TWO: THE LIFE MAP

The Life Map is a tool useful primarily for children who have been in the foster care system prior to adoptive placement, or, in the case of international adoption, for children who have memories of life in an orphanage or foster home. It is helpful for children as young as four years through adolescence. Making a Life Map is helpful in reconstructing the child's placement history. The Life Map can communicate a number of important life events that are often lost when children experience a number of moves. These life events include:

• where the child has lived
• how long he lived there
• the people, pets, places that were important to him
• why he had to move
• how he felt about the moves

The child should be an active participant in the drawing of the map. He should be encouraged to draw it in any manner he chooses. The key purpose of the Life Map is to generate open discussion about the child's history, to give the parents the opportunity to talk about and clarify any of the child's misconceptions, to provide support for painful feelings, and to provide reassurance about his new parents.[3]

The Life Map

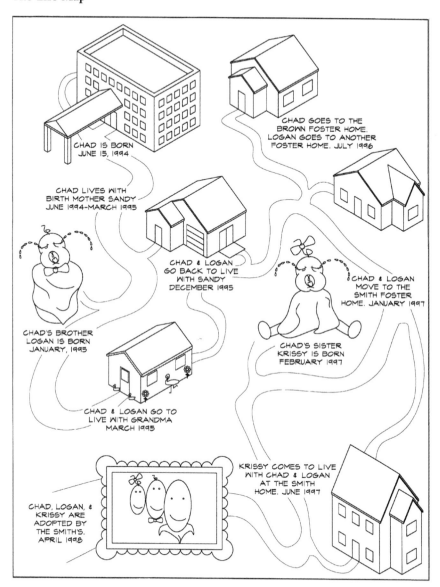

CHAD IS BORN
JUNE 15, 1994

CHAD GOES TO THE
BROWN FOSTER HOME.
LOGAN GOES TO ANOTHER
FOSTER HOME. JULY 1996

CHAD LIVES WITH
BIRTH MOTHER SANDY
JUNE 1994-MARCH 1995

CHAD & LOGAN
GO BACK TO LIVE
WITH SANDY
DECEMBER 1995

CHAD & LOGAN
MOVE TO THE
SMITH FOSTER
HOME. JANUARY 1997

CHAD'S BROTHER
LOGAN IS BORN
JANUARY, 1995

CHAD'S SISTER
KRISSY IS BORN
FEBRUARY 1997

CHAD & LOGAN GO TO
LIVE WITH GRANDMA
MARCH 1995

KRISSY COMES TO LIVE
WITH CHAD & LOGAN
AT THE SMITH
HOME. JUNE 1997

CHAD, LOGAN, &
KRISSY ARE
ADOPTED BY
THE SMITH'S.
APRIL 1998

The Life Map Narrative

Chad was born on June 15, 1994, and his brother, Logan, was born on January 15, 1995. Two months after Logan was born, they went to live with their grand-mother. They eventually returned to live with their mother, Sandy. However, things did not work out at home, and they went into foster care. Chad went to the Brown foster home, and Logan to another one. In January 1997, both Chad and Logan moved to the Smith foster home. Their sister, Krissy, was born and came to live with them at the Smith foster home when she was four months old. In April 1998, the Smiths adopted Chad, Logan, and Krissy.

TOOL THREE: THE CHILD'S ECO MAP [4]

The Eco Map is a valuable tool for a child in foster care and adoption. It was originally developed by the staff of Branch County Department of Social Services, Coldwater, Michigan as a tool to open communication between a child and his caseworker. It is used with foster and adopted children to guide them in understanding the reasons for their placement and to understand the role of different people in their lives.

To use the concept, give the child a copy of the Eco Map and crayons or markers. Encourage the child to do the writing and coloring himself as the various areas of the map are discussed. The Eco Map is designed to alternate less psychologically loaded questions with ones that are more difficult.

1. *Why am I here?* Encourage the child to share his own explanation to himself about why he is in foster care/adoption. If the child says something like, "Well, you put me here; you answer the question," the parent or worker might respond by saying, "It is important for you to understand why the placement decision was made, but I'm also interested in your thoughts. We will discuss both."

2. *Social worker*: Children are often confused about the agency people in their life. Let the child know what their job is—that is, to work with him and his new parents toward building a happy adoptive family.

3. *Courthouse*: Briefly describe the hearing process and the role of the judge.

4. *Homes*: Encourage the child to identify one of the homes as his birth home and one as the foster home, with pathways to both. A third home can be added when necessary (e.g., if the child has contact with two birth parents who do not live together). Encourage the child to talk about similarities and differences in the two homes and parenting styles. Although children commonly focus initially on the physical attributes, let them know that, through time, the two of you will be comparing them in terms of the interactions. Describe the roles of foster parents.

5. *Siblings*: Finding out about sibling relationships is important whether brothers and sisters are placed together or not. Many children find separation from siblings to be as painful, or even more so, than separation from birth parents.

6. *I feel_____*: Encourage spontaneous verbalization from the child.

7. *Things that bug me*: Let the child complete this. Younger children frequently respond to the visual cue by indicating "bugs" that bug them. Children will usually expand on their dislikes if encouraged to do so.

8. *School*: Encourage the child to talk about previous school experiences and the feelings he has about going to a new school while he is in foster care.

The Eco Map

1. WHY AM I HERE?   2. SOCIAL WORKER   3. COURTHOUSE

4. HOMES   5. SIBLINGS   6. I FEEL

7. THINGS THAT BUG ME   8. SCHOOL   9. I WORRY ABOUT

10. THINGS I LIKE TO DO   11. DREAMS   12. FRIENDS

9. *I worry about_____*: Encourage spontaneous responses.

10. *Things I like to do*: Let the child talk both of the things he enjoys and things that others do that make him happy. The responses can be used to help foster parents initiate positive interactions with the child.

11. *Dreams*: These can be either nighttime dreams or daydreams. The former frequently help identify fears and worries; the latter, hopes and dreams.

12. *Friends*: Talk with the child about friends and how he might keep in contact with them, as well as discussing how he might go about making new friends in the new neighborhood and school.

TOOL FOUR: THE FAMILY TREE

The Family Tree, a modification of the more commonly known family tree, has a unique purpose. According to Dr. Fahlberg:

The Family Tree can help children organize all the people who have been an important part of their lives. The biological family can be identified as the roots of the tree. These "roots" (the biological family) cannot be seen, but they anchor the tree, just as the biological family provided the child with a genetic heritage, and will always be part of her. The child's foster or kinship families can be represented on the trunk of the tree, as they have helped the child grow. The adoptive family may be represented on the upper trunk, branches, leaves, fruit, and flowers. Through this activity, the child learns she does not have to choose between families and she can come to understand how each family played an important role in her growth and development.[5]

TOOL FIVE: THE FAMILY COLLAGE

The Family Collage can be a fun activity for a child and parent to assemble. A collage is a collection of pictures that are placed on a large piece of paper or cardboard. In adoption work, Goodman suggests gluing the pictures to a cutout of the body outline of the child. The collage is used to represent past, present, and future events in a child's life. The child is instructed to use photos, cut out pictures from magazines, or draw pictures that to him represent important people or events and his wishes for the future.[6]

TOOL SIX: BIBLIOTHERAPY/VIDEOS

Bibliotherapy means "helping with books." Parents can broaden children's understanding of the circumstances of their adoption through the use of stories, other literature, and videos. As children read the stories of others, they can see how other youngsters in similar circumstances confronted difficulties and overcame them. They can also see how children who had the same life experiences faced loss, disappointment, separation, and fear.

When selecting books for children, parents should consider the following:[7]

1. *Take into account developmental age as well as the child's reading level.* Preschoolers enjoy stories with colorful pictures and simple conversation. Older elementary youngsters enjoy stories with mystery, plot, and intrigue. Teens usually pick

The Family Tree

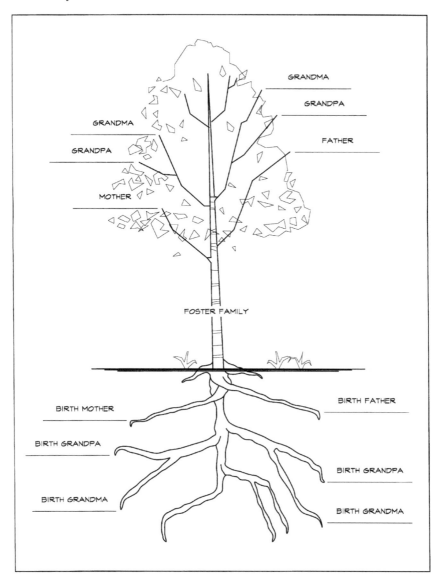

books that are relevant to their concerns, such as identity, dating, decision making, and parent-teen struggles.

2. *Choose reading material or videos that address a child's apprehensions.* Those apprehensions could include leaving a foster family, loss of birth parents or siblings, or living in a transcultural family. Vera Fahlberg points out that most G-rated movies for children deal with loss.[8] Movies/videos such as *Bambi* or

Annie, to cite just two, can open up discussion between parents and children about feelings of separation and loss.

3. *Parents should learn how to explore feelings and attitudes by asking appropriate and timely questions.* Those personal questions can be couched by asking how the child thinks the hero or heroine felt and how the child would feel if he/she were in the same position.

A suggested reading list can be obtained by visiting Tapestry Books on the Internet at www.tapestrybooks.com. Adoptive Families of America (1–800–372–3300) also provides an extensive reading list for children.

Parents can use the next five tools to encourage interactive communication from children ages four to ten:

- Let's Make a Phone Call
- Let's Tell a Story/Let's Write a Story
- Can You Tell Me What They Think? (Using dolls and puppets)
- Pick a Feeling Card
- Who Do You Go to for What?

TOOL SEVEN: LET'S MAKE A PHONE CALL

The use of pretend and play is especially helpful for children who are developmentally between the ages of four and seven. One helpful game is playing telephone. Vera Fahlberg observes that very young children often do not respond to direct questioning. She suggests that using the toy telephone game, when combined with pictures of adults from whom the child is separated, can be helpful in gaining information that direct questioning would not elicit. It also helps parents to correct wrong information or wrong thinking.[9] The following example shows how to play the game:

Casey, age six, had been in foster care for two years before being adopted by her foster parents. Her birth father had died and her birth mother, who already had severe mental health issues, became totally ineffective and was unable to parent a young child and keep her safe. Using the telephone, Casey pretended to call her birth mother. Before making the call, her adoptive mother asked her to think about questions that she wanted to ask her birth mother. When Casey "placed" the call, she asked her mother if she was still mad at her and why she couldn't come back to care for her. Casey's adoptive mom took on the role of her birth mother and said to her, "Casey, I was never angry at you. I was very upset that your daddy died. When he died, I became very sad. There were many days I didn't get out of bed. You weren't safe during those times. I couldn't take care of myself well and I knew that I couldn't be the mommy that you needed.

You now have a mommy and daddy who can take good care of you and keep you safe."

TOOL EIGHT: LET'S TELL A STORY/LET'S WRITE A STORY

Another creative technique is guiding children to communicate their thoughts and feelings about their life experience. Fahlberg calls this joint storytelling: "The child is asked to choose a favorite animal and name him. Then the adult starts telling a story about the animal that reflects the child's history. After several sentences, the adult asks the child to continue the story. In this way, the child has the opportunity to share emotional reactions to life events as well as his perceptions and desires for the future."[10]

Why is storytelling helpful? In *Working with Traumatized Children*, Kathryn Brohl notes that storytelling is "an effective way to address traumatic memories, [to monitor] responses and to teach problem solving. Storytelling also bypasses resistance by speaking to, as well as offering solutions to, overcoming a trauma without directly discussing the trauma."[11] The following example shows how to play "Let's Tell a Story."[12]

Benjamin, age four, had been living in interim care for close to a year because he had been severely physically abused by his mother's boyfriend. He had developed a close, loving relationship with his foster parents. Benjie had weekly visits with his teenaged birth mother, who was no longer with the same boyfriend. The plan was for him to be returned to Mother's care shortly. His caseworker, Mrs. Shields, wanted to know more about how Benjamin viewed the past abuse and whether or not he perceived his mom as now able to provide adequate physical safety. She decided to use joint storytelling to facilitate her communications with Benjie. She knew that with the younger child it is frequently necessary for the adult to ask some leading questions during the storytelling.

Mrs. S.: Once upon a time there was a bunny named Ben. When he was just a baby, Bunny Ben lived with his mommy and his grandma. How do you think things went for Bunny Ben when he was a baby?

Ben: Bunny Ben was happy with his mommy and grandmother.

Mrs. S.: Then what do you think happened?

Ben: Then they moved.

Mrs. S.: One day Bunny Ben's mommy and grandmother had an argument and Ben and his mommy moved. They moved in with some friends of Bunny Ben's mother. How do you think things went for Bunny Ben then?

Ben: Sad.

Mrs. S.: Was Ben sad a lot? Was he missing someone?

Ben: He was *very* sad for his grandma. There was a mean man.

Mrs. S.: When Bunny Ben was very sad, he cried a lot. Mommy's friends did not like to hear crying. One of them would get so frustrated that he would spank Bunny Ben so hard that it really hurt him. It is not okay for adults to hurt children. One day some neighbors heard Bunny Ben crying very hard. They called some adults who help bunny families who are having problems. One of the adults came to visit Bunny Ben's family. Bunny Ben had lots of bruises on his bottom. The man who had spanked him was very angry at everyone. Bunny Ben needed to be in a safe place where he wouldn't be hurt. How do you think Bunny Ben felt when he moved to a new place?

By continuing the story, Mrs. Shields encouraged Benjie to talk about his feelings in interim care and about his thoughts and feelings about the upcoming move back to Mother's care. She learned that he missed his mom and wanted to spend more time with her. However, Mrs. Shields also learned that he was less worried about physical harm in the future than sad about anticipating the separation from his foster family. Like most children his age, the story solution he chose was for Mommy Bunny to move in with Bunny Ben and his foster family.

Mrs. Shields then modified the ending to the story, acknowledging that Bunny Ben would like one ending, but that none of the adults thought it would work out for them. Instead, they decided that he should go live with Mommy Bunny but frequently visit with his foster family so he wouldn't miss them so much.

This same type of story can be used to help children verbalize their feelings about the adoption experience.

Older school-age children often enjoy writing their own story. The story that follows was written by a ten-year-old African American boy, Mike, after his adoption into the Caucasian family of his first grade schoolteacher.

Tom-Tom the Round Pumpkin

Once upon a time, Tom-Tom the jack-o-lantern was born on a mountain. But he was abandoned by his real mother. That made him feel sad when she couldn't take care of him anymore. He decided that he was too young to be alone so he went to find a new family. He looks and looks. He was sad and lonely while he looked for a new family. It made him act bad. Everyone thought he was a *bad behaving* pumpkin.

Then one day when he had turned 8 years old he found a new family of pumpkins. They didn't exactly look like him because they were oval shaped pumpkins and he was a round pumpkin. But they were still pumpkins anyway even though they looked a little funny on the outside.

Now he is ten years old and is a happy, *good*, silly, little pumpkin. He doesn't even notice their shape anymore. Life is good for Tom-Tom.[13]

TOOL NINE: CAN YOU TELL ME WHAT THEY THINK?— DOLL AND PUPPET PLAY

This "play" technique is quite helpful to communicate about adoption with the preschool or young school-age children, ages three to seven. The activity has four purposes:

1. to teach or clearly illustrate the facts of the child's history;

2. to elicit feelings and perceptions from the very young child;

3. to correct misperceptions (often related to magical thinking of children in this age range) or fantasies; and

4. to express feelings, wishes, or dreams of the "characters" involved in the child's past or present.

The parent can use small Fisher-Price figures, other small dolls, or puppets to represent important figures in the child's past and present. The parent explains to the child that they are going to play out a story. Identify the characters, using the real names of the child, birth parent, adoptive parent, siblings, and others, or use fictitious names but actual circumstances of the child's adoption. Allow the child to control and speak for the "child" doll to elicit his or her perceptions and feelings. Parents should never "correct" feelings, but they can "correct" the actual events in the story by saying, "Let's play the story this way—I think this is the way the story might have happened." This play technique allows learning through a visual, experiential activity that can be repeated many times over (children will thoroughly enjoy the attention and the activity as well as the ability to add more details and figures as they mature). Children who have difficulty understanding language will especially benefit from seeing a reenactment of their life. This play therapy technique may provide a safe opportunity, for both the parent and child, to express fears, anger, sadness, and good wishes for the future held naturally by all members of the adoption triad. Expression of these feelings occurs through a character, thereby creating an emotional comfort zone for all involved.

The number of figures or puppets used should be adjusted based on the child's age and developmental capacity to keep track of different characters in the story. A reasonable rule of thumb is to allow only as many characters as the child's age, plus one. That is, a four-year-old can accommodate a story with five characters.

Parents should not feel compelled to illustrate every detail in excruciating accuracy during the first play session. Initially, it is important only to understand the child's perception, "where the child is" in beginning to make sense of his or her adoption story. As the parent and child continue to "play the story" during subsequent sessions, the parent should address the following issues, one aspect at a time.

- Understanding what placements have occurred in the child's life
- Answering questions about siblings, birth parents, and other attachment figures
- Understanding reasons for the child's separation from the birth family
- Exploring feelings about the child's separation from the birth family
- Understanding other separations that have occurred in the child's history (orphanages, kinship families, foster families, previous adoptive placements)
- Exploring feelings about the child's separation from these placements
- Understanding the reasons behind the adoption plan made by agencies and courts or by the birth parents
- Understanding why the adoptive parents wanted the child
- Understanding the child's future with the adoptive family
- Exploring the child's wishes/dreams for the future in relation to siblings, birth parents, and other kinship or foster families with whom the child has connections
- Helping the child understand that his birth parents wish him to be happy and successful in his new family; they want him to make them proud of him
- Helping the child to understand that he can love and be loyal to many persons and families at the same time

TOOL TEN: PICK A FEELING CARD

A tool very familiar to therapists is also helpful for parents: the Feeling Faces. These cards can be purchased at educational stores or made at home. The cards reflect a variety of emotions that children may experience at various times in their lives. They can be used in conjunction with discussing the Life Map and in "Let's Tell a Story." A simplified sampling of common emotions that can be placed on the cards for younger children might include happy, sad, scared, angry, lonely, or confused. For older children, once they can read, a fuller range of emotions can be written on a single card:

• happy	• ashamed	• scared
• sad	• relieved	• confused
• frustrated	• hopeful	• angry
• guilty	• rejected	• lonely
• unloved	• excited	• powerless
• hopeless	• furious	• ignored
• worried	• depressed	• satisfied
• concerned	• embarrassed	• stubborn

The Feeling Faces

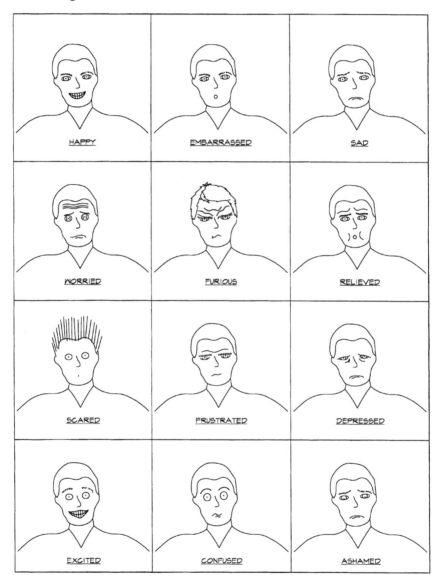

Katherine's Story

Katherine, a nine-year-old foster child, had been in therapy for a number of months. Her therapist released her, informing her caseworker, Sue Pelleg, that the child no longer needed her services.[14] Sue wasn't convinced due to the child's extensive background of abuse, and knew that Katherine needed more work before her upcoming adoptive placement, as shown by the following incident:

One afternoon, Katherine was in my office and started rummaging through my "goody bag." She pulled out my puppets and my face cards. She looked at me and said,

"I am going to tell you a story about this bunny who is getting adopted. This card (the angry face) is the bunny's daddy. This card (the grumpy face) is the bunny's mommy. One day the bunny and her worker (holding up a smiling face) went to court. The baby bunny knew that today the judge would make a decision about her adoption. The mommy and daddy bunnies came crashing into court. They were yelling and screaming at each other. The baby bunny was really scared. Just like this (holding up the scared card). The bunny wanted her daddy and mommy to go to jail for all the things that they did to the baby bunny and so they couldn't come back and hurt her. The baby's worker (holding up the smiling face) asked the baby bunny how long should the bunny mom and dad go to jail. The baby bunny answered, 'until they get a heart.' "

For Sue, the use of the feeling cards revealed much anxiety and fear for Katherine, emotions another therapist said were not present. Sue was able to help Katherine deal with her concerns now that they were out in the open. She credits the use of feeling cards and the puppets for helping this youngster come to terms with emotions she didn't have words for.

TOOL ELEVEN: WHO DO YOU GO TO FOR WHAT?

Children, even young children who have been institutionalized, have been severely neglected or abused, or have experienced multiple moves, have developed a mental blueprint of themselves and the adults in their world. In *Troubled Transplants*, Richard Delaney and Frank Kunstal write that maltreated children often view themselves as unsafe, worthless, and weak. Those same children, according to Delaney and Kunstal, view the adults in their world as unresponsive, unreliable, and dangerous.

James Anthony developed a tool that is particularly helpful for parents (and caseworkers) in eliciting children's perceptions of the adults in their world.[15] It can be used early in placement for children ages four to ten to help parents gain an understanding of the child's thoughts and feelings about adults important in the child's past and how those perceptions impact present and future relationships.

The parent develops three series of cards. The first series has stick figure drawings of family members—mother, father, grandmother, grandfather, older or younger siblings, aunts, uncles, foster parents, and so on. The last card in the first series, Mr. Nobody, should show a man's back. The cards should represent significant people in the child's past.

On each card in the second and third series, the parent writes a single sentence. In the second series of cards, each begins with the words "This is who I go to when I. . . ." This set of cards is used to help the child initiate interaction. In the third series of cards, which addresses interactions initiated by others in the child's life, each sentence starts with the words "This is who comes to me when they. . . ." The parent or child reads the card and places it on the appropriate person. This activity helps parents to develop an understanding of how children perceive others in their life—in a positive or negative manner.[16]

First Series of Cards: Significant People in the Child's Life

Second Series of Cards—"This is who I go to when . . ."

> This is who I go to when I am hungry.
> This is who I go to when I feel sick.
> This is who I go to when I fall down.
> This is who I go to when I want to share something happy.
> This is who I go to when I want to share something sad.
> This is who I go to when I am very scared.
> This is who I go to when I want a hug.
> This is who I go to when I need to share a happy secret.
> This is who I go to when I need to share a scary or sad secret.
> This is who I go to when I have a question about schoolwork.

Third Series of Cards—"This is who comes to me when . . ."

> This is who comes to me when they want to share something happy.
> This is who comes to me when they want to do something fun.
> This is who comes to me when they are mad.
> This is who comes to me when they are sad.
> This is who comes to me when they want a hug.
> This is who comes to me when they want me to do something (for example, chores, watch younger siblings).
> This is who comes to me when they want something from me.

Finally, along with the communication tools described above and adapted for use with older children, preteens and older teens can be encouraged to communicate their thoughts in writing.

TOOL TWELVE: WRITE A LETTER OR JOURNAL

Teens often go underground with their feelings—at least in their willingness to talk with adults. Sometimes the only way for an adolescent to communicate is through letter writing or journalizing. The following letter was written by a teen to her birth mother at the suggestion of her adoptive mom. The letter would never reach the birth parent in this particular case, but Tasha was willing to share it with her adoptive parents. It gave them tremendous insight into her feelings and perceptions about her earlier life experience.

Dear Barbara,
    In just a few short days, I will be sixteen years old. Sixteen. Does that seem possible to you? It has been many, many years since I saw you. The last memory I have is at that agency. Mom and dad have pictures of that last visit. I was around four. I hope now that you are happy. Are you? I'm not, not totally anyway. Happiness is what I wish for every year when I blow out my birthday candles. When you signed on that dotted line and gave me away, you blew out the candles. Why did you do that? Was it your wish for happiness?
    In these 12 years I have lived with a wonderful mom and dad. They have tended to and kissed my scrapes and scratches, helped me with homework, listened to my excited chatter (mostly about boys), taught me to drive the family car (I will be getting my license next week). I love them for what they mean to me. I know what I have done these years. I know what my parents have done. But, mother, what have you done?
    Everyone tells me that sixteen is too young to find you. They tell me that I am just not ready yet. I disagree. I have many questions that only you can answer. Why should such a large part of my life be missing? You blew out the candles? I had no choice. Why must I suffer?
    Your daughter, Tasha

Another helpful activity for teens is journaling. Keeping a running diary helps adolescents to formalize thoughts and feelings that are difficult to talk about. Carol, who was adopted as an infant, used her journal to chronicle her struggles with adoption issues. The following entries are in the form of a letter to her birth mother.

From Carol's Diary, December 30, 1997, Age Fifteen

today is my birthday. at 2:26 am you gave birth to me. does it mean anything to you that so many years ago you gave birth to a child? well, here i am—thinking about you. are you thinking about me? it is only fair that you should be thinking of me, but how am i to know.

From Carol's Diary, December 30, 1998, Age Sixteen

it has been a difficult birthday to enjoy. thoughts of you dominated me all day. i feel like i walk around with a big label taped to my blouse. the label screams

"ADOPTED," hushed voices whisper "given up," "thrown away" "adopted, adopted, adopted." i walk around, like today in the stores and it feels like everyone can see right through me and knows all about me.

SUMMARY

Knowing how to encourage a child to communicate about the issues of his past is a challenge for parents. Utilizing the tools discussed in this chapter will hopefully enable parents and children to open doors to healthy family communication.

QUESTIONS

1. In what ways is a lifebook valuable for an adopted child?
2. What challenges do you see in putting together a lifebook for your child? How can you overcome these challenges?
3. What other tools do you see as particularly helpful?
4. Are there any tools that you do not completely understand how to use?
5. What other tools have you used that are not discussed in this chapter?

NOTES

1. Denise Goodman, "Seven Reasons Why Children Need a Lifebook," in Jayne Schooler and Betsy Keefer, *Mystery History: Helping Adopted Children Understand the Past*. A training curriculum for foster and adopted parents. (Columbus, Ohio: Institute for Human Services, 1998).

2. Schooler and Keefer.

3. Judith Rycus and Ronald Hughes, *Field Guide to Child Welfare* (Washington: D.C. CWLA Press, Columbus, Ohio: Institute for Human Services, 1998).

4. Adapted with permission, from Fahlberg, *A Child's Journey Through Placement* (Indianapolis: Perspectives Press, 1991), 341–42.

5. Rycus and Hughes, 978.

6. Ibid.

7. Jayne Schooler, *The Whole Life Adoption Book* (Colorado Springs: Pinon Press, 1993), 136–37.

8. Vera Fahlberg, phone interview, July 13, 1999.

9. Fahlberg, *Child's Journey*, 356.

10. Ibid.

11. Kathryn Brohl, *Working with Traumatized Children* (Washington, D.C.: CWLA Press, 1996).

12. The story is taken entirely from Fahlberg, *Child's Journey*, and is used with permission of the author.

13. Beth Anthony, "A Place for Mike." *Guideposts Magazine*, July 1999. Used with permission.

14. Sue Pelleg, LISW, MSSA, has had extensive experience working with children, first as an elementary school teacher then as a caseworker and therapist.

She is currently Manager of Welcome Home, Cuyahoga County Ohio Early Childhood Initiative Program.

15. As cited in Fahlberg, *Child's Journey*, 46.

16. The questions and the cards were adapted from and added to Dr. Anthony's suggested list.

CHAPTER TEN

Transracial or Transcultural Adoption: Talking About Adoption Within a Minority Family

Race is one of those "forbidden" topics, much like death or sex. We know it's there, but we feel uncomfortable talking about it. One person of color noted, "Race is the first thing noticed, and the last thing talked about."

Many families who adopt children of a different race or ethnicity struggle to find ways to help their kids develop a positive racial identity. Parents who may have only observed racism and discrimination now find themselves a "minority family" and must learn to deal with those issues themselves. Even more important, through effective communication about racial and cultural issues, they can help their children cope with unfairness, stereotyping, and discrimination. This chapter offers practical insights and describes tools needed by families as they face this unique adoptive experience.

OVERVIEW OF TRANSRACIAL AND TRANSCULTURAL ADOPTION

Race and culture are not synonyms. Race, on the one hand, refers to physical characteristics which are, of course, genetically transmitted. Culture, on the other hand, is created by people and is transmitted through socialization or learning. "Culture is a system of values, beliefs, attitudes, traditions, and standards of behavior that govern the organization of people into social groups and regulate both group and individual behavior."[1] Culture helps assure the survival of both the group and its members.

Transracial placement refers to the placement of children of one race with an adoptive or foster family of another race, for example, the placement of Asian or African American children with European American families. Transcultural placement is the placement of children from one cultural group with an adoptive or foster family whose cultural background is different. Examples of transcultural placements would include adoption of children of one religious culture or socioeconomic group into a family of a different religion or socioeconomic group. Transcultural placements would also include, for example, the placement of Eastern European children with American families. The children and families share the same race, but have experienced different cultures. It can be argued that *all* adoptive and foster placements are, to a greater or lesser degree, transcultural in nature; virtually no foster or adoptive placements would be identical in culture to the practices, values, belief systems, and codes of conduct of the birth family.

However, relatively few adoptions are transracial. There are no definitive sources of data about the incidence of transracial adoption within the United States. A survey completed in 1995 by the Child Welfare League of America indicated that in 1993 only 4 percent of all adoptions were transracial.

HISTORY OF TRANSRACIAL PLACEMENTS

During the first half of the twentieth century, most adoptive "matches" were based on physical characteristics, religious background, and ethnicity. Transracial placements were extremely rare. During the late 1950s and early 1960s, some agencies, particularly those based in large metropolitan areas, began transracial placements of children. Adopt-a-Child in New York City and Minority Adoption Recruitment of Children's Homes (MARCH) in San Francisco were both created in the 1950s to place waiting children of color in white adoptive homes. In 1961 Parents to Adopt Minority Youngsters (PAMY) was founded in Minneapolis.[2]

During the remainder of the 1960s and during the next decade, the incidence of transracial placement of children increased as the numbers of young white children available for adoption decreased. Lists of prospective parents waiting for young white children became longer and longer for a number of reasons. The stigma attached to unmarried parenthood was greatly diminished by the sexual revolution of the sixties, and birth parents no longer felt social coercion to make adoption plans for children born out of wedlock. Further, abortion became legal with the Supreme Court decision *Roe vs. Wade*, thereby providing a safe alternative way of dealing with untimely pregnancies. As the availability of young white children diminished, prospective adoptive families began to take another look at waiting children, often children of color.

In 1972 the National Association of Black Social Workers questioned the wisdom of placing children of color in white homes, stating that white parents did not have the skills to prepare nonwhite children to cope with a racist society. In response to this criticism, numerous studies have been undertaken to validate or critique the practice of transracial placements. These research projects have come to conflicting conclusions, "proving" both that transracially adopted persons have well-developed racial identity and positive self-esteem, and transracially adopted persons have struggled with identity confusion, and lack a sense of belonging in either the majority or minority cultures.

While social workers and parents remain widely and passionately divided on this controversial issue, the incidence of transracial placements has been steadily increasing. In 1994 the Multiethnic Placement Act (MEPA) was passed by the U.S. Congress. This act, amended in 1996 by the Interethnic Placement Act (IEPA), states that no foster or adoptive placement of a child can be denied or delayed based on race, color, or national origin. Likewise, no family can be denied the opportunity to adopt or foster based on race, color, or national origin. To discriminate in placement decisions based on these criteria is a criminal violation of an individual's civil rights. It is likely that this legislation will drive the rates of transracial adoption even higher within the next few years.

HISTORY OF INTERNATIONAL PLACEMENTS

World War II left many European children orphaned, and American families provided homes for many of these children. By the 1950s, the number of homeless European children had dwindled, but new conflicts in Korea, and later Vietnam, created pools of children who needed families. The 1980s brought an increase in adoptions from Central and South America and India, while conflicts and political upheaval in Eastern Europe have led to adoptions of children from Romania, Russia, and Bosnia during the 1990s. Further, social policies attempting to reduce population growth in China have limited families in that country to one child. Chinese families who wish to have male children care for them during old age have surrendered female children for adoption. As a result of all these social and political factors, the number of international adoptions has grown steadily over the past few years:[3]

1990	7,093
1991	9,008
1992	6,536
1993	7,348
1994	8,195
1995	9,679

1996	11,316
1997	13,620
1998	15,774

The primary sending countries for children adopted internationally in 1998 were:[4]

Russia	4,491
China	4,206
Korea	1,829
Guatemala	911

As both transracial and international placements become more common, many adoptive families will need to learn to talk with their children about racial and cultural issues in addition to adoption issues. The work of Gail Stenberg and Beth Hall in their book, *An Insider's Guide to Transracial Adoption* (web site: www.pactadopt.org), stands out in addressing these issues and has informed the ideas presented here. The racial and cultural issues of identity formation and positive self-esteem add an additional layer to the task of parenting. Visualize the tasks of transracially parenting adopted children as an onion. The "heart" of the onion is the job of parenting any child, understanding normal child development, and responding appropriately to all the needs of the child. The next layer of the onion represents the generic adoption issues, involving separation from the birth family and the resulting grief, fear of abandonment, lack of trust and control, and so on. The final layer of the onion, for the transracial adoptive parent, is the layer of skill needed to parent a child of a different racial and/or cultural background than one's own, helping the child understand and feel good about who he or she is, and helping the child cope with the baggage of living in a world that does not tolerate diversity well.

While it can be tempting to announce, "I don't see color, I only see the child," parents must remember that everyone else in the community will see both. Ignoring racial and cultural issues, like the proverbial ostrich with its head in the sand, leaves children ill equipped to build a positive racial and cultural identity and without the survival skills necessary to be successful adults.

BUILDING SELF-ESTEEM

Understanding Racial Identity Formation

One's sense of the world, as well as success in negotiating that world, is largely interpreted through the sense of self, through identity development. Identity can be defined as an individual's personal, coherent sense of self. Identity development involves the adoption of certain personal values, attitudes, feelings, characteristics, and behaviors in addition to identification with a larger group of people who share similar characteristics.[5]

Identity formation for all *persons of difference* (including, for example, persons with disabilities, persons of minority races or religions, persons who are gay or lesbian) becomes more complex. Persons of difference are often subject to prejudice and discrimination. Furthermore, they must learn to function within a bicultural context. That is, persons of difference must learn to adjust within the majority culture in school, work, and many daily living activities, and they are also expected to function easily within the culture reflected by their difference (deaf culture, racial or ethnic culture, Jewish culture, to name a few). The task of learning to cope with prejudice and discrimination and the task of forming a bicultural identity can lead to identity confusion, conflict, and various forms of anxiety and sociological dilemmas.

The challenge of living with a bicultural identity is documented in the work of the Institute for Human Services in Columbus, Ohio.

This duality is difficult to comprehend by persons who have never experienced social oppression. Persons of difference struggle between their cultural norms and the norms of the majority. This is especially difficult for children of difference. This awareness doesn't occur all at once, but rather, gradually during school-aged, pre-adolescent, and adolescent years. Youth are confronted with being part of, yet apart from, *in* a larger social environment, but not *of* it, included at some level, and excluded at others. This duality is at the heart of the identity struggle and generates powerful feelings of rage and indignation.

Parents and families of adolescents of color must be aware of this struggle. This insight will allow the parents and families to understand the nature of the youth's behaviors, attitudes and beliefs. Providing support and encouragement in a nurturing environment and multiple opportunities to model other youth and adults who have established healthy identities will facilitate the identity process for youth.[6]

STAGES OF RACIAL IDENTITY FORMATION

All persons experience stages in the formation of their racial identity. Persons of difference (persons of color) have an identity formation complicated by external factors. Incidents of prejudice, discrimination, and stereotyping create critical incidents during the process of identity formation. If, for example, children are confronted with discrimination, they will compare what they have been told to what they have experienced. This can trigger a deeper exploration of their racial identity and may challenge previously held beliefs. The following model was developed

Racial Identity Formation

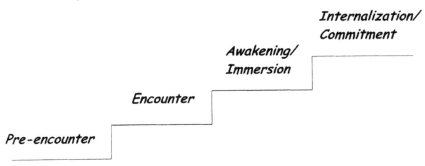

by Thomas Cross.[7] It describes four stages of racial identity formation for persons of color. The degree of discrimination experienced and the level of contact and comfort with the culture of difference will impact progress through these stages of identity formation.

Stage One: Pre-encounter. I'm a Person of Color, but Who Cares?

Individuals in this stage of racial identity formation lack interest in the concept of race. Young persons are likely to interpret the world from the perspective of the majority culture, and they see no reason to challenge the views and codes of conduct of the majority culture. They may even think and behave in ways that communicate a devaluation of their own culture.

Stage Two: Encounter. Racism Hit Me Right Between the Eyes, When I Wasn't Even Looking!

Individuals have experienced one or many critical incidents inconsistent with their earlier beliefs. A critical incident can be a single encounter with a racist or oppressive experience or an accumulation of more subtle experiences with racism. Some examples of critical incidents would be name-calling, exclusion from groups or activities, or exposure to episodes of stereotyping. These critical incidents cause young people to question and reexamine previously held beliefs of the dominant culture. They may experience confusion about their own cultural group as well as the dominant culture. Youth may begin to develop new ideas and positive stereotypes about their own racial group as well as negative stereotypes about the dominant culture and/or other groups.

Stage Three: Awakening/Immersion. I Need to Know Where I Come From.

Youth in this stage have searched for their identity and are committed to their racial/ethnic roots. This stage reflects the polar opposite of the pre-encounter stage. Youth at this stage of development are likely to reject the norms and practices of other groups and completely embrace the norms, values, and codes of conduct of their own racial group. Youth immerse themselves in the dress, language, friends, music, art, foods, and other manifestations of their cultural identification and reject those of other cultures. Confrontation and bluntness become the norm, and individuals in this stage may even decide that "all whites are devils." Immersed persons may avoid contact with those in the majority group. Persons in this stage of identity formation may also have confrontations with others in their cultural/racial group who are not thoroughly immersed or as confrontational with differences as they are themselves.

Stage Four: Internalization/Commitment. I Can Look Beyond Myself.

Individuals in this stage are secure and self-confident about their difference. After the intensity of the immersion stage, individuals develop a more balanced, integrated perspective on racial identity. Persons in the final stage of identity formation can appreciate and even assimilate traits from other racial/ethnic groups. Still grounded in their own cultures, individuals in this stage move toward a more pluralistic perspective. Here is how James Baldwin described the internalization/commitment phase:

Not one of us knows how to walk when we get here. Not one of us knows how to open a window, unlock a door. Not one of us can master a staircase. We are absolutely ignorant of the almost certain results of falling out of a five-story window. None of us comes here knowing enough not to play with fire. Nor can one of us drive a tank, fly a jet, hurl a bomb, or plant a tree.

We must all be taught that. We have to learn all that. The irreducible price of learning is realizing that you do not know. One may go further and point out—as any scientist, or artist, will tell you—that the more you learn, the less you know, but that means that you have begun to accept, and are even able to rejoice in, the relentless conundrum of your life.[8]

Robin's Story

Robin, now twenty-six years old and the mother of three boys, was born to a Caucasian woman addicted to heroin. During the pregnancy, Robin's mother took methadone, a prescription drug used by treatment centers to "wean" addicts from heroin. Robin was born addicted to methadone and had to remain in the hospital for ten days following her birth. Her birth father was African American. Robin was placed in the foster home of Dot and Bob, Caucasian parents who, for many years, fostered children with special needs. Dot and Bob ultimately had two children by birth, a daughter older than Robin, and a son who was younger. Her foster parents adopted Robin when she was only one and a half years old. They continued to foster children with special needs, including many children of color, over the next twenty-five years.

Today, Robin remembers noticing that she was darker than the others in her family when she was about three years old. She feels that her parents handled the racial issues well because they were always open to questions and shared information honestly. As a young child, she went to bed crying at night because she idolized her older sister and wanted to be white like her. As Robin got older, particularly during the middle school years, the racial issue became larger. Robin remembers being embarrassed, at times, when she was in public with her family because her parents and siblings were white. When with her family in the community, her adoption became public information to even the most casual observer. Dot recalls that Robin really did not understand until she was about eleven years old that her birth mother was white. This information had been shared with Robin when she was much younger, but she did not comprehend that information until she was in middle school. Dot commented on Robin's anger "that we hadn't told her," or at least hadn't told her in a way that could be absorbed by her. Dot remembers that some of the African American girls rejected Robin when she was a middle school student because her choices for hair and clothing styles were not "appropriate" in their eyes. Robin wore her hair in an Afro and did not want her mother to touch it. The African American girls considered this hairstyle out of date and teased her about her appearance. Most of her friends during this time were white. The most significant single critical incident occurred when a carload of teenage boys passed Robin while she was walking on an isolated road in a white neighborhood. The boys yelled racial slurs at Robin, and she remembers feeling very angry and afraid. She considered responding, but felt outnumbered and powerless. She ran home and shared her feelings with her parents. During this time, Robin often fantasized about going to live with a black family, feeling that they would understand what she was going through. Her mother had an African American friend and co-worker who was extremely important to both Robin and Dot.

When Robin was in high school, she became reacquainted with a grandfather who was married to an African American woman. Robin spent two summers with her grandparents, but she and her step-grandmother were not able to "connect." Robin was very outspoken, and she functioned very much as a white child. Her grandmother could not accept Robin's "white" behavior.

Dot believes the area where she was least proficient as a transracial adoptive parent was in understanding the importance of looking good in the African American community. Robin did not like to have her hair braided or relaxed, and Dot allowed Robin to wear her hair in a "natural." Dot believes now that Robin's journey through adolescence would have been easier if she had pushed the issue of hair care as a parenting issue and not a grooming issue: in other words, who takes charge, when, and with what consequences. When and to what degree does a parent allow the child to be in control of hair, clothes, and behaviors, and when does the parent take charge of those decisions? "Our philosophies gave control of those issues to the kids in most situations. Our son's long hair and black leather jackets had one set of consequences—Robin's 'Afro' had another. I believe hers was more damaging on a long range basis because of the way the community dealt with it. The issues are more complex than knowledge about hair care, and, in my view, are not well understood across cultures. The senses of what puts our children at risk or in danger are different."

Dot does feel that her neighborhood was not as integrated as she would have liked, but the adoptive parents ensured that Robin attended integrated schools. In fact, they struggled with decisions about sending Robin to an excellent private school designed for learning disabled students, but chose to send Robin to the public school so that she would not be the only child of color in her classroom. The high school Robin attended was in a metropolitan community and was the magnet school for students who spoke English as a second language. As a result, Robin attended school with a very diverse group of students.

Dot also believes that fostering children of many different races was helpful for Robin, as she was not always the only person of color within the family. Further, routine interaction with several African American foster parents was profoundly important in helping Robin understand and feel good about African American families, and African American women in particular. In addition, these informal cultural consultants were helpful advisors to Dot and Bob as they marshaled Robin through critical incidents involving her schoolmates and others in the community.

Today, Robin identifies herself as a person of mixed racial heritage. She sees herself as neither black nor white, but as biracial. Her friends are almost exclusively African American. She lives in an African American neighborhood, and she does not feel comfortable dating white men. She sees herself becoming more "black" as she matures in many of her cultural practices—she has picked up African American mannerisms, styles of speaking, parenting practices, and so on.

Dr. Denise Goodman, adoption consultant and trainer, notes:

Achieving identity congruence in the face of oppression and discrimination is a major challenge. Successfully navigating through these obstacles takes psychological and sociological stability, especially for children. Foster/adoptive families of persons of difference must first be aware of the struggle the youth faces. This will bring an understanding of the nature of the youth's behaviors, attitudes, and beliefs.[9]

STRATEGIES FOR ENHANCING POSITIVE CULTURAL IDENTITY

Be a Bridge

Your child needs to belong to groups that you cannot belong to. "So when you can't be the direct provider of culture, be a bridge to the culture your child needs to be part of, a culture you can't be part of yourself. Please don't feel discouraged by his participation in a culture that does not include you. The connecting links you can forge will not only support him but will expand your family life in ways that will continue to unfold throughout your lives. Nothing could be more positive."[10]

Remember the story of the ugly duckling? Could the mother duck who raised a swan have taught her baby to swim like a swan or to sound like a swan or to act like a swan? Of course not—she was a duck. She could certainly teach him everything she knew about how to act like a duck, but she couldn't know how to be a swan. Even if she had read 1,000 books about swan history and habits, she still wouldn't have been an authentic swan; she'd be a duck who knew a great deal about swans. That baby swan had to learn from other swans how to be a swan. In the same way, the foremost challenge you face as an adoptive parent is that you will not be able to provide directly for all your child's essential needs, no matter how hard you try and no matter how much you want to. You will not be able to provide personally for your child's need to belong to his culture. Culture is not something you learn about in books. Culture is something you live. You become part of it by living in the experience.

And if you are parenting a child of a different race from your own, you will not be able to provide directly for your child's need to build a positive racial identity. You will never become a member of your child's race or genetic family, no matter how many books you read or how much soul food or chilies or dim sum you eat or how educated you become about the history of her race.[11]

Get Help from People from Your Child's Cultural Group.

You cannot parent any child alone. When parenting a child of a different race or culture, you must aggressively seek help from persons of that child's culture.

Mary was sitting on a park bench, watching her biracial daughter play happily on the swings with several other children. Her daughter Crystal would periodically run back to Mary, "checking in," to be secure her mother was safely nearby. An attractive African American woman, a complete stranger, approached Mary and asked if she could come to her home that evening to fix Crystal's hair. Surprised, Mary accepted this offer of help. That evening, her newfound friend came to her home, put a tablespoon of Vaseline in Crystal's hair, and began to braid it. The following morning, Mary, as instructed, took out the braids, and she found that Crystal's hair looked more beautiful than it ever had before. Her friend continued to provide "cultural consultation" to the adoptive family as Crystal grew up. Crystal and other children of color in this large adoptive family benefited greatly from this woman's willingness and commitment to play a role in her development of self-esteem and positive racial identity.

Beth Hall and Gail Steinberg, authors of *An Insider's Guide to Transracial Adoption*, remind parents:

The best tool you can develop as a parent of a child of another race is a healthy ability to challenge your own assumptions about what you need to do and about what your child faces. Even though, in every possible way, you are your child's parents and she is your child, she will be living in a different world than you do. You will not be able to provide for all her needs yourself. Once you give up that expectation, you can begin the process of providing.[12]

Make sure your child understands the "rules" of his birth culture as well as the rules of yours.

All cultures have codes of conduct, styles of language and dress, and values that have served to foster the continuation of the culture and the survival of its members, as well as a sense of group cohesiveness. Your child, even more so than other children of color, lives in a bicultural world and must learn the skills to negotiate and navigate successfully in both cultures. Understand that you are not the best authority to teach the survival skills your child needs to navigate within his cultural milieu, but make sure that he has the opportunities to learn these skills at school, at church, in neighborhood groups, and with friends of the family.

STRATEGIES FOR TALKING WITH YOUR CHILD ABOUT RACE AND RACISM

Listen More; Talk Less

As the authorities in the family, parents often feel that they are appropriately providing guidance and instruction for their children only when they are doing the talking. Yet all effective leaders and teachers have learned the art of listening. Before teaching and guiding, parents must first understand where the child is in his experience, perception, and development. To understand those issues, parents must hear before they speak. Further, parents need to learn more about their child's reality to understand when they can provide help themselves, and when they need to seek help from others. "Parents may tell themselves they feel comfortable raising a child across racial lines, but when faced with issues that threaten their child's well-being, feelings of uncertainty, anger, and perhaps shame can arise. Don't assume your feelings are the same as your child's. Don't overload the situation with your input. If you bring race into every situation to the exclusion of everything else, your child may avoid talking about race with you at all costs. The best advice is: Listen More; Talk Less. *You need to understand your child's experience, not direct the action.*"[13]

Ask Open-Ended Questions

To understand the child's perceptions, parents should not ask questions that can be answered with a monosyllable. Parents should ask, for example, "How did school go today? What happened?" instead of "Did you have a good day?" Use these open dialogues as a barometer to learn more about your child's experiences and stage of identity development.

Don't Turn Into a Psychological Dentist, Extracting Feelings as if They Were Bad Teeth"[14]

Parents should not constantly search the horizon for racial or cultural problems that do not exist for the child. It is possible to *over*respond to the racial and cultural issues faced by adopted and foster children. Parents should not insist on the racial issue throughout every conversation with the child. "Encouraging your child to talk when she says, 'I'm okay, leave me alone,' may be overload. It's possible nothing is really wrong. We sometimes assume that superficial answers to our anxious questions mean the child is concealing painful emotions, but we may be looking for something that isn't here. On the other hand, don't assume that because there is no discussion, there are no problems. Trust your intuition and everything you know about your child, but don't overreact or invade your child's right to be the star of his or her personal drama by taking it over for yourself."[15]

Create a Code Word or Gesture for Dealing with Rude Remarks in Public

When strangers or casual acquaintances make ridiculously rude remarks in the presence of the child, many families find it helpful to communicate their desire to terminate the encounter through use of a secret code word or gesture. Any member of the family experiencing discomfort can use the word or gesture to let others know that they can no longer abide the stranger's ignorance or rudeness. Children enjoy being a part of the "in group" that knows and uses these codes and can benefit from the camaraderie, implicit support, and fun of using these codes in public. These code words or cover stories can stop the escalation of an unpleasant encounter into a critical incident.

COMMON THEMES THROUGHOUT DEVELOPMENT

Preschoolers

Children begin to notice racial differences as early as two years of age, and most often by the age of three. Transracial adoptive parents of preschoolers and early school-age children are often troubled when their child expresses the desire to be "white like you." Parents become concerned that this statement indicates a rejection of the child's racial or cultural identity. However, it is not unusual, in a society dominated by white people and images, for children of color, even those being raised in same race or birth families, to express a desire to be white or lighter skinned. It is important, however, that children of all ages (and children raised in all types of families) be exposed to diversity and be able to see people other than those in the media who look like they do.

School-Age Children

Transracially adopted children of school-age years may feel teased or excluded by their peers because of racial differences, or because they are different by virtue of transracial adoption: a child of color living with a white family. Children this age should be empowered to resolve their own problems as much as possible. Parents should ask a child about a critical incident, his or her feelings at the time, and possible responses that might have been used. Parents should help children explore both the immediate and long-term consequences of the potential responses. Children should be helped to explore whether it would be better to handle a similar situation differently in the future, or if they should respond in the same way if confronted with such a problem again. For example, in a dialogue with Robin about her critical incident (boys yelling racial slurs at her on an isolated road), Robin's potential responses might have included:

1. Engage in a confrontation by yelling back at the boys.
2. Respond through an obscene gesture.
3. Run home without responding.
4. Continue to walk as if the encounter did not happen, without engaging in any verbal exchange.

Robin and her parents could explore each of these alternatives, and any others that present themselves, to determine if she chose the most appropriate response at the time. The consequences of the first two alternatives might have been an escalation of the critical incident in an unsafe environment, jeopardizing Robin's safety. Running may also have led to escalation, prompting the boys to chase her, and the act of running may have sent a message to both the boys and Robin that she could not protect herself from verbal assaults. The final alternative, the one chosen by Robin at the time, seems to have the fewest negative consequences; therefore, her parents could support her in her ability to handle a difficult situation with both grace and good judgment. At the conclusion of such a teaching dialogue, parents should ask if the child feels there is anything the parents should do. The child should be secure in parental support, but allowed to handle unfairness without adult intervention whenever possible. Through these incidents and the "teachable moments" that follow, children can develop more sophisticated survival skills and a sense that they can cope with discrimination in the future.

Adolescents

Issues related to self-image and dating often surface for the transracially adopted teenager. "The development of body image and the successful assimilation of that body image into the psyche is an essential element of adolescent identity formation. It is critical for the development of positive body image that teens of color have role models that reflect body styles similar to their own. If a teen has no such personal experience, he will be at the mercy of the media's representations of people of the child's race or ethnicity."[16]

Dating can be problematic for transracially adopted teens, who may find barriers in dating others who are white, but may feel uncomfortable with, or lack access to, potential dating partners of color. Discussion and exploration of feelings about dating are critical for the transracially adopted teen. "The important thing in putting talk into the air is not whether the teenager responds or agrees, but that he or she hears the talk," Randolph Severson comments. "The psyche is such an extraordinary 'continuous learner' that it cannot help but assimilate every new datum of information in its lifelong quest for truth."[17]

SUMMARY

Foster and adoptive parents should celebrate the rewards that diversity through transcultural and/or transracial parenting brings into their lives. Few persons of a majority race or culture have the tremendous opportunities for personal growth afforded to those individuals who benefit from this challenge.

Robin's mother, Dot, has the following advice for a new generation of transracial adoptive parents:

• Be honest and open; it's the unknown that kids can't handle.

• Stay closely integrated in the child's culture. Seek out relationships and connections that will assist your child in maintaining an understanding of and attachment to his or her culture.

- Understand that you are not a white family with some members of other races. You are now a family of color. Remember that as you make choices about neighborhoods, schools, churches, etc.

- It might be preferable, if adopting/fostering across racial lines, to adopt or foster more than one child of color.

- Don't isolate yourself. You need to socialize and interact with other foster/adoptive families, preferably those with racially mixed families. It is extremely helpful to have other parents to talk with about the issues of raising a child of color to have a positive self-esteem and racial identity.

QUESTIONS

1. In what ways does your family differ culturally from your child's birth family?

2. Do you see your family as a minority family? If yes, how has that affected your entire family?

3. At what stage of racial identity formation is my child? Why?

4. Has your child experienced critical incidents? How has he been affected? How have you been affected?

5. What kinds of discrimination might your child experience? Do you feel comfortable assisting your child in coping effectively with discrimination? Where can you find help?

6. Do you need to seek assistance from your child's birth culture to learn ways to enhance your child's self-esteem and positive racial identity? Where might you find that kind of assistance?

NOTES

1. Denise Goodman and Daniel Houston, "Cultural Issues in Permanency Planning," Tier II Adoption Assessor Curriculum, Ohio Child Welfare Training Program, Columbus, Ohio, 1998, 10.

2. Ibid.

3. U.S. Immigration and Naturalization Service and U.S. Department of State. Evan B. Donaldson Adoption Institute, www.adoptioninstitute.org.

4. Ibid.

5. Goodman and Houston.

6. Ibid., 26–27.

7. William Cross, *Boys No More* (Beverly Hills: Glencoe Press, 1971).

8. Quoted in Gail Steinberg and Beth Hall, *An Insider's Guide to Transracial Adoption*, (San Francisco: Pact Press, 1998), 28.

9. Goodman and Houston, 30.

10. Steinberg and Hall, 52.

11. Ibid., 51–52.

12. Ibid., 52.

13. Ibid., 99.

14. Ibid., 100.
15. Ibid., 393.
16. Ibid.
17. Ibid.

CHAPTER ELEVEN

Kinship Foster Care and Adoption: Telling the Truth When It's "All in the Family"

Many foster and adoptive families are created when a child is removed from the care of his or her parents and placed with close or extended family members. In fact, relative adoptions are historically the most common form of adoption, since most cultures encourage the adoption (formal or informal) of orphaned children by extended family members. Kinship care creates an unusual challenge for a family: telling the child the truth about the past when that truth involves a close family member. This chapter will discuss the joys and hazards unique to kinship care and ways to keep communication sensible, sensitive, and healthy.

HISTORY OF KINSHIP ADOPTION

"A study by Kari Sandven, Ph.D., of the Riverside Medical Center in Minneapolis, Minnesota, and Michael D. Resnick, Ph.D., of the School of Public Health at the University of Minnesota, found that the acceptance of informal adoption dates back to the kinship structures of ancient African cultures. It was customary then for aunts and uncles to help raise one another's children, creating the tradition of shared rather than exclusive parenting. Three generations of family lived together, and there were flexible boundaries that emphasized the clan over the nuclear family. The concept 'It takes a village to raise a child' began here."[1]

While the numbers of kinship placements have been increasing dramatically in recent years, the phenomenon of both formal and informal kinship placements has always existed in this country. A formal kinship adoption is one facilitated by an attorney and/or agency, with an adoption legalization in court. An informal kinship placement occurs when a relative or close family friend steps in during a family crisis to care for children who are orphaned or otherwise in need of nurture and stability.

An informal kinship placement, while statistically much more stable than agency foster placements, may or may not be permanent, and the placement does not involve institutions such as child protective services agencies, courts, and so on. Informal kinship placements have occurred often in minority cultures, where distrust of formal institutions is more prevalent and where family crisis might be precipitated due to higher levels of poverty. It is not uncommon in the African American community, for example, to see a grandmother or great-grandmother caring for children, or an aunt or close family friend assisting with care of children. Such informal networks also exist within many other cultures, including the Latino community. "In the South Texas community where I was raised, there was an informal system of intra-family adoptions that undoubtedly evolved in response to family and community needs," says Irma Herrera, director of Multicultural Education and Training Advocacy, Inc., in the San Francisco area. "Adoption was our way of distributing the burdens and benefits within a community."[2]

Adoptive parents involved in either formal or informal kinship adoption share the same responsibilities as those in nonkinship adoption.

• They are to nurture and care for their kin children;

• They are to assure that the children's needs are met; and

• They are to help establish a plan to connect the children to safe, stable, nurturing relationships intended to last a lifetime, when they cannot be reunited with their birth parents.

Many informal adoptive kinship families have strong reservations about a formal adoption of the children in their care. In fact, 85 percent of kinship foster families studied did not want to formally adopt the children. Most of them believed that it wasn't necessary because "they are already family." Others thought that it would create conflict within the extended family and create problems with the birth parents of the children. Despite these reservations about formal adoption, most kinship families remain firmly committed to the care of their children. Seventy percent indicated that they would allow a child to remain with them either "as long as he/she wants to" or "until he/she is able to take care of him/herself."[3]

Unfortunately, the system of informal kinship adoption has been faltering under societal pressures during the last two decades. Azizi Powell, former director of Black Adoption Services for Three Rivers Adoption

Council in Pittsburgh, Pennsylvania, says, "The black family's mutual aid system of informal adoption is breaking down under the pressure of crack, prison, poverty, middle-class success, death, and do-your-own-thing individualism. There are a lot of motherless children unable to go home to kin."[4]

ADVANTAGES OF KINSHIP ADOPTION

There are powerful advantages for those children separated from birth parents who find permanency in kinship adoption. Whenever children must leave the'ʀ birth parents, the trauma of separation is softened when they can remain with people, places, and cultures familiar to them. Further, research on kinship placements indicates that children who are placed with kin have fewer moves and more stability than children in the child welfare system usually experience. A study by the Child Welfare League of America concluded that only 23 percent of children placed with relatives were not able to continue living with them after three years, compared with 58 percent of children in nonrelative foster care. In New York City, where half of all children in foster care live with relatives, a task force on kinship care found that kinship parents were more likely than traditional foster parents to care for large sibling groups of children, further reducing the trauma of separation from the birth family.[5]

Children in kinship adoptions may have more opportunity to stay in touch with their birth parents, particularly if birth parents continue to remain involved in functions with the extended family. As a result, children in kinship adoptions may not feel totally cut off from their past, may not, in other words, feel that much of their history is a mystery. And relatives may be less fearful than other adoptive parents of unknown factors within the child's genetic background.

COMMUNICATION CHALLENGES OF KINSHIP ADOPTION

Challenge One: Familiarity Breeds . . .

One of the most significant advantages of kinship adoption, the relationship with the birth parents, can also present significant challenges to kinship adoptive parents. If adoptive parents know (and perhaps dislike or disrespect) the birth parents, will they be able to perceive the child as a person in his own right? Will they be constantly looking for evidence that he is "just like" his birth father? Will he have the same weaknesses as the birth mother? Furthermore, kinship adoption can include many of the same feelings and dynamics as an ugly, bitter divorce. Can, for example, kinship adoptive parents, who may have suffered themselves as a result of the behavior of these birth parents, present the birth parents in a positive light to the child? Can kinship adoptive parents, who have very strong feelings at times about the birth parents, talk with their children about the birth father without calling him "your *!?*//* father?" "This is an issue, of course, for all adoptive parents, even when they are not relatives," says Lois Melina, editor of *Adopted Child* newsletter. "But it's more complicated with family members. It's easier, for example, for a non-relative to speak compassionately about a birth parent who is an alcoholic than for a family member who has experienced firsthand the birthparent's violence when drunk, inability to take responsibility for his actions, expectations that he will be forgiven (for his offenses) when he is sober, and refusal to seek help."[6]

Challenge Two: Loss of the Dream of One's Child as a Parent

Beth Brindo, an adoption expert at Bellefaire Jewish Children's Home in Cleveland, Ohio, comments that grandparents who adopt must grieve the loss of the vision of their birth children as parents. They will not be able to enjoy watching their children raising children. The bitterness that might accompany this grief can spill over into their communications with their adopted children about their birth parents and the circumstances surrounding their birth, poisoning the children's understanding of their roots and their own self-esteem.

Kenneth and Claudia's twenty-year-old daughter, Sandra, was their greatest joy and their greatest heartache. Right after high school, Sandra had become involved in an abusive relationship and refused to leave it. By the time she was nineteen, she was the mother of a beautiful son. However, the drugs and alcohol present in Sandra's apartment took precedence over her care of Mickey. Nothing other than the drugs would get her attention. Kenneth and Claudia made the heartbreaking decision of reporting their only daughter to the protective service agency in their town—so that young Mickey would be safe. Sandra's live-in boyfriend talked her quickly into signing Mickey into the full and legal custody of her parents.

Challenge Three: Establishing Boundaries

Many kinship adoptions are also open adoptions. The birth parents often know where the children are, and they continue to relate, if not to the children, to the extended family. As in all open adoptions, adoptive parents must set some boundaries about the type of contact, timing of contacts, who holds parenting responsibility and decision-making authority, how and when information is to be shared, and so on. In kinship adoptions, setting boundaries can be even more difficult, creating increasingly complicated ripples, because the adoptive parent is functioning as the parent to the child as well as being the grandparent, aunt/uncle, niece, sibling, or other relative of the birth parent. The desire to "keep peace in the family" can sometimes interfere with creation of healthy boundaries so important in open adoption relationships.

Challenge Four: Family Gatherings

Some extended families can become fractured as members "choose sides" if and when adoption-related conflict occurs. In kinship adoptions where parental rights of birth parents were involuntarily terminated, this fracturing can become particularly problematic. Such fissures can present more than the usual family or holiday reunion stress. If disagreements exist about how to communicate with the child about the adoption, for example, the holiday gift exchange can become quite emotionally charged. Or if adoptive parents have tried to keep the adoption secret, it is highly likely that cousins or others within the family will use family gatherings to leak this information to the adoptee. This is hardly an ideal way to learn about one's adoption history.

Challenge Five: Keeping the Family Secret

Finally, one would expect kinship adoptions to be more open than adoptions arranged for nonrelated persons. However, according to Beth Brindo and other post-adoption specialists, the reverse seems to be the case, at least anecdotally.[7] Kinship adoptive parents seem *more* likely than nonrelated adopters to keep the facts of the adoption secret. Because the parties involved are "all in the family," there can be an increased tendency to withhold or distort information in an attempt to "protect" family members from shameful or painful scenarios.

Many individuals who grew up in kinship adoptions are surprised to learn, as adults, that they were adopted, and that "Aunt Susie" was really the birth mother. In other cases, while honest about the facts surrounding parentage, some kinship adopters avoid the topic of adoption altogether within the family. Many informal kinship adopters have had minimal contacts, or none at all, with adoptive parent support organizations, agency training programs, or social workers. Left to handle a delicate situation without support or knowledge, many resort to avoidance as the path of least resistance.

Darlene grew up with her aunt and uncle in an informal kinship adoption. She knew that she was adopted, and she regularly visited with her birth mother (the sister of the uncle raising her). However, she had never met her birth father, and she had no information about him. Whenever Darlene asked her adoptive mother or her birth mother about her birth father, she was told that she was "better off" to know nothing about him. In fact, she had never even seen a picture of him. The circumstances surrounding Darlene's birth (she was born out of wedlock, fathered by a man considered "beneath" the mother's family) were a matter of embarrassment to the mother's family—the subject of Darlene's father became a forbidden topic within the home. Darlene was left to imagine dreadful things about her father, and about herself. She spent a considerable amount of energy during her childhood and adolescence fantasizing and wondering about her birth father, and she was fearful, as a young adult, of forming close relationships involving commitment and permanency with men.

PRINCIPLES OF TALKING ABOUT KINSHIP ADOPTION

Be the Parent.

"Adoption within families is not without its own unique challenges," says Sharon Kaplan Roszia, co-author of *The Open Adoption Experience* and a national expert on adoption. "In family adoption, everyone has two relationships to the child. The child's birth relatives are also his adoptive relatives. Adoptions within a family have 'strings attached' that reflect underlying issues in the family. Nonetheless, the child will not be confused about who his parents are as long as the adults are not confused and act accordingly."[8] That is, *the adoptive parent is the parent*. This is not a divorce situation, in which two parties who do not live together will be co-parenting the child. Children living in kinship adoption have one set of parents: the adoptive parents.

Adopted People have a Right to Know the Truth about their Parentage. Be Honest.

Kinship adoptive parents may be reluctant to share information about a painful episode in the family's history, an episode that may have included drug addiction, criminal history, extramarital affairs, or other potentially embarrassing scenarios. And they may be particularly reluctant to share information with a child who developmentally lacks discretion about repeating this information outside the family or asking questions of other family members. Kinship adoptive parents have an unusually difficult balancing act on the tightrope of adoption communication. The parties involved in the troubling circumstances that led to the separation of their children from their birth parents are family members, people who will be a part of the children's future as well as their past. The principles of imparting the information, however, remain the same, regardless of the difficulties involved in the task (see Chapter Seven). Honesty is paramount, and children are not "protected" by lies, omissions, or distortions. And if the adoptive parents try to protect the birth parents, or themselves, through untruths or half-truths, the children will suffer due to damaged trust, unrealistic fantasies, and anxieties about an unpredictable future.

Regularly Discuss with Birth Parents Ways in Which Communication Will be Handled with the Child. Adapt These Communications Appropriately as the Child Matures.

It is likely, in kinship adoptions, that birth parents will have some contact with the children. To ensure that communication given to the children is accurate and clear, make a plan with the birth parents, and review it regularly, on strategies to be used with the children in explaining the adoption situation to them. Birth parents will be more helpful in collaboration on clear communication if they have some degree of "buy-in" about the why's and how's of adoption communication. In discussing a communication plan with the birth parents, adoptive parents should regularly remind birth parents that they both have the same goal: healthy, well-adjusted children. There may be some disagreement about methods needed to achieve that goal, but communication will be much healthier, as well as more open and more effective, if parties have discussed those issues and come to some areas of agreement about what information will be shared, at what point, and using what language. Because the children's developmental stages, and therefore their ability to understand adoption-related circumstances (see Chapters Five and Eight), will change over time, these communication plans should be routinely readdressed with birth parents.

Make Sure that Other Significant Persons in the Extended Family are "On the Same Page" as the Adoptive Parents Regarding Adoption Communication.

Kinship adoptive parents must learn to communicate effectively with both the child and the birth parents. As in all open adoption situations, it is essential that communication philosophies and strategies are clear to both the birth and adoptive parents, so that a unified, clear message can be sent to the child. Differences of opinion about techniques or strategies will occur over time, as they invariably do with two parents living together and raising children together. However, kinship adoptive parents and birth parents should try to focus on the needs of the children and the shared purpose of both birth and adoptive parents: raising children who feel good about their family and themselves, who will be able to function as healthy, productive, and content adults.

Learn What Services and Supports Exist for the Child and Family, Regardless of the Association (or lack of one) with an Agency.

Adoptive families are eligible for adoption subsidies, financial supports for families caring for children with special needs. When family members adopt formally, they too are eligible for these subsidies. Adoptive families should contact their local child protective services agency to learn more about the financial support available to them and their children. A Medicaid card to cover health care expenses for the children may be a part of the adoption subsidy.

When families adopt relatives informally, the child may be eligible for Temporary Assistance to Needy Families (TANF; also includes a Medicaid card) through the local Department of Human Services. Further, the nurturing family might be licensed to serve as foster parents through a child protective services agency and receive foster care board rates to assist with the cost of raising children. Children in the care of relatives may also be eligible for Supplemental Security Income (SSI) through the Social Security Administration.

Finally, ten states have developed programs for subsidized guardianship to help kinship parents who are willing but financially unable to care for children in need of placement. Under these programs, kinship adoptive parents do not have to meet state requirements for licensure as foster parents, but they receive a monthly payment for the support of the children. Kinship adoptive parents, formal and informal, should explore all avenues to support in their endeavor to provide a safe, permanent home for children. Certainly, all the support needed by families is not financial. Kinship adoptive parents also need help with special educational needs, counseling, parenting children with special needs, day care, health care, and so on. Many excellent support groups are forming for grandparents raising grandchildren, and adoptive parent support groups are a rich informational resource for families raising children with a wide variety of special needs. Local child protective services agencies can be contacted for more information about support groups, therapists, and resources within the community.

Jessica's Story

Eighteen-year-old Molly, a freshman in college, unexpectedly became pregnant. Her large Irish Catholic family was embarrassed by the pregnancy and strongly encouraged Molly to make an adoption plan for the baby. Molly's mother contacted her niece, Virginia, to ask if Molly could live with her during the remainder of the pregnancy. Virginia was thirty-five years old, single, and working as an attorney. Virginia, happy to help one of her favorite relatives, describes the five months with her pregnant cousin Molly as one of the best times in her life.

Molly was planning, through her physician, an adoption for her unborn child with a young married couple. After several months of having young Molly live with her, Virginia began to think about adopting the baby herself. She had always wanted to adopt, but she felt reluctant to propose such a plan to Molly, fearing she would be pressuring the young woman to make a decision that might not be best for her. Just as the last trimester of the pregnancy was about to begin, however, Molly asked Virginia if she would consider adopting the baby. Virginia was thrilled and talked with her extended family about the plan. All agreed that Virginia made a good living, was ready to parent, and should proceed with the adoption. Virginia became the Lamaze coach for Molly and was present in the delivery room for the birth of a wonderful little girl, later named Jessica.

Even though Virginia knew the birth mother very well, contact between the adoptive mother and the birth mother was limited for several years. Molly needed time to grieve her loss, and Virginia needed time to become secure as the parent to little Jessica. Molly came to see the baby when Jessica was eight months old, and Virginia remembers feeling a strong connection to Molly. However, she felt some concern about a completely open adoption. Openness in adoption practice was relatively unusual in the mid-1980s, when Jessica's adoption occurred. Virginia was content to continue a "semi-closed" adoption, one in which she knew the birth mother but had very limited contact with her.

When Jessica was two years old, Virginia married, and her husband adopted the baby. The family was ultimately expanded by the additions of a birth child and another adopted child.

All of Virginia's siblings knew about the adoption and the identity of the birth mother, and Molly's siblings also knew of the situation. Others in the extended family did not know that Jessica was the birth child of Molly. They were only aware that Virginia had adopted her oldest child. This secrecy had the effect of diminishing Virginia's contact with her aunt. Contact between them became somewhat uncomfortable. It seemed that the birth grandmother didn't know quite how to respond to a child who was both her great-niece (by adoption) and her grandchild (by birth). This distance in the relationship between Virginia and her aunt was difficult for Virginia to accept because they had always been close in the past. Virginia's mother had died when she was only twelve years old, and her aunt had stepped in to fill an empty space in her life. While the addition of Jessica to her home brought tremendous joy to Virginia's life, it brought with it a significant change in another important relationship.

While Jessica grew up knowing that she was adopted, she did not know the identity of her birth mother. By the time she was five years of age, questions about her birth mother began to emerge. She wanted to know why her birth mother had not kept her, what she looked like, and her name. Virginia felt uncomfortable withholding information from her bright, inquisitive youngster. She talked to two other parents who had open adoptions and was heavily influenced by one who commented, "After all, we don't own our children." After much soul-searching, she decided it was time to call Molly. The birth mother decided that, if a more open relationship between birth mother and child would help Jessica, she would consent to risk revealing the family "secret" by opening the adoption.

Molly and Virginia met to consider the decision they were making; if they openly told Jessica about her birth mother's identity, the information could not later be retracted. Jessica remembers meeting her birth mother for the first time when she was six and one-half years old. Virginia, Molly, and Jessica all baked cookies together, and, not surprisingly, the cookies did not come out very well!

Since the original meeting, Jessica and Molly have had sporadic contact. Jessica was nine years old when she last saw her birth mother at a family reunion. At that time, Molly promised to stop by the family home and see Jessica before the night ended. Molly did not keep her promise. Jessica was extremely angry and felt that Molly chose to be with her boyfriend instead of with her.

Jessica was later upset by another comment made by her birth mother, who told her, "If I could take back my decision to surrender, I would. If I could do it all over again, I would have kept you." Jessica was very troubled to hear her birth mother express feelings that Jessica should not be with her adoptive family; it made her feel that perhaps she was not where she was meant to be.

Jessica began experiencing tremendous anger toward her birth mother. Due to Jessie's feelings of confusion and anger, the adoptive family sought the help of a post-adoption support group. Jessica acknowledged that the group experience was very helpful in sorting out her feelings about adoption and her birth mother.

As a result of Jessica's rage, the adoptive family decided to avoid the next reunion. Jessica, however, talked her parents into attending the family get-together. Molly did not attend this reunion, and the situation was not uncomfortable for any of the adoptive family members.

Virginia acknowledges that her kinship relationship with Molly has sometimes made it difficult to establish boundaries with her. The birth and adoptive mothers have been able to talk candidly about their feelings, and have successfully resolved many of these issues. The birth and adoptive mothers have always shared a positive relationship. In fact, as she emphasized when confronted with Jessica's anger toward her birth mother, Virginia would always have strong affection and respect for Molly. Molly is still single (marriage plans did not materialize) and currently has a master's degree. She works with adolescents as a school guidance counselor.

When asked about the pros and cons of kinship adoption, Jessica stated that if her birth mother and birth grandparents were not part of the family, she would not always see them and feel uncomfortable. She would not have worries about family loyalties, and she would not wonder how it would feel to have her picture taken with the "birth" branch of the family tree at reunions instead of with her adoptive branch of the family. Virginia commented on the changes in her close relationship with her aunt, also Jessica's birth grandparent. On the other hand, Jessica is able to get most of her questions answered (though she still has little information about her birth father), and it is comforting to know that she can locate and see her birth mother whenever she chooses to do so.

Virginia has the following advice for other kinship adoptive parents:

• Be honest with the child. Don't withhold or distort information.

• Open the adoption from the time of the placement.

• Know where boundaries are and keep them clear to all involved.

- Remember that you are the parent.
- Be sure that you have the support of the extended family.

QUESTIONS

1. What are some advantages of kinship adoption to your child?

2. What have been some of the communication challenges you have faced in talking about the adoption with your child? With the birth parents? With the extended family?

3. What are some boundaries you have had to maintain? Are there others you need to develop for the health of your child or your family?

4. Do you feel that you are the parent? Does the birth parent understand that you are the parent?

5. Do you need additional support or services in raising your kinship child? Do you know where to get this support or service? If not, who can you ask to find out?

NOTES

1. "Keeping the Family Tree Intact Through Kinship Care" (Washington, D.C.: National Adoption Information Clearinghouse, 1999), 1.

2. Ibid., 2.

3. Ibid.

4. Jesse Thornton, "Permanency Planning for Children in Kinship Foster Homes," *Child Welfare* (September-October 1991): 593.

5. "Keeping the Family Tree Intact," 2.

6. Ibid., 3.

7. Beth Brindo, Bellefaire Jewish Children's Bureau, personal interview, July 23, 1999.

8. Ibid.

CHAPTER TWELVE

Opening a Closed Adoption for School-Age Children: Questions Most Asked by Parents

Marsha sat down for the third time this week. She had a letter to write. She just didn't know what to say and how to say it. She was writing to her eleven-year-old son's birth mother and sending the letter through the agency. Jeremy had joined Marsha and Dale's family when he was two days old. Their adoption was typical of adoptions at the time: closed. Totally confidential. No information. No contact. For the last six months, Jeremy has been expressing a need to learn more about his birth mother. For the last two months, he has been saying that he needs to see her.

When the need to open up a closed adoption surfaces in the life of a child, several questions must be addressed before moving forward. This chapter answers fourteen questions often asked by adoptive parents when contemplating opening a closed adoption.

QUESTION 1: WHAT ARE OPENNESS IN ADOPTION AND OPEN ADOPTION?

To understand what opening a closed adoption means, it is important that parents clearly understand the different degrees of openness possible within adoptive relationships.

What Closed Adoption Means: No identifying information is shared between the birth family and the adoptive family. This is also called *confidential* or *traditional* adoption. Information may be given to the agency to update the records, but is not intended for transmission to either party.[1]

What Openness in Adoption Means: Openness in adoption refers to a continuum of openness within relationships that can exist between members of the birth family and the adoptive family of a child. Openness may include knowledge about the "other" family of the child, the birth parent's selection of an adoptive family for the child, contact through a third party, or ongoing visitation. The relationships may exist among the child, the adoptive family and the birth parents, or among the child, the adoptive parents and birth siblings, and the grandparents, other relatives, or kinship figures (including former foster parents).

What Open Adoption Means: Open adoption means that everyone involved in the process, whether adoptive or birth parent, is open to meeting and talking with each other both prior to and subsequent to the placement. How much communication and contact will occur is impossible to say. But in an open adoption, the assumption exists that there will be as much communication as possible within the limits of courage, compassion, and common sense.[2]

Continuum of Contact

Totally Closed: No Contact	Mediated Contact: Family works through agency	Totally Open

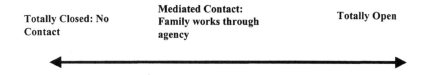

Totally Closed: No Contact: John, a three-year-old child, is placed into his adoptive family. Only nonidentifying social/medical information is given to the family. The family plans no contact with the birth family.

Mediated Contact—Family Works Through Agency: Cassie is eight years old. She has a lot of questions that her family cannot answer. When she joined her adoptive parents as a one-year-old they were given very little information. Her adoptive family contacts the agency to ask social workers to work with the birth family in exchanging information, pictures, and so on. It is all to go through the social worker at the present time. No last names are exchanged.

Totally Open: Betsy and Kenneth are ten-year-old twins. Victims of child abuse, they were adopted at age four from the local protective services agency. They have had no contact with their birth family since that time, although the families had contact with each other when the children were in foster care. Each family knows the names of the other. About six months ago, the adoptive family received word that the abuser (their father) had died and that their mother had stabilized. Their agency worker felt that the mother had a clear understanding why she would never be able to parent her children. The family begins writing letters to her and will eventually plan for phone calls. Within a year, they hope the children can visit with their birth mother.

QUESTION 2: HOW DO I KNOW MY CHILD IS READY? WHAT AGE IS BEST?

For Sharon Kaplan Roszia, an expert in the field of adoption, the question isn't simply about the child. "When assessing readiness to open an adoption, the question is not about the child's readiness, but the readiness of the adoptive parents," Roszia asserts. "Children take their cues from their parents. When the parents think it is a good idea to grow up knowing all of life's connections, most children will follow suit. In my opinion, the earlier those connections are made, the better for the child."[3]

QUESTION 3: MY CHILD HAS ASKED TO MAKE CONTACT FOR A NUMBER OF YEARS, AND WE ARE FINALLY DOING IT. HOW CAN WE ADDRESS HIS EXPECTATIONS AND CONCERNS?

Adults who have searched for their birth parents often have high expectations for the experience. Some youngsters who hope to have contact with birth parents do, too. The following questions can be used to explore your child's expectations.

1. What do you expect that you will feel like when you hear from your birth mother (or father) the first time?
2. What do you expect that you will feel like when you see your birth mother (or father) for the first time?
3. What do you expect your birth mother (or father) to say to you?
4. What do you expect will happen in the future with them? Do you expect to see them regularly? Never see them again?
5. What do you want to ask him/her?
6. Who do you want to be there when you meet her/him the first time?
7. Where do you want to meet her/him the first time?
8. How do you think you are going to feel after meeting her/him?

If a child is not good at addressing his feelings and expectations, suggest that he draw a picture of the first meeting and then explain the drawing. (See Chapter Nine for other tools to draw out a child's feelings.)

QUESTION 4: ARE FEARS AND APPREHENSIONS AS ADOPTIVE PARENTS A NORMAL PART OF THE PROCESS?

Yes, opening a closed adoption can be a fearful, uncertain step for families. "Adoptive parents do have fears related to opening an adoption," Roszia states.

One fear comes when birth fathers who were out of the picture suddenly reach out for contact. What happens is that adoptive parents remember the terrible things they heard about the father and want nothing to do with him. They are left with remnants of an old image.

What I tell my families is that they must update the image. Engage in honest conversation with those who know him and if possible with the birth father himself. Make a decision as to what level of openness is appropriate for the child after this.[4]

QUESTION 5: WHAT IF THE UPDATED IMAGE OF THE BIRTH FATHER OR BIRTH MOTHER OR FAMILY IS NO DIFFERENT FROM BEFORE?

People can change, but sometimes they don't. Even if the circumstances of the birth father or birth mother remain the same as at the time of the adoption, Roszia suggests that adoptive parents generally have new tools to deal with some degree of openness. "Adoptive parents have themselves grown and have come to a better understanding of people— why addictions happen, or even how to deal with mental illness. They find themselves better equipped to talk with their child, who is now older and [to] help them with understanding and expectations for the birth family contact. Life experiences and maturity generally provide those new tools of managing birth family issues and contacts."[5]

QUESTION 6: WHAT OTHER CONCERNS DO ADOPTIVE PARENTS FACE?

Another concern parents have for opening the adoption is the influence of the birth family on the child. As Roszia points out, "There may be a vast difference in lifestyle and values that will conflict with those of the adoptive family. Families must keep lines of communication open—not in a judgmental sense, but as an opportunity for the child to see and express the differences he witnesses."

Not only is the influence of the birth family a question for the child, but the child may be confused by lifestyle differences themselves. Roszia comments that if there is some level of contact with the birth family, the child in the adoptive home may experience sadness or survivor's guilt when in contact with siblings in less desirable circumstances.

Working off an old image, fearing influence, and worrying about guilt are three matters that confront adoptive parents. Roszia-cites one more: "The bottom line for many adoptive parents in hesitation about any level of openness, especially in older child adoptions, is the fear that there will be a damage in their child's relationship with them. They fear that the child will feel less a part of the family and that they will feel less a parent."

In their excellent book, *The Open Adoption Experience*, Lois Melina and Sharon Kaplan Roszia point out significant gains rather than losses for the adoptive parent/child relationship.

- "For some children, having contact with their birth parent forces them to confront extremely painful events they experienced at their birth family's hands." By facing those issues, fantasies are dispelled, grief work begins, and the child eventually is able to move on in forming other significant relationships.
- After removal from the traumatic experiences in the birth home, children can more easily move to a level of forgiveness for their birth parents. Once that happens, they can also see good things about them. With some level of contact, children often are able to see ways they are different from their birth families. The understanding that their lives are changed for the better frees them to make more positive choices.
- Resisting attachment to a family for a child adopted at an older age can create a powerful block to positive relationships or attachment in the adoptive home. One reason for that resistance is the loyalty they feel compelled to keep for their birth parents. When parents encourage some level of contact, even if it is very occasional, and even if it is just a letter, children receive the message that it is still okay to love their birth parents—that they can learn to love both sets of parents.[6]

QUESTION 7: WHAT ARE SOME QUESTIONS THAT PARENTS CAN EXPLORE TO ASSESS WHERE THEY ARE EMOTIONALLY IN THIS PROCESS?

Some of the following questions will guide parents in talking about openness with a trusted, supportive friend. These will help parents assess their own expectations and worries for opening up their child's closed adoption.

1. What are my wishes for my child in opening up this adoption?[7]
2. What are my worries about contacting this birth parent?
3. What are my expectations for this relationship?
4. Do I have the ability to perceive the needs of my child in order to set boundaries for the birth parent?

5. Do I have the ability as the adoptive parent to assess the capacity of the birth family members to respect boundaries?

6. Do I have the ability to set boundaries?

7. Do I have a supportive, objective person to help guide us through this?

8. Do I have the ability as the adoptive parent to maintain a sense of entitlement even though the birth family is involved?[8]

QUESTION 8: IF PARENTS DO OPEN THIS ADOPTION, WILL THEIR CHILD ESCAPE HAVING TO FACE THE ISSUES OF ADOPTION FOUND IN CLOSED ADOPTION?

Developing some level of openness and contact with the birth family does not erase the pain adopted children sometimes experience in relation to issues of loss, rejection, abandonment, shame, or guilt. What it does do for the child and his adoptive parents, according to Roszia, is move the work to the front end of the child's life, instead of waiting until the time of search and reunion. "It is short-term pain for long-term gain," Roszia asserts.

Abby's Story

Abby just turned sixteen. She is the daughter of Don and Martha Kammer and the younger sister of Elizabeth. The Kammers live in central Idaho. Abby is bright, inquisitive, and her parents' joy. She is quite the typical adolescent, interested in dancing, talking on the phone, gymnastics, talking on the phone, getting her hair to look just right, and talking on the phone.

Abby entered her adoptive home at the age of four months. Martha and Don first met her when they visited the foster home where Abby lived and felt an immediate connection. Abby is biracial. Her birth mother is Caucasian. Her birth father is African American. Throughout Abby's life, the Kammers have been open and honest about Abby's racial, cultural, and social history.

The family's journey into openness in adoption began when Abby was three and one-half years old. They made the decision to begin contact with her birth mother. Opening the closed adoption has indeed been a journey, a process.

The following scenarios walk through different seasons in Abby's open adoption experience. By observing Abby, her adoptive parents, and her birth mother, other adoptive parents can gain a perspective on the issues and concerns that arise. They can also recognize the opportunity some level of openness affords in creating an atmosphere of open and honest communication around the issues of adoption.

Scenario One: At Age Four

Event: Bubbly, energetic Abby is excited. Today is her birthday. She will finally be four. Also, something else is about to happen. Today her birth mother, Allison, will be coming to her party. Abby has heard of Allison all of her young life. Abby has talked with Allison on the phone, and now she is coming in person.

The day goes exactly as planned. Allison, rather nervous and shy, comes in quietly and gives Abby a hug. She stays long enough to have cake and ice cream and then slips out.

The next day, Allison stops by the house to ask a question. "May I take Abby out to lunch at McDonald's by myself?" Martha, Abby's adoptive mother, responds, "Let me think about it. Give me a call on Friday morning."

After Allison leaves, Abby approaches her mother. She has overheard Allison's request. She quietly asks her mother, "If I go to McDonald's with Allison, can you and Beth [Abby's older sister] come, too?"

What might be Abby's anticipated feelings?

Abby, at four, does have a budding understanding about adoption. Why? Because it is concrete. Allison is there in person and they meet. Abby can understand that Allison is her birth mother. Her hesitation about going with Allison, however, is probably more a developmental issue than an adoption issue. Very few children her age would go with a stranger—even to McDonald's.

Other feelings or questions might be sprouting in her mind, but at four, she may not be able to verbalize them. These questions, related to her racial and cultural heritage, may arise because Abby may recognize and acknowledge

- that her birth mother is not the same color as she is;
- that her birth mother and her adoptive mother are the same color;
- that her birth mother may talk and act very differently than her adoptive family, and those differences make talking to her awkward and difficult.

The fact that Abby now experiences a level of openness in her adoption doesn't erase the questions and feelings. It moves them to the front end of her life, where she and her parents can deal with them openly and concretely.

Scenario Two: At Age Nine

Event: Allison, Abby's birth mother, has been part of her life now for over five years. Abby sees her about once a month. On this particular occasion, the whole family is camping, and Allison is invited out to the campsite for dinner. After dinner, Allison and Abby take a walk around the campground. During the walk, Abby asks her birth mother a question.

"Allison," she says, "why did you give me away?"

Allison responds, "Abby, no one can just give a child away. There were a lot of things wrong in my life at that time."

"I know, that is what my mom told me," Abby counters. "But why did you give me away?"

What might be Abby's anticipated feelings?

By the time many adopted children reach the age of nine, they have moved developmentally in their thinking to conclude that their adoption means that they were given away. Children who experience openness in adoption encounter much the same feelings. Abby is dealing with issues of rejection at an early stage. The benefit of now having openness is that Abby can direct that question to the person who is the best one to answer it—her birth mother.

Other feelings or questions now also developing in her thinking are connected to her racial and cultural background. These lingering questions, which she can now verbalize, may arise because she is able to

- recognize her different racial identity, and
- wonder if she was "given away" because she does not look like her birth mother.

The fact that Abby now experiences a level of openness in her adoption doesn't erase the questions and feelings. It moves them to the front end of her life, where she and her parents can deal with them openly and concretely.

Scenario Three: At Age Twelve

Event: Beth, Allison, and Abby enjoy doing things together occasionally. Allison has been part of Abby's life for eight years. On this particular evening, the three of them have just returned from the movies. When they reach home, Beth jumps out of the car and scoots into the house. Abby lingers a few moments.

"Allison, I need to ask you a question. Is my birth father black? When can I meet him? Does he want to see me? Why doesn't he ever call? Who else in your family is black?"

Allison has avoided any reference to or conversation about Abby's birth father. She has been dreading the moment that this question would come up because she will have to tell Abby that her birth father died. Allison never shared that piece of information with Abby's adoptive parents.

"Yes, Abby, your birth father was black. He came from a big family with lots of brothers and sisters. They don't live around here. The reason that he doesn't call is that he died a few years ago."

Abby grows quiet and opens the door to get out of the car. "Oh," she whispers. "I just wanted to see someone I looked like."

Abby never tells her mother about this conversation. Allison mentions it a few days later, in a casual conversation with Martha, Abby's adoptive mom.

What might be Abby's anticipated feelings?

As Abby matures, questions related to the pain of adoption continue to emerge. She is feeling a sense of loss related to the fact that she doesn't know anyone that she looks like—her birth father, now dead, was never a memory for her. She perhaps is also struggling with rejection from her absent birth father as well as budding issues of identity development. A curious issue is the fact that she asked her birth mother a question she has grown up knowing the answer to—"Is my birth father black?" This feeling is possibly related to trust—just checking to see if the story her parents told her was the truth.

Questions connected to her racial and cultural background are far more obvious. They emerge because

- she is entering a normal stage of identity development, which for her includes her racial and ethnic identity;
- she is perhaps struggling to integrate her black and white identity—she doesn't look like anyone in her birth mother's or adoptive family;
- she may be subjected to teasing at school or in the neighborhood because she is biracial; and
- she may perceive that she was "given away" because she is "different."

The fact that Abby now experiences a level of openness in her adoption doesn't erase the questions and feelings. It moves them to the front end of her life, where she and her parents can deal with them openly and concretely.[9]

QUESTION 9: WHAT SHOULD BE THE PROCESS OF OPENING UP THIS ADOPTION?

Opening up an adoption for a school-age child must happen in stages so that the child understands incrementally what is happening. Although children are impatient, says Patricia Doemer, author of *How to Open an Adoption*, "taking the time to get acquainted improves the chances of a long-term relationship."[10] Doemer suggests that the process begin with letter writing, talking on the phone, and then, eventually, face-to-face contact. She notes that the process can take up to six months to a year before the first face-to-face meeting.

QUESTION 10: WHAT ARE SOME SPECIAL AREAS OF CONCERN OF WHICH PARENTS SHOULD BE AWARE?

Cultural Issues

Birth and adoptive parents may represent different cultural perspectives: different socioeconomic levels, different levels of education, different ethnicities or races, different ages, and so on. These differences will create potential conflicts in several areas, including how boundaries and privacy are handled, parenting practices, communication patterns, and handling grief related to adoption. If birth and adoptive parents can be coached to understand the cultural differences, they will be more successful in communicating effectively with a minimum of conflict.[11]

Birth Siblings Still in the Birth Home

Occasionally, adopted children will meet birth siblings who are now in the home of their birth parents. Adoptive parents must realize that jealousy, sadness, and anger about not being part of the birth family are a normal grief reaction. This does not signal that the child wants to move in with the birth family. Expressing support and empathy toward the adopted child will allow him to share his thoughts and feelings.[12]

QUESTION 11: ARE THERE ANY CIRCUMSTANCES UNDER WHICH AN ADOPTION SHOULD NOT BE OPENED?

Yes, there are circumstances under which it is not in the best interest of the child to open a closed adoption. The issue of safety for the child is the primary reason for not opening contact. In cases where a threat of violence or a capacity to do harm is present, working through the agency to gain updated information from the birth family is essential.

QUESTION 12: WHAT HAPPENS IF, AFTER OPENING THIS ADOPTION, THE BIRTH FAMILY BACKS AWAY? WON'T THE CHILD BE DEALING WITH ANOTHER LAYER OF REJECTION?

In a perfect world, this wouldn't be an issue; it wouldn't happen. However, we do not live in a perfect world. Parents can use this painful opportunity to talk about the feelings birth families may encounter when facing the issues of opening up an adoption.

- Birth parents may have trouble dealing with their feelings around the adoption, especially when the adoption occurs as a result of involuntary surrender through the public system. There still may be a lot of blame directed at the agency, and responsibility for the birth parents' part in the circumstance is denied.
- Members of the birth family may not support the opening of the adoption. The birth parent would have little or no support for opening the adoption when discouraged from doing so by relatives.
- Birth parents may find the questions from the child too difficult and too painful to answer. It would be much easier to avoid the relationship altogether than to try and work through the varied emotions encountered by all parties.
- The sense of guilt for "failing" one's child may be too overwhelming to process. Not continuing the relationship would help the birth parent to put the guilt on a back shelf.

QUESTION 13: WHAT ABOUT INTERNATIONALLY ADOPTED CHILDREN? WHAT OPTIONS ARE AVAILABLE TO THEM? HOW SHOULD THE SUBJECT BE APPROACHED?

Susan Cox, Vice President of Public Policy and External Affairs for Holt International Children Services, feels strongly that opening up an adoption for an internationally adopted child can be very difficult emotionally for that child.

The reality of search and reunion (opening a closed adoption) is that it is extremely complex and intense. It is the deeply held view of many international adult adoptees with the experience of search behind them, that while they believe search is positive and the right of every adoptee, those who search should be emotionally mature and prepared. The feelings and emotions experienced during the search process are so powerful, complicated and overwhelming, that they can be difficult to understand and process.[13]

What issues make opening a closed international adoption far more complex than domestic adoption? Cox cites two:

1. *Language*: Every communication must go through a translator. There is always a filter. Countries where international search is taking place do not share English as a first language. It is necessary to locate a resource who can translate communications, and is also competent in sometimes reading between the lines of answers that are given, or perhaps withheld. Finding someone sympathetic to the objective of search, who does not have their own political or

ideological agenda, and can objectively present information and facts is critical.[14]

2. *Culture*: There is a huge cultural component when communicating with the birth family of another culture. People in different cultures do not process things in the same way. People in different cultures do not express feelings and emotions the same way. In some cultures dealing with issues such as those involved in opening up an adoption is far too personal.

Cox favors opening adoption for internationally adopted children, but feels that timing is critical. She suggests that opening up an adoption for a minor child should be done only when there are special circumstances. Cox, however, is a strong advocate for homeland tours—a return to the child's birth country—for minor children. A trip to the homeland will give children an opportunity to visit important places, such as the sending orphanage or child care center, and perhaps even to meet people such as caregivers or care center staff who knew them as babies. The following areas can be explored as families prepare their child for a homeland tour:

1. Sit down and talk about what information the family already has about their child, the birth circumstances, and the birth family.
2. Ask questions about the child's expectations. (Questions used earlier in the chapter can be adapted here.) Additional questions might include:
   a. How do you think you will feel when everyone you see looks like you?
   b. How do you think you will feel when you return to the orphanage?
   c. How do you think you will feel when all you hear is your birth language and don't understand it?
3. Talk to the child about what cultural differences will be encountered—from food to sleeping arrangements. For an older child, this can be a fun research project to do before going.

Is a homeland tour helpful for an internationally adopted child? Ask eleven-year-old Joshua Barr.

Josh's Story—Making a Trip to the Homeland

Joshua Barr, a delightful, inquisitive eleven-year-old, was adopted from Korea when he was just a few months old. No information about his family was in the file. From the time Josh was an infant, the Barrs have created an environment that would tie him to his culture and homeland. However, they knew that someday their inquiring son would need to connect to his homeland in hopes of finding answers to questions that they couldn't give him.

On June 27, 1998, Josh and his father, Jim, joined a homeland tour group for a two-week trip to Korea. The following is a brief look at the trip from Josh's perspective.

Q. How did you prepare to go to Korea?

A. I spent a lot of time reading about the country from books at the library.

Q. How did you picture the country before you went?

A. I thought it would be very, very big and it was! [Josh lives in a small rural county in southeastern Ohio.]

Q. What surprised you most about Korea?

A. It was so crowded. My town isn't crowded at all. It was kinda scary, because everyone looked like me and if I got lost, how would I be found? I couldn't believe how fast the subways were. They were so crowded. One thing I wondered about when I got on the subways was if one of those people is my birth mom or dad.

Q. What was your most enjoyable memory?

A. One of the first nights we were there, we had a real Korean meal. It was at the Holt agency where I was adopted. I got to meet the doctor who gave me my shots when I was just a baby. Another neat memory was a trip up Mt. Sorak. We first went on a trail and then it got real steep and we had to use a cable built into the side of the mountain. It was awesome!

Q. What do you remember about Korean housing and food?

A. Most of the houses we saw were one-story houses. The food was different, for sure. For breakfast we ate garlic bread and salad. I tried all the neat foods. I ate a whole cup of charcoaled silkworms. I ate the eyeballs of fish—raw—and squid with soy sauce dumped all over it. I tried snails at one meal for an appetizer. They were good!

Q. A trip like this can be emotionally difficult for anyone. What was difficult for you?

A. All the time before I went, I thought a lot about meeting my birth parents. I had really hoped I would get to do that. But that didn't happen. We went one afternoon to a home where girls stay that are having a baby and placing that baby for adoption. Those mothers talked about how impossible it was to keep a child as an unwed mother in Korea. That helped.

Q. What else happened that was meaningful for you?

A. Some kids did get to meet their birth mothers and I was happy for them. One of the girls was nineteen, and she met her birth mother at a hotel where we were staying. She introduced her to us. That was awesome for us!

Q. How do you think this trip helped you?

A. It made me very proud of Korea. I understand more about the history of the country. I do understand now why my birth mother made an adoption plan for me. I also got to meet some other kids my age and a little older that were adopted from Korea, too. I do hope that when I get a little older, I can go back there again.

QUESTION 14: WHAT PARENTAL CHARACTERISTICS ARE FOUND IN FAMILIES THAT FIND SUCCESS IN OPENING A CLOSED ADOPTION?

"One of the primary characteristics is that adoptive parents have confidence in their own parenting abilities and styles," says Martha Nabor, an adoptive parent and an adoption professional with International Adoption Services Center in Maine. "They do not need to always second-guess themselves about discipline or boundary setting."

Another characteristic Nabor cites that is helpful is that these parents need to be able to take risks:

Open adoption relationships require risk taking. Adoptive parents with these ongoing relationships need to be able to function without all the answers upfront and clear. You don't know all the answers when it comes to working out these types of arrangements.

A final characteristic is that these adoptive parents are aware of and sensitive to the core issues of adoption that impact not only their child, but the birth mother as well. Open adoption does not eradicate the grief, loneliness, and guilt for these birth mothers. It eases, but not erases.[15]

SUMMARY

When opening up a closed adoption, it is critical that both adoptive parents and the adopted child have the opportunity to assess the following with an objective, supportive person:

1. What are the expectations?
2. What are the fears?
3. What are the wishes and worries?
4. How will we handle disappointments and setbacks?
5. What parental characteristics best fit successful relationships when opening a closed adoption?

QUESTIONS

1. How would you describe the current level of openness in your adoption?
2. What are some of the questions you can use to address your child's expectations about opening up the closed adoption?
3. What are your own wishes and worries for this experience?
4. What type of support do you have from your extended family, friends, or adoption agency?
5. Discuss why you agree or disagree with the recognition that opening up a closed adoption does not completely erase some of a child's pain regarding adoption?

NOTES

1. Harold D. Grotevant and Ruth McRoy, *Openness in Adoption: Exploring Family Connections* (Thousand Oaks, Calif. Sage Publications, 1998), 28.

2. James Gritter, *The Spirit of Open Adoption* (Washington, D.C.: Child Welfare League of America, 1997), 19.

3. Sharon Kaplan Roszia, phone interview, July 7, 1999.

4. Ibid.

5. Ibid.

6. The points were adapted from Lois Melina and Sharon Kaplan Roszia, *The Open Adoption Experience* (New York: HarperCollins, 1993), 332.

7. The worries and wisher concept was developed by Martha Nabor, International Adoption Services Center, Gardiner, Maine. It is used in *Openness in Adoption*. A training curriculum developed for the Ohio Child Welfare Training Program by the Institute for Human Services, Columbus, Ohio by Nancy Burley, Denise Goodman, Betsy Keefer, Cheryl Reber, and Jayne Schooler (1999)

8. Ibid.

9. Ibid.

10. Patricia Doemer, *How to Open an Adoption* (Royal Oak, Mich.: R-Squared, 1998).

11. *Openness in Adoption*.

12. Susan Cox, "Search and Reunion in International Search" available through Holt International Children's Services, P.O. Box 2880 (1195 City View), Eugene, Oregon 97402; Phone: (541) 687–2202 and phone interview.

13. Ibid.

14. Ibid.

15. Nabor.

CHAPTER THIRTEEN

Adolescence—Chronic but Not Terminal: Keeping Lines of Communication Open

Adolescence is difficult for all children, regardless of how they joined their families. The circumstances surrounding adoption add another layer of adjustment to two tumultuous tasks: identity formation and separation from the family. In searching for an identity, most adolescents experiment with a variety of personas. They alternately shun and embrace family values, codes of conduct, career choices, and expectations of themselves. When children have more than one family (and multiple fantasy families) on which to base their self-concept, the struggle to form an identity becomes much more complicated. Further, children who have lost families already may find emancipation from their port in the storm, the adoptive family, extremely difficult.

Studies and statistics have "proven" both that adopted teens are well adjusted and that they have adjustment problems. Some studies report that adopted adolescents fare at least as well as, if not better than, their nonadopted counterparts. For example, 715 adoptive families with adolescents adopted as infants were studied in 1994 by Benson, Sharma, and Roehlkepartain to determine the level of success in key developmental tasks of adoption—formation of identity, attachment to family and others, quality of family life, and psychological well-being.

Adopted adolescents in this study were as likely as their nonadopted siblings to express high self-esteem and positive concepts of identity. A little more than half of the sample wanted to know more about their birth parents, and two-thirds of the sample expressed the desire to meet their birth parents. Infants placed before one month of age showed the highest indicators of attachment. The adopted adolescents in this study demonstrated successful adjustment at a rate that equals that of other adolescents. On some indicators, the adopted adolescents ranked slightly higher than a comparison sample of public school adolescents.[1] Other studies report that adopted children engage in delinquent and dysfunctional behavior at significantly higher rates than do children who were not adopted.

J. Lynn Rhodes found, in a study done in 1993 of 380 adopted children and 290 birth children, a strong pattern of dysfunctional behavior in approximately one out of every four of the adopted children. While all of the problem behaviors existed in both birth and adopted children, they occurred with much greater frequency and intensity in adopted children.

The behaviors reported most frequently by the adoptive parents were rejection of authority, lying, cruelty to other people, refusal to accept responsibility for or consequences of actions, school performance below ability, lack of long-term friends, manipulation, difficulty with eye contact, stealing, refusal to follow parental guidelines, and self-control problems. Other behaviors seen more frequently in adopted children than in birth children were inability to give or receive affection; self-destructive behavior; phoniness; problems with food; thinking about fire, blood, or gore; superficial attraction to and friendliness with strangers; substance abuse; and promiscuous sexual activity. It is important to note that children studied were primarily adopted as newborns, with 44 percent being adopted by thirty days of age, and 87 percent adopted by one hundred eighty days of age.[2]

Another study, completed by Illinois State University, focused on adoptive families at risk of dissolution. It found that the serious problems of many adopted children with special needs "endure long after adoptive placements become legal, and despite traditional therapeutic efforts to ameliorate them. For many children, these problems escalate with age."[3] In reading many research studies on the adjustment of adopted adolescents, parents and professionals have difficulty making sense of conflicting results. All should agree, however, with Victor Groza, who observes, "For the most part, adoption has been a very successful social arrangement. . . . Most studies support the notion that adoption outcomes are overwhelmingly positive."[4]

However, we are aware that adopted children are particularly vulnerable to the stresses of adolescence. They frequently experience trauma related to separation from birth parents and other caretakers, early abuse and neglect, stressed attachment and lack of trust, identity confusion, transcultural assimilation, poor self-esteem, and struggle for control. The adoptive family can be equally stressed through disappointment, inappropriate guilt, unmet and/or unrealistic expectations for themselves as parents and for their child, helplessness, and lack of understanding of the child's grief and anger.

In spite of attempts at research, the scope of the problem is difficult to measure as a result of sealed adoption records and inadequate reporting within the mental health community, often oblivious to the role of adoption within the struggle of some youth and their families. While the debate will continue to rage, the Child Welfare League of America estimated in 1987 that 14 percent of all adolescents in substitute care are adopted. This statistic is quite significant, as an estimated 2 percent of the general population consists of adoptees placed with nonrelatives.

Carrie's Story

Carrie, age fifteen, had been placed with her adoptive family at the age of six. She was placed by a public child protective services agency who placed her three biological sisters in three different adoptive homes. While the girls maintained some telephone contact, they were rarely able to visit one another. The children had been removed from two alcoholic parents who neglected the girls over several years. Carrie had adjusted remarkably well with her empathetic, supportive adoptive parents until she was thirteen years old. As she was entering adolescence and middle school, Carrie began to underachieve in school, to select "lowlife" friends and to experiment with numerous bizarre identities, to reject her adoptive parents' attempts at affection and support (interpreting these as attempts at controlling her), and to display alarming anger toward her birth parents. The adoptive family wisely sought the assistance of post-adoption professionals who assisted Carrie in understanding, if not accepting, her birth parents' addictions and poor parenting skills. Carrie returned, with the help of her adoptive parents and therapist, to the placing agency, which gave her additional information about her history. This information helped her to sort through her identity confusion without constant, and often self-destructive, fantasies and experimentation. While Carrie continued to be preoccupied with concern about her sisters, she made progress in grieving for the life they would have shared together if the birth parents had been stable enough to provide for their care. The assistance Carrie and her parents received in communicating about the past enabled Carrie to cope with her history in less destructive ways. She could directly address her anger, experience sadness for her lost life with her birth family, and emancipate several years later as a young woman who had endured significant losses and was able to anticipate a promising future.

COMMUNICATING WITH ANY ADOLESCENT

Virtually all parents of teenagers find communication and conversation to be trying, at the very least. Adolescent boys often grunt in monosyllables, seeming more unable to complete a sentence than they have been since they were two years old. Adolescent girls, while certainly able to talk for hours with their peers, find it impossible and exasperating to converse with parents, who "don't understand *anything!*"

Deborah Clark writes about communication with adolescents on a parent-to-parent forum. "It is during this period that communication seems to consist more of the slamming of doors, tears, sulks and angry outbursts than of actual rational talk. Parents and professionals know that this is the most difficult time for parents and children alike."[5]

Haim Ginott, who wrote *Between Parent and Teenager* remarks:

Our only consolation (or perhaps half a consolation) is that here is a method to his madness. His behavior fits his developmental phase. The purpose of adolescence is to loosen personality. His personality is undergoing the required changes: From organization (childhood) through disorganization (adolescence) to reorganization (adulthood). Adolescence is a period of curative madness, in which every teenager has to remake his personality. He has to free himself from childhood ties with parents; establish new identifications with peers, and find his own identity.[6]

The following principles will assist any parent in communicating with adolescents:

Choose Your Battles Wisely. You May Have to Lose Some Battles to Win the War.

The teenager's job description is to challenge authority, test values, and create his own credibility/competence, often by belittling that of his previously accepted experts: his parents. He will create conflict in the process of these endeavors, and the wise, secure adult knows when to engage in conflict and when to let it slide. If the youth's "baiting" behavior does not endanger himself or others, adults may wisely allow natural consequences of poor choices (if you don't turn in your homework, you have to attend summer school) serve as the most effective teachers. When adults are forced by circumstances to intervene with guidance and protection, they should cool off so that instruction and limits are not given in anger. It is hard to learn from someone who is enraged. Ginott reminds us that "wise parents know that fighting a teenager, like fighting a riptide, is inviting doom. When caught in [a] cross-current, expert swimmers stop struggling. They know that they cannot fight their way to shore. They float and let the tide carry them, until they find a firm footing. Likewise, parents of teenagers must flow with life, alert to opportunities for safe contact."[7]

Avoid Criticism; Focus on Positives.

Some parents make a career of criticizing their children, believing that such criticism will enable their teenagers to achieve a level of perfection that the parents were unable to accomplish themselves. "For their own good," they remind their teenagers of imperfections. It is natural for all parents to focus attention on behaviors that need to improve and ignore those that are acceptable. How many parents open a report card full of A's, with one C−, and remark, "Why did you get that C−?" Any animal behaviorist can assure us that positive reward and praise are much more effective in shaping behavior than constant rebuke and punishment. If you want your teenager to talk with you, don't bombard him with "helpful" suggestions for improvement. Instead, look for opportunities to give him positive feedback, not only when he has done a perfect job, but also when he has improved over his last performance.

Encourage and Respect Independence; Allow Your Teenager to Make Some Mistakes Without Creating Dependency Through Parental Intervention.

Resist the temptation to "help" your teenager too often. The wise parent can tell the difference between a teenager who is about to make an insignificant mistake that can be corrected easily and a teenager who is about to plunge headlong into a disaster that cannot be remedied. Help should be available, but given only when really needed. Repeated "rescues" can become enablers for continued dysfunctional behavior. Child psychologist Ginott explains:

In adolescence, dependency creates hostility. Parents who foster dependence invite unavoidable resentment. Teenagers crave independence. The more self-sufficient we make them feel, the less hostile they are toward us. A wise parent makes himself increasingly dispensable to his teenagers. He sympathetically watches the drama of growth, but resists the desire to intervene too often.[8]

Respect the Teen's Privacy.

Teenagers begin to emancipate from their families years before they actually move out of the home. Teenagers accomplish this distancing behavior by drawing very firm, clear boundaries around their privacy. They place signs on their bedroom doors, informing siblings and parents that they are no longer welcome. They write poetry, make entries in diaries, and have long conversations with friends, all of which are inviolate from family intrusion. Teenagers may even resent casual, caring questions from concerned parents such as "How was school today?" as an intrusion into their privacy, their personhood. These boundaries are a normal part of adolescence and should be treated with reasonable respect, not interpreted by parents as indicators of rejection.

Keep Guidance Short and to the Point. Focus on the Present, not the Past.

Parents communicating with teenagers should avoid the temptation to preach incessantly during long lectures about problem behaviors. In his book *The One Minute Manager*, Kenneth Blanchard recommends that supervisors in a work setting tell employees in one minute or less what they have done wrong, and what needs to be done to correct the problem. Parents could learn much from this book about talking with teenagers about problematic behaviors. When approaching your adolescent about a behavior that needs to change, think about your willingness to talk about your own deficiencies for extended periods of time. Keep it brief and end the discussion with a positive expectation for improvement.

As in marital relationships, healthy communication depends on keeping the present problem in perspective. Avoid a tendency to bring up past "sins"—they will not add any power to your position. A focus on the past only makes you appear unreasonable and ridiculous, someone who can be much more easily ignored by a recalcitrant teen.

Don't Catastrophize or Label.

When children make poor choices, it can be a short leap for many parents to make dire predictions about their future: "You will never get into college." "You will never get a good job." "You will be living under the freeway overpass in a refrigerator box." While parents may experience many of these fears and firmly believe in the imminent realization of them, such anxiety almost always reflects a gross exaggeration, and the situation is never improved by sharing these viewpoints with the child. More appropriate messages that will help teens improve their behavior and learn to be self-sufficient are: "That was a mistake. I know you will do better next time." "Let me know if I can help you solve this problem. We may be able to talk it through together and come up with a solution that makes sense." These messages keep the focus on the problem (and its solution) and don't label the child as a failure.

Don't overreact.

"Although it's tempting to blurt out they're grounded for life when they've done something outrageous, sometimes it's best to take a moment to cool down. Overreacting tells your teen not to come to you when they have a problem because they fear your anger or unfair punishment."[9] Talk with your parenting partner, an understanding grandparent, a friend with children of a similar age. They may be able to help you see your parenting problem from a new perspective.

Don't Minimize the Teenager's Pain.

Adolescents experience life in extremes. Daily life for them is a roller-coaster ride of the highest highs and the lowest lows. When they are in pain, the pain is extreme. While parents with greater experience and maturity recognize that sibling squabbles, invasions of privacy, slights from friends, disappointments, or rejections from the current "significant other" are not as life-altering as they seem to the adolescent, parents can provide significant support and can enhance communication through reflective listening, a technique of listening intently to another's story or problem and responding only with a summary of the situation and the reflected feelings. Solutions to or evaluations of the problem (or, even worse, a denial of the problem) are *not* offered. The following interchange is an example of reflective listening:

Teen: I hate Stacy!! I told her a secret, and she blabbed it to everyone else! I can't ever go to school again. Everyone there thinks I am an idiot.

Parent: You must be angry and embarrassed that Stacy did not keep your confidence. It's really disappointing when someone lets you down.

Timing is Everything.

When limits must be set or parental "correction" is required, the timing of the correction is critical to its success. Remember that the role of the parent is to teach independence, and the function of discipline is in teaching, not in punishment. When emotions run strong in either the teenager or the parent, conditions for a teachable moment are hardly optimal. When teens are overwhelmed with difficulties, they are not open to learning. When parents are enraged or panic-stricken, they cannot serve as teachers and mentors. Sometimes the most important part of communication is the ability to defer discussion until everyone is rational. The most mature comment to the teenager who finally comes home two hours after his midnight curfew to face a worried, sleep-deprived, and angry parent might be: "I am too worried, exhausted, and upset to talk about this now. In the morning, we will talk about the consequences of your lack of consideration for me and your lack of respect for family rules. Right now, we are all going to bed."

HOW TO TALK ABOUT ADOPTION WITH AN ADOLESCENT

As adoption adds a layer of complexity to adolescence, it adds a similar layer of complexity to parenting. The adoptive parent has more sensitive information to communicate and needs an even higher level of skill to keep communication open and productive.

Share Full History Prior to Adolescence.

Again, timing is important in communication. If a teenager is adopted, he needs all the facts about his history *before* he enters adolescence. Parents can withhold some facts for a time until a child is sophisticated enough to hear them (see Chapters Seven and Eight), but too long a delay in withholding information erodes trust and sets up the teenager for self-destructive fantasies.

Assist the Teen in an Information Search.

Adolescents struggling with identity formation may need to revisit either the agency that facilitated the placement or their country of origin, if the adoption was international, to get as many facts about their history as possible. Sometimes these interviews or trips can do little more than assure the teenager that information is really not available and that the adoptive parents are not withholding information.

Assess the Need for More Openness in the Adoption Relationship.

Some teens may need more openness in their adoptions as they become more sophisticated. They may wish to correspond, without identifying information, through an agency intermediary, with their birth family members. They may benefit from asking directly for answers to their questions. Some teens may need to see pictures of their birth parents and/or siblings so that they can see someone who looks like them. And some teens may need to meet their birth parents to ask questions, be sure that birth parents or siblings are safe, and express their feelings directly about the adoption. Decisions about opening the adoption should be made with the help of a post-adoption counselor and should be made slowly. Chapter Fourteen addresses how to open up an adoption for an adolescent.

Learn the Skill of Reflective Listening.

Adoptive parents should become particularly adept at the skill of reflective listening. Adopted teens need empathy and can rarely find it among their nonadopted friends. Adoptive parents should allow the child to express his feelings of rage or grief and respond only with understanding and support, without judgment of either his parents or him. He is entitled to his feelings, and his experience of the adoption is real to him, regardless of whether his perceptions match those of the adoptive parents. Reflective listening is not an easy art, because we want to "fix" the pain felt by people we love.

Don't Overreact to Overacting.

Remember that adolescence is a time of high drama, and the "players" (adolescents) frequently overact, making extremist statements. The "directors" (parents) must not overreact to these histrionics, and they must learn to translate the extremist language into dialogue that makes sense. It is much easier for parents to respond appropriately to hurtful comments made by their adopted teens if they understand that all teenagers are very dramatic, and that much of this drama masks feelings of rejection and fear of future abandonment. Here are some common examples of statements made by adopted adolescents (with appropriate translations):

Dramatic Overacting	Possible Translation
I hate you! I wish you had never adopted me.	Are you going to keep me, no matter what?
I want to go live with my birth family.	I want more information about my birth family. Can you help me find out more?
I can't wait until I'm eighteen. I am out of here as soon as I am old enough!	I am afraid to leave home. Does adoption end when I turn eighteen? If I leave, can I come back?
I don't want to talk about adoption. Why do you always bring that up? I never even think about it!	I need to know if you love me as much as a child who was born into this family. I'm afraid you don't love me, and neither does anyone else, including my birth family.
You can't tell me what to do! You're not even my real mother!	Are you really my mother?

Adoptive parents must learn to respond to the translations, the "real" dialogue beneath the words used by an angry adolescent.

Honor his Roots to Enhance his Self-esteem.

Remember that one's need to feel good about one's identity is based largely on one's roots and heritage. Help the adopted teen to discover the positives in his history as well as the negative aspects that may have led to his separation from the birth family.

Recognize the Teen's Fantasies, but Tell the Truth.

When your teen shares with you a belief about his history that you know to be untrue, ask him where and how he got his information. His beliefs may be imbedded in a cloudy memory or may have no basis other than his wish for a history that is more dramatic and appealing than the real one. Offer to share the information the agency has already given you, or ask if the teenager would like to begin an information search with your assistance. The adolescent needs to have an accurate history, but needs to get this information gently and with parental support.

Help the Teen Construct a Realistic Vision of his Adoption if Facts are Unavailable.

If adoptive parents don't know all the facts and cannot get answers due to the nature of the circumstances around the adoption, look for "most likely scenarios" to share with the teenager. That is, if a child is abandoned or comes from a country that collects limited social history from the birth family, try to get information about the situation in that country or at the period of history surrounding his separation from the birth family. The child needs assistance in building a "fantasy" that is as close to the reality of his adoption as possible.

Use Support Groups for Adopted Youth as a Springboard to Assist the Teen in Talking about Adoption.

Remember that adopted youth often have difficulty talking about adoption with their parents. They may assume that the adoptive parents will be hurt if they know how much the child thinks about the birth family. Support groups for adopted youth can be an extremely helpful tool, as teenagers will talk and listen to other kids when they will not communicate with adults.

PARENTING STRATEGIES FOR THE ADOPTED ADOLESCENT

Develop a Short List of Nonnegotiable Rules.

Just as adoptive parents need to choose their battles, they also need to prioritize rules. That is, adoptive parents should think about what is most valued in the family and develop a small number of inviolate rules that support those values and principles. Examples are: "We value education. Therefore, in our family, the rule is that you must go to school until you graduate from something." "We value your safety. Therefore, in our family, all members must inform the family where they are at all times and when they are expected home. If your plans change, you must call home to inform us of the change. Between the ages of sixteen and eighteen you have a 12:30 P.M. curfew on the weekend and a 10:30 P.M. curfew on week nights." Parents should keep rules to a minimum (three to five is a reasonable number), but let teens know that the few rules that do exist are *not* negotiable. Consequences for violation of these rules should be predetermined and automatic (again, *no* negotiation).

Beyond the Nonnegotiable Rules, Allow the Teen to Exercise Control and Decision making Whenever Reasonable.

Adopted children and youth often struggle with issues of control, as significant decisions regarding their lives have been left to birth and adoptive parents, social workers, judges, government bureaucrats, and so on. Adoptive parents should allow their older adopted children to exercise as much control as possible. Adopted teens can exercise control when given freedom to make choices within guidelines provided by the parents. Demanding compliance with parental time frames, dress codes, standards of academic performance, and so on only creates conflict and reduces the likelihood of appropriate behaviors.

Don't Personalize the Teen's Anger.

Adoptive parents should try to understand that their child's anger is directed toward the separation from the birth family and is not aimed at them. The child may express rage toward the adoptive parents because they are available and because they are "safe" targets. Human nature compels us to feel anger when confronted with the anger of others, and parents may be tempted to respond with more anger to the rage felt by an adopted teen because of grief, loss of control and trust, and fear of future abandonment. The wise adoptive parent must be able to withdraw from the teen's angry outbursts, physically and/or emotionally. These outbursts must become storms that the parent learns to sidestep, allowing them to pass by and dissipate. Adoptive parents cannot allow their teen to create havoc within the family by accepting the adoption-related rage personally and responding in kind.

Remember the Teen's Need to be Different from the Adoptive Family.

The teen's need to create an identity separate from that of the adoptive family will likely be stronger than the need for individuation among nonadopted children. Don't panic if the teen experiments with identities that are similar to those of the birth family. Modeling after the birth family is normal and to be expected; don't begin to catastrophize and predict that the child "will wind up in prison like his father or pregnant at age fourteen like her mother."

Be Alert for Signs of Distress in the Child Following Losses and Transitions.

Adolescence is a time of tremendous change. School transitions occur as the child moves into middle school, on to high school, and perhaps even on to college or emancipation. All of these transitions can prove particularly difficult for a teenager who has experienced little permanency or security. Furthermore, adolescence can bring many real or imagined rejections (abandonments): a boy is dumped by his girlfriend, a girl is not accepted into the most popular clique at school, a boy or girl does not make the team. These rejections can be devastating to a young person who already believes that he is not worthy of love because his own birth parents could not or would not keep (love) him. Adoptive parents must be aware of the intense impact of these blows to his self-esteem and must *initiate* conversation and show support for the shaken youth. When such rejections occur, the youth needs to feel the unconditional support and love of his parents. Greg Louganis, the Olympic diving champion, once commented that he used to get very nervous before a dive until he remembered, "No matter how I dive, I know my mom will always love me."

Maintain your Commitment.

Perhaps the most significant thing an adoptive parent offers his/her child is maintenance of commitment and permanency. Children and teens can be angry, too preoccupied with adoption issues to achieve success in school, too afraid of failure to achieve success in sports or other endeavors. They may experiment with bizarre identities or even proclaim their strong desire to leave the adoptive family. The steady, enduring commitment of parents to the child and adoption can yield unimaginable healing during the turbulent years of adolescence. Remember that adolescence is chronic, but not terminal, both for you and your child.

CONCLUSION

Adolescence can be a difficult time for any family. Having an adolescent in the family creates a period of imbalance for all family members, not just for the adolescent whose identity is emerging. Many parents with adult children assure us that nothing challenged them to grow more as individuals and as parents than mentoring their child during adolescence. While navigating the turbulent waters of parenting teens, it is easy to forget that there is, indeed, light at the end of the tunnel . . . that adolescence is, fortunately, time-limited. The reward in surviving as the parent of an adolescent (and very happily, the vast majority do), is that survivors will experience one of the greatest joys of the life span: watching your child blossom into a young adult. The surprises and joys that accompany this blossoming are well worth the struggles necessary to the "pruning" and "shaping."

QUESTIONS

1. What questions have been asked by your teenager about his or her adoption? Birth family?
2. Do you sense that your teen might be asking in nonverbal ways for more information about his or her history? In what ways does your teen "act out" the need to know more?
3. Do you feel you need additional information to respond appropriately to your teen's need for information? If so, what plan do you have to get that information? How can you involve your teen or young adult in getting it?
4. What have you communicated well with your teen regarding his or her history? Where would you like to improve?
5. What are three ways you can improve communication with your adolescent?

NOTES

1. P. L. Benson, A. R. Sharma, and E. C. Roehlkepartain, *Growing Up Adopted: A Portrait of Adolescents and Their Families* (Minneapolis: Search Institute, 1994).

2. J. Lynn Rhodes, *Dysfunctional Behavior in Adopted Children* (1993) as quoted on www.lrhodes.com/adoption2.html.

3. S. L. Smith and J. A. Howard, "The Impact of Previous Sexual Abuse on Children's Adjustment in Adoptive Placement" *Social Work* 39, no. 5 (September 1994).

4. Interview with Victor Groza, editor of *Clinical and Practice Issues in Adoption*, 1998.

5. Deborah Clark, *Teen Talk*, www.parentingteens.com/commun.html.

6. Haim Ginott, *Between Parent and Teenager* (New York: Macmillan, 1969), 2S.

7. Ibid., 33.

8. Ibid., 38.

9. Frances Reza, "Are You an Approachable Parent?," *Parenting Today's Teen*, www.parentingteens.com/commun5.html. 5/25/99. Kayena Communications.

CHAPTER FOURTEEN

Opening a Closed Adoption—
The Teenage Years

> By the time I was fourteen, I felt angry, alone, and left out. All my
> friends, of course, knew their backgrounds. They weren't adopted. I
> didn't have even one clue. Everyone in my world kept me guessing.
> I just want answers to questions I am just beginning to think about.
>
> Raylynn Becker, age sixteen

Any adolescent, whether born into a family or adopted into a family,
faces certain development tasks. In addition to incredible physical
changes, adolescents go through turbulent mental and emotional trans-
formation. As their thinking processes deepen, they shift from the tan-
gible preoccupations of childhood, during which they focused only on
things they could see or experience, to a view of life on a high level.[1]
Adolescents begin to ask profound questions such as Who am I? What
am I going to do with my life? and even What is the meaning of life?

Adopted teens are no different. They struggle with the same questions,
but perhaps with a difficult dilemma. Denying who you are as an individual is a major part of being an adolescent. Like everyone else, adoptees need to know where they came from in order to begin to develop
a sense of who they are. Because they lack the basic knowledge of their
biological roots, teenage adoptees who have grown up in a closed adoption have a harder time trying to form their own identity.[2] As most
adopted adolescents struggle with life's normal transitions, they do so

under the shadow of a history about which they know little or nothing, and therefore do not fully understand.

Throughout this chapter, the diary of Carol Wallenfelsz, who chronicled her adolescent struggles, will give insight into the heart cries of many adopted teens. As this chapter stops along the way to revisit her confusion and pain, it will also discuss a teen's identity dilemma, examining the stages of identity formation and the first signs of an active search. A visit with an adoptive family who opened a closed adoption, considerations of issues for both parents and teens, and suggestions on how best to proceed will conclude this journey into opening a closed adoption for adolescents.

From Carol's Diary: December 30, 1987, 2:18 P.M.

seventeen years ago, mother, seventeen years. at 2:26 mother, you gave birth to me—december 30, 1970. so what are you doing now? i mean, does it mean anything to you that so many years ago you gave birth to a child? and here i am—wondering about you. it's only fair that you should be thinking of me. but what is fairness? who's to say?[3]

WHAT IS THE IDENTITY DILEMMA?

Rebecca's tremendous musical talent was the joy of her adoptive parents. Just like her adoptive father, Rebecca could pick up any stringed instrument and make it sing. Rebecca's confusion as she matured was, "Who am I most like—my birth family or my adoptive family?" She could play instruments like her father and brothers, yet she looked nothing like them. "Who am I really?," she wondered. She had no idea.

Establishing one's identity is not something that happens only during a certain period in life, according to adoption therapist Joyce Maguire Pavao.

Identity issues are an ongoing process, they don't just start in adolescence. However, the teen years are certainly the major developmental zone for identity formation.

It's true that for every young person, they are trying to figure out who they are not—and who they are. They are trying to play different roles, experiment with different looks, and figure out who they are along the way.

I think that for adoptees, especially when there is little to no information about where they came from, there is an awareness that they don't really have the genetic information to do that kind of sorting out of their identity. They are basing it on their family of intimacy—their adoptive family, but that's not necessarily where their abilities, interests, and traits have come from.[4]

For some, the struggle for identity brings about major behavioral changes.

Casey, age seventeen, was nearing graduation and trying to decide what direction to take in her life. Casey knew little about her adoption, except that her birth mother was a teenager living on welfare. Struggling with attempting to find some type of identity, Casey made some poor decisions. Just before graduation she announced to her parents that she was pregnant. In spite of their acceptance of the crisis and their support, she moved into the apartment of the baby's father. She had chosen an identity on which to build her life. She would be just what she thought her birth mother to be.[5]

Settling one's identity is more difficult for an adopted teen. "For most children," Maguire Pavao explains, "the people around them are mirrors in which they measure themselves until the adolescent years. At that point they look in the mirror and see themselves. They become more and more aware of how different they are. I think it is a complicated process for adoptees during the teen years. It is at this point they begin to realize they do not know another person in the world genetically related to them."

From Carol's Diary: January 13, 1988, 12:52 A.M.

it is 12:52 in the morning, mother. is it right that thoughts of you dominate me even when I should be getting my rest? i guess it just goes to show that thoughts of you do dominate me—even at the oddest time. how can i not be dominated? i'm dominated by the face i've never seen, the voice i've never heard, the love i've never felt—yet, i live to please you; to be you.

should i be angry with you? sometimes i want to be, but i think i'm afraid of losing you if i become angry. isn't that crazy. i'm afraid of losing something that i've never had. i don't know if i'll ever be able to be the "me" i am. i'm too worried about being you, pleasing you, loving you.

HOW IS IDENTITY FORMED?

Erik Erikson coined the term "identity crisis" to describe the time during adolescence that teens begin to question "Who am I?" According to David Brodzinsky, identity formation is not as simple a process as that popularized by Erikson's followers. "Most of us don't achieve a uniform Identity with a capital I; instead we come to think of ourselves as different 'I's' in different contexts. We might have an occupational identity, a religious identity, an identity having to do with interpersonal communication or basic values or other aspects of our lives," Brodzinsky says.[6] To achieve an identity, "an individual must integrate these various aspects of the self with each other over different points in time. For the adoptee, there's another element. The self as a family member is an important component . . . but the adoptee has two families: the one she knows and the one she doesn't know."[7] How can an adoptee find answers when she has been separated from the people and information that will give her those answers?

As an adopted youngster enters the adolescent years, according to psychologists such as James Marcia of Simon Frazer University, identity crisis can be resolved in one of four ways: identity achievement, moratorium, identity foreclosure, or identity diffusion.

One. Identity Achievement

Identity achievement happens when a person consciously experiences a crisis and tries to resolve it by exploring alternative roles. The identity achiever asks herself, "What do I believe in?," and then tries on different values and ideologies. After a period of time, she makes a commitment to a particular identity and a particular set of values. For those who experience identity achievement, this usually occurs in very late adolescence or the early twenties.

Two. Moratorium

A person in moratorium also asks the question "What do I believe in?," but for various reasons she puts off making a commitment to any particular path. Remaining in moratorium, according to Marcia, is not a permanent solution, since it is inherently destabilizing and uncomfortable. Eventually this person moves on to identity achievement or identity diffusion.

Three. Identity Foreclosure

This type of identity formation involves a person who looks as if she has achieved a solid identity because she has made a commitment to a set of values or a role in life. However, this decision occurs before the individual has really had a chance to experience a "crisis" or other alternatives. Often it is done in an effort to please other family members. Marcia gives as an example of identity foreclosure the individual who goes into the family business because it is expected.

Four. Identity Diffusion

This teen is a person who not only avoids confronting the identity "crisis" but is unable to make a commitment to any particular route, such as a career or set of values. "Identity diffusion comes about because a youngster lacks either a support system that would allow her to ask troubling questions or a parent figure sufficiently appealing to identify with. The child moves through adolescence unsure of what she wants, unwilling to confront the options, unable to identify with a nurturing figure because none is available."[8]

Brodzinsky strongly feels that the adopted adolescent who experiences identity achievement has grown up in a family that allows adoption discussions and helps the teen move toward a resolution about how "being adopted does or doesn't fit into an overall sense of themselves."[9] Gaining information about one's past appears to be a large part of the overall picture for identity achievers. However, gaining that information by opening contact between the adolescent and the birth family has its own unique set of circumstances. After revisiting Carol's diary, considerations to be examined by adoptive parents will be discussed.

From Carol's Diary: February 22, 1988, 8:41 P.M.

over the weekend, mother, i met a woman who, not long ago, put her baby up for adoption. she cried, "i'll never see her. i'll never see my baby." the tears, how they poured from her eyes and from her heart. mother, how i longed to reach out to her, but the moment came and the moment passed, so on paper i wrote to her: believe me when i tell you that your child loves you for i am your child and i love you.

i felt you, mother, through her, i felt you. i clung on to her to let her know that her baby loves her, because mother, i love you. every morning i look in the mirror and i see you. i seem to be at a loss of words. everyone says that i was so loved, so loved and had to be put up for adoption. that's hard to grasp. just because the woman so loved her child and still does, doesn't mean you do. i must keep that in mind. i'm afraid to get too close, to get my hopes up too high. you let me down once before, why shouldn't you now?

A VISIT WITH A FAMILY WHO MADE AN IMPORTANT DECISION

Making the decision to open up an adoption between birth family members and an adolescent is an important one. Many factors come into play, including whether it was an adoption plan or court-ordered removal (as in the case of an older child's adoption). The availability of information, the age of the teen, and the emotional health of the teen are other considerations in the decision process.

Adopted as an Infant—Andrea's Story

In her preteen years, Andrea Mitchell showed little interest in the whole subject of adoption. She knew of the circumstances of her birth and how she joined her adoptive family. Her parents attempted to answer her questions, but the question of searching was usually avoided or redirected. They were afraid they might lose her. As she neared her middle teen years, Andrea began to ask more penetrating questions for which her parents had no answers.

As time went on, they noticed a dramatic change in their sensitive child's behavior. She became increasingly depressed and withdrawn. Attempts at getting her to talk were unsuccessful. Andrea's problem hit a crisis level. One morning when Andrea failed to get out of bed for school, her mother, Cynthia, knocked on her door. When there was no answer, she cracked the door open to find her daughter apparently asleep. As she walked over to awaken her, her foot crushed a pill bottle on the floor near the bed. Attempts to rouse her failed. Cynthia rushed to call for emergency help and then her husband, Peter, at work.

Fortunately for Andrea and her family, her suicide attempt was unsuccessful. Following her recovery, the entire family entered therapy. One theme consistently recurred from Andrea: "There's this feeling inside, like a huge, gaping hole that has always been there. It just doesn't go away. It feels like a part of me is missing."

On strong recommendation from the therapist, the Mitchell family initiated a search for Andrea's birth family. Her parents petitioned their local court for assistance and received valuable information. They then contacted a search organization in the area that specialized in such undertakings.

Within several weeks, her birth mother was located and gave permission for the contact. The family met her in a park, about one hour from their home. Since that day, Andrea has kept in contact with her birth mother sporadically. She doesn't plan to establish an ongoing relationship with her at this point in her life. In her own words: "Dad and Mom are my parents. They have loved me and cared for me. Meeting Patricia was the most important thing I could have done, for it enabled me to close the book on a past I never really knew. It filled in an incredible sense of emptiness that was gnawing away at me. I feel complete and whole."[10]

CONSIDERATIONS FOR ADOPTIVE PARENTS

Many adoptive parents, like Andrea's, have resisted the idea of searching because they feared the loss that might occur. But they may realize that the loss in other ways can be much more dramatic and hurtful.

Opening contact between the adolescent and the birth family has its own unique set of circumstances. Adoptive parents need to examine the following considerations.

Consideration One: Is This Issue Important for Teens? First Signs of an Active Search.

Do adolescents think about their birth history? Do they have an interest in meeting birth parents? The answer is yes to both questions, according to the Search Institute's study *Growing Up Adopted: A Portrait of Adolescents and Their Families*, completed in the spring of 1994. Forty percent of the adolescents studied wanted to know more about their birth history (60% girls, 45% boys). When asked if they had an interest in meeting their birth parents, about two-thirds (65%) responded affirmatively. The primary motivation for meeting birth parents varied:

• To find out what they look like (94%)

• To tell them I am happy (80%)

• To tell them I am okay (76%)

• To tell them I am glad to be alive (73%)

• To find out why I was adopted (72%)

When examining this list of motives, it appears that the desire to meet birth parents is more than an inquiry into personal history. It is also a wish to connect and deliver a message of affirmation.[11]

Many teens wish to give their parents a message of affirmation. Many others struggle with painful issues of feeling rejected, feeling different, and feeling isolated that perhaps can only be resolved by searching for information and/or eventually entering into a reunion experience.

How does an adoptive parent know what to do? Is information enough? How does one know it's the right time to open up the adoption? What part should the adoptive parents play?

With over twenty years of experience in the adoption field, Joyce Maguire Pavao sees adolescence as a very normal time to do a search, at least for information, noting:

Most of the adolescent populations we've been working with over the last ten years were adopted into families who were given very little information about the birth parents. At that time, the adoptive parents probably didn't care about it, they just wanted their baby.

Now that the child has gotten older and asks questions, these same parents want help with those answers. As we work with parents and teens, we encourage them, if they have the inclination, to go and at least ask for non-identifying information. It is their right to have that information. The child is trying to form an identity, and he needs that information to help with that. Most likely at this point in time, there's a great deal of interest in just finding out information.[12]

Consideration Two: Timing and Process Are Important.

• Behavior may signal struggle around the issue.

• Never open an adoption without the teen's active involvement.

For some adopted teens, information about their birth parents, their background, and their beginnings is enough. For others, the need is far greater. Occasionally, according to Brodzinsky, a young person's changing and disruptive behavior may be a search in disguise. Maguire Pavao observes that, in making a decision to open a closed adoption for a teen, it's important to pay attention to the cues offered by the adolescent:

If the parents go about opening up an adoption without the child's knowledge or involvement, it can also work in a very negative way. They may not be ready. Behavior is the language of kids. Some teens are very verbal and can tell the parent exactly what is going on. But there are teens who act out in various ways. Some kids run away to other families as if they are trying on different families. Then there are children whose behavior is becoming more and more difficult and worrisome to the parents. These youngsters could be crying out with their behavior for answers and connections.[13]

Kara, at sixteen, began running away. When she finally opened up to her parents, she said she was in a desperate search for her birth parents. She always went to the same place across town, a place she knew her birth mother had once been. She had the thought that maybe someone she would run into would know her birth parents.

Consideration Three: Parental Involvement in the Process. What Part Should Parents Play?

- Recognize the importance of the search issue for the teen.
- Tell the child that he or she has permission to go beyond just thinking about it.
- Enter into the child's pain and confusion through sensitive listening.
- Give the child a mission to do in the search process.[14]

"I believe that all adoptees search," comments Kay Donley Ziegler. "However, there are levels to it—some just think about it, some talk about it—some may take action and make specific plans to do it. Not everyone ends up in the same place, needing to do the same thing."

Adoptive parents can play an important role, according to Ziegler. "They can help their young person move from thinking about it to talking by being willing to be open about it." They can ask questions that communicate to the youngster that he has their permission to get beyond the silence of just thinking about doing a search to talking freely about his thoughts and concerns.

Ziegler believes that an important solution for the family faced with this decision is to join with the child. "Entering into your child's pain by tuning [in] with sensitive listening and support can intensify attachment in the relationship. I encourage parents to analyze what is going on. If they don't have a healthy sense that this is normal for an adopted teen, they will get defensive and push him away. By far it is better to join with him, not in his hare-brained schemes, but in suggesting a family project where each one can take part in helping him find the answers he needs."[15]

Another thing parents can do, Ziegler says, is start reading about the subject. Getting familiar with the subject as a normal and natural outgrowth of growing up adopted will set the apprehensive adoptive parent at ease. "Parents can also gain a lot by tapping into adoption support groups and learning how other parents have dealt with the issue. Parents don't have to go to war with their child over this. They can, instead, join their child in his battle, his search for himself."[16]

Maguire Pavao readily agrees. "Parents who feel the behavior is signaling this is a critical time can give their child some mission to do in the search process, because that is probably what they are up to subversively. Why not do it up front and together and see what comes of it? In some cases, the fantasies are far more dangerous than the reality."[17]

Consideration Four: Discuss the Anticipated Emotions, Questions, and Situations that Might Arise.

Adolescent adoptees may experience

- anger
- depression
- fear of rejection
- high expectations

Making the decision to open an adoption for an adolescent is a critical turning point in the life of an adopted person. It is important for workers and family members to be aware of the intense dynamics within the experience.

Anger

The process of opening an adoption can trigger a great deal of buried anger. Blocked from expressing unwelcome feelings about adoption when younger, teen adoptees often find their emotions vaulting to the surface in incredible anger, even rage. At whom is the anger aimed?

- The birth mother—Why couldn't you keep me?
- The birth father—Where were you?
- The agency—Why couldn't you help my birth mother?
- The adoptive parents—Why couldn't you tell me more? What are you hiding from me?

Depression

Some adoptees may be dealing with the losses generated by adoption for the first time. For some reason, the possibility of talking with their birth mother, getting a letter from her, or even seeing her is enough to invoke incredible sadness. "When a teen adoptee meets a birth parent," says Maguire Pavao, "he is often unprepared for the depression that comes with that. One reason is that there is a lost history. You meet the person after 16 years or so and realize you missed all those years."[18]

Fear of rejection

Some teen adoptees may appear quite ambivalent about opening the adoption. At the root of that ambivalence may be the fear that the birth parent will not respond. They fear the possible hurt and pain that may come with such a rejection.

High Expectations

Some teenagers moving into this experience develop high expectations, such as that the birth parents will welcome them wholeheartedly, that their feelings around adoption, if negative, would be healed, and that everyone will become one big happy family. It is important that before opening an adoption for an adolescent, the worker and the family explore the teen's expectations.

Parents need to recognize that these feelings may manifest differently in children based on the child's cultural socialization. Some cultures believe that any display of personal feelings should be low-key or even suppressed and that an individual should be stoic when faced with stressful situations. Other cultures may encourage the free expression of feelings, which may range from verbalizations to behavioral responses. Parents should be cautioned about interpreting the child's behavior without confirmation from the child.

From Carol's Diary: December 30, 1988, 5:52 P.M.

i am legal now, mother. that doesn't really mean much. it's been difficult to enjoy my birthday. this has definitely been the best birthday and the worst birthday i ever had—probably for all the same reasons. thoughts of you have dominated me all day. i walk around with this label on me, mother, the label screams

"ADOPTED." hushed voices whisper "eighteen years ago," "julia" "given up," "adopted, adopted, adopted." i walk around, like today, in the stores and it feels like everyone can see right through me and no one can see into me.

PRINCIPLES OF PROCEEDING FOR TEENS AND THEIR FAMILIES

Making the decision to move beyond getting nonidentifying information to opening up the closed adoption is a critical one for an adolescent. Maguire Pavao suggests keeping in mind the following as principles:

One. Involve a supportive, objective individual.

It's helpful to have a consultant—whether a search and support group or a therapist acting as a consultant, not as a therapist. The family can have someone objective helping them with their communication. No matter how much adoptive parents "intellectually" get it and believe they are doing the right thing for this child, many struggle with it emotionally. They worry about what they will find. They are very nervous and protective.

Two. Talk about the stages of the search and what reactions teens may encounter.

Families need to be aware of and talk about some of the stages of the search and responses from others the teen may experience. Many searchers get pretty obsessed with the search. It becomes like a detective story. For people on the outside, it might look like a soap opera. For the people on the inside, it is real life. As the search progresses, it's pivotal to realize that the journey is as important as the destination and can't be trivialized.

Three. Be aware of sensitivity to rejection and feelings of loss.

Rejection (or what appears like rejection) and loss create great sensitivity for all searchers, and teens are no different. People pull back. People say they are going to call and don't. The birth mother and the adoptee are going through pretty complicated feelings.

Adolescents comprehend the loss issue, of course, on a different level, and how deeply the loss is felt depends on the person. Teens conduct searches in different ways. At thirteen or fourteen they may do a search for their roots just for concrete information. In their twenties, they may go back and do it all over again a different way. Some teens are just not ready to search at a deeper level, but they do want to connect.

Four. Offer administrative assistance.

Sometimes a teen may say he wants to search, yet a year later, he's taken no action. At that point, adoptive parents can offer administrative assistance—like calling a lawyer or writing the agency. Youngsters generally have no idea how to do those types of things. Parents can become the "secretary" for their youngster and do some of the legwork, but the teen needs to feel in charge. He must decide what he wants to do and when, and must know that at any time he can put the brakes on.

From Carol's Diary: March 31, 1992, 4:48 P.M.

dear mother,
   i haven't written a journal entry like this to you for quite some time—maybe a year. i write now out of a sense of obligation. i think. i am not sure. in january of 1991, i received background information on you and the adoption. i contacted them with the hope of getting whatever information possible. i remember receiving it. i cried—out of fear of what i would discover; out of joy to finally have discovered something. i had planned to write you after i read it, but i wanted time to process it and react rationally. so i waited.

Carol—The Rest of the Story

When Carol was eighteen years old, she gave her name to a search group, hoping to receive the help she needed. At that time, she was told she couldn't search because of her age.

On April 10, 1993, the search agency contacted her with vital information. On April 26, 1993, Carol spoke to her birth mother for the very first time. Carol writes of her experience:

It wasn't long before I held the telephone in my hand looking at it knowing the woman who gave birth to me, the woman who caused me such pain and such anger, the woman who I waited twenty-two years for—was on the other end. I looked at the woman who conducted the search and who first spoke to my birth mother and I whispered, "What do I say?" "Say hello," she said. Hello. That seemed absurd to me. Hello? My first word to my birth mother was going to be "hello?"

Well, I did say "hello" and what we said after that I really can't remember. I do know I didn't wait long to say, "I love you."

What happened after that is something only a dreamer can dream up and only a miracle can make come true. Mary and I are so happy to be a part of each other's lives. I know now that stubborn streak does come from her. And my creative talents, my love for the arts—her too. My dentist was wrong, my chin comes from my birth mother, not my adoptive father. All those years I spent looking for a curly, dark-haired woman, my birth mother spent looking for a straight, blonde-haired little girl. But there is no question whatsoever we are mother and daughter.

My parents have remained supportive through all of this. They deserve the "Parents of a Lifetime Award!" I have tried to be sensitive and supportive of them. I realize this impacts them as much as it does me.

Although this reunion is a very big thing to me, my family remains my family, even if none of us look alike. My three adopted brothers are my brothers as much as any brothers could be and my adoptive parents are truly my mom and dad.

FURTHER ADVICE ABOUT OPENING AN ADOPTION

Betsie Norris of Adoption Network Cleveland offers this perspective on adolescents and open adoption:

From my experience with adolescents, I would say that while many are at a peak in their adoption issues, only some are self-aware enough to know this. There are many reasons for "stuffing" adoption issues during this stage: Adolescence is a time when people want to be the same as their peers, not different; separating from family, the normal task of adolescence, is difficult enough without acknowledging the adoption overlay; loyalty and dependence issues may be at a high point, to name a few.

Many teens will not talk about adoption, they may act it out instead. Many will deny it is an issue if asked. There are multiple ways to address and work on adoption issues without focusing on adoption, per se.

The teen years may or may not be a good time to . . . begin communication with birth family members. If a decision is made to search, it is important that this be a family decision that everyone involved is comfortable with. In most cases, I would say that this should be initiated by the adoptee. Always, it must be agreed to by the adoptee.[19]

Jane Nast, President of American Adoption Congress, says of her personal experience:

We participated in the opening of our son's adoption when he was thirteen years old. I had a lot of fears in the beginning. I was scared. I was afraid he would want to return to his birth family. However, it was a wonderful experience for all of us. What better time for this to happen than when our son was looking for identity and answers to questions we couldn't give him? When he took biology in school, he didn't have to pretend. He knew. David has said to us that opening up his adoption was the best thing that ever happened to him.[20]

SUMMARY

Opening an adoption for teens has its own set of unique considerations. These include:

- How important is this issue for the teen?
- What will be the timing? What will be the process?
- What will be the parental involvement in the process?
- How will the family deal with the anticipated emotions, questions, and situations that might arise?

QUESTIONS

1. How important do you feel some level of birth family contact may (or may not) be for your adolescent?
2. What concerns do you have for your teen?
3. What concerns do you have for yourself and other family members?
4. Discuss the emotions often found in teens during the search process as they might relate to your teen.
5. Discuss the principles of proceeding to open up your teen's adoption as they relate to your family.

NOTES

1. Jayne Schooler, *Searching for a Past* (Colorado Springs: Pinon Press, 1995), 167.
2. Karen Gravel and Susan Fischer, *Where are My Birth Parents? A Guide for Teenage Adoptees* (New York: Walker and Company, 1993), 12.
3. The entries from the diary kept by Carol Wallenfelsz as a teen. She now writes and speaks on adoption issues throughout southwestern Ohio. Jayne Schooler, *Searching for a Past* (Colorado Springs: Pinon Press, 1995), used with permission.
4. Personal interview with Joyce Maguire Pavao, July 1994.
5. Jayne Schooler, *The Whole Life Adoption Book* (Colorado Springs: Pinon Press, 1995).
6. David Brodzinsky, Marshall Schechter, and Robin Marantz-Henig, *Being Adopted: Lifelong Search for Self* (New York: Doubleday, 1992), 166.
7. Ibid.
8. Ibid., 169.
9. Ibid.
10. Quoted in Schooler, *Searching for a Past*, 172.
11. Peter L. Benson, Anu R. Sharma, Eugene Roehlkepartain, *Growing Up Adopted: A Portrait of Adolescents and Their Families* (Minneapolis: Search Institute, 1994), 26.
12. Quoted in Schooler, *Searching for a Past*, 168.
13. Ibid., 169.

14. Ibid., 176.
15. Ibid.
16. Ibid.
17. Schooler, *Searching for a Past*, 176.
18. Ibid.
19. Ibid., 178.
20. Jane Nast, phone interview, August 7, 1999.

CHAPTER FIFTEEN

Communicating about Adoption in the Classroom: Teaching the Teachers

Greg, age fifteen, was a tenth grade biology student. He and his brother, not biologically related, were both adopted by the same family as infants. They had one sister, much younger, who was born into their family. Greg's biology teacher, Mr. Sparks, was teaching about heredity and eugenics. He had explained the concepts of dominant and recessive genes, and, to illustrate these concepts, he told the students to make a chart of all the members of their families. The students were instructed to chart which family members had earlobes and which did not. Mr. Sparks would then use these charts to show the students the principles of heredity. When Greg went home to complete the assignment, he discovered that he was the only person in his adoptive family who had earlobes. He charted his family's ears, as instructed. The following day, Mr. Sparks held up Greg's paper for the entire class to see how miserably he had failed at the assignment. "Look at Greg's homework! This is absolutely impossible! You obviously weren't paying attention yesterday!" Mr. Sparks was the one who had not been paying attention. While Greg's chart was not biologically possible, the teacher overlooked the fact that many families are created by social, not biological, ties. Mr. Sparks ignored the existence of blended families, adoptive families, foster families, and kinship families.

Not surprisingly, this embarrassing episode for Greg resulted in a critical incident that ignited anger and confusion about his identity as an adopted person. The assignment, by itself, caused Greg to acknowledge that he was different from everyone else in his family. The public ridicule by the teacher added insult to injury. The insensitivity of this teacher created several difficult months for Greg and his adoptive family.

Many adoptive families can tell similar stories about problems created by teachers who do not understand adoption and do not know how to address the topic in a sensitive way in the classroom. Teachers are hardly malicious people who seek to harm children. The harm occurs out of ignorance.

This chapter presents information that adoptive and foster parents can share with educators in their communities. After all, children spend a significant part of their lives at school, and the messages given at school about adoption can have a tremendous impact on children's attitudes toward, and understanding of, their histories. In any discussion about adoption communication, teachers cannot be overlooked as a powerful resource to help children better understand adoption, develop positive attitudes toward both birth and adoptive parents, and further self-esteem and positive self-identity.

Adoptive and foster parents may present information about adoption-sensitive communication to teachers on an individual basis or through in-service training workshops with entire schools or districts. Adoptive or foster parents may wish to address the issue as a single concerned parent, or they may wish to use an adoptive parent support group to develop a workshop to be presented at teachers' meetings or conferences. The goal is to help educators understand ways to better communicate about adoption and foster care with all of the children in their classrooms.

SHARING ADOPTION HISTORY WITH THE SCHOOL

Many adoptive parents struggle with the issue of telling the school/teacher that their child has been adopted into the family. They struggle with such questions as:

- Should we tell the school/teacher that our child is adopted?
- If so, when should we tell it and to whom?
- How much history should we disclose and to whom?

A concern about adopted children being labeled as problem children has some basis in research.

In 1987, Freidman-Kessler of the Fielding Institute (Santa Barbara, California) asked 121 Caucasian female teachers to evaluate the behavior, personality and intentionality of a child described in a vignette. Half of the children were identified as being adopted. The study found that the severity of the wrongdoing of the child in the vignette was the most important factor affecting the teacher's judgment of the child's behavior, personality traits, intentionality, and the designated punishment. However, the researcher found adoption affected, to varying degrees, the teachers' determination of the child's attractiveness, aggressiveness, callousness, disagreeableness, and how intense the punishment should be. Nineteen graduate students in education were asked to give their first impressions of adopted children. The responses were overwhelmingly negative.[1]

Of course, many families have adopted transracially or internationally, have adopted older school-age children, or live in small communities where the adoption is common knowledge. None of these families will struggle with the decision to share adoption information with the school. The adoption is obvious to everyone in the community. In these situations, adoption information must instead be managed in a positive way. This chapter will provide parents with some resources to help teachers learn more effective ways of addressing the issue of adoption and foster care.

Other families who adopt younger children of the same race wonder if the teacher should be informed at all that their child joined the family through adoption. This issue is a thorny one, because, once the school is told of the adoption, the information cannot be retrieved. When adoption history is not obvious, the decision to share the information is final, and made when the child is only a few years old and unable to make an informed choice. Some of the arguments for and against sharing adoption history with the school include the following:

Parents Should Share Adoption History Because:

The child should not be "ashamed" that he is adopted. Secrecy implies and reinforces shame.

Educators and other children need to learn more positive attitudes about adoption and foster care. If these circumstances are hidden, others have no opportunity to become more aware and sensitive.

If educators have not learned about adoption, they are more likely to thoughtlessly give assignments or make remarks that could be hurtful to adopted children.

If educators are unaware of issues, they cannot possibly cope effectively with behaviors related to adoption. An educator would be unaware that a child is angry or sad because of grief or identity confusion related to adoption.

Parents Should Not Share Adoption History Because:

The child will be identified and labeled in a negative way.

The child owns his history, and that history should not be shared outside the family before he can make an informed decision about doing so. To share his past is a violation of his rights.

The other children in the class will learn about the child's adoptive history and will torment him with insensitive comments.

Adopted children already feel "different." Making an issue of the adoption reinforces that sense of being different. It is possible to insist *too much* on the issue of adoption.

Clearly, the arguments on both sides of this issue are compelling. Adoptive parents should make decisions about sharing adoption history with their eyes open, aware of the ramifications of their choice. If parents decide that adoption information should be shared, the teacher should be explicitly reminded that adoption information is to be held in professional confidence, and not shared with anyone who does not have a need to know. Finally, if parents decide to share adoption history with the school, information in this chapter may be helpful to the teachers who instruct their children.

TIPS FOR PARENTS ADDRESSING GROUPS OF STUDENTS OR TEACHERS

If adoptive parents speak with children or teachers to help them overcome media images of adoptive families, they should speak about adoption in general terms. They should *not* share their own children's personal histories. Those personal histories belong to the children and are not open for public examination.

Talks with students will, of course, need to be directed at the developmental level of the children. Even very young children can understand, however, that families are formed in many ways. Patricia Irwin Johnston, adoption author and expert, wrote in *Adoptive Families Magazine*:

You might begin by helping children understand that families come together and their members are "connected" in more than one way. Blood and genes (e.g., a birthmother and her birthdaughter) relate some family members to one another. Law (e.g., a husband and wife) forges some family members' connections. Still other family members share no genetic ties or legal connections but are members of the same family by social custom (e.g., a man and his mother-in-law). Sometimes what binds together a group of people as members of the same family is neither genes nor law, but the love they feel for one another (a stepparent's mother, who serves as a "Grandma" or a parent's close friend who becomes "Aunt Sally"). Families expanded by adoption may not share genes, but they are connected by love, by social custom, and by law.[2]

If a child is uncomfortable with his or her own parent making a presentation to his school (either to peers or teachers), the parent might consider asking another adoptive parent (from another school or district) to make a presentation on adoption. However, children or teens old enough to make informed decisions about the subject of adoption can be involved in designing either a presentation or a panel discussion of peers whose lives are touched by adoption for teachers and/or students.

CREATING PROFESSIONAL AWARENESS: ADDRESS COMMON PITFALLS FOR TEACHERS

The Family Tree

Experienced adoptive parents can assure educators that the single most dreaded school assignment made by teachers is the family tree, often assigned in the third grade. The family tree assignment often occurs at about the time children are developmentally able to understand what adoption means, what it means to be born to one set of parents, but raised by another set. Concerns and fears about the "real parents" crop up at this time, and the family tree assignment throws many an adopted eight-year-old into feelings of confusion, anxiety, and divided loyalties. While a family tree assignment can be very difficult for adopted or foster children, if handled with sensitivity and creativity, the assignment can be helpful to them in understanding all the important persons in their histories (the most significant point of the assignment for all children).

When making the family tree assignment, for example, teachers can acknowledge that trees, and families, have many branches. All of the children should be given the flexibility to represent their important "branches" in ways that make sense to them. For example, some adopted children benefit from drawing a tree that represents the birth family in the roots, foster families in the trunk, and the adoptive family in the leaves. (See Chapter Nine).

This type of flexibility and sensitivity helps not only adopted and foster children, but children who live with stepparents, grandparents or other kin, and single parents. In fact, the assignment itself is not problematic unless it is given with an expectation of rigidity, of a "right and wrong" way to represent families. Adopted and foster children given an opportunity to represent only one family on their tree will, of course, struggle with which family to draw. The struggle leads to a conflict of loyalty which is entirely unnecessary. Messages to foster and adopted children, both at home and at school, need to clarify for the children that they are allowed to love, and feel good about, all of the families in their histories.

The Baby Picture

Other children or teens have difficulty when they are asked to bring baby pictures to display for an assignment or for the high school yearbook. Teachers or yearbook editors find it fun to have students guess whose baby pictures are included in a class or school collage. Some adopted and foster children have no baby pictures, and such an assignment can emphasize this gaping wound in their histories.

Writing a Family History

Elementary teachers often assign children to write family or "back-yard" histories. These autobiographies may be challenging for children who are uncertain about their histories or who have histories they do not want to share in a public forum. Children who find themselves with a difficult family history to write will need sensitivity from both parents and teachers in better understanding their histories, making appropriate decisions about information to be shared, and making decisions about shortened "cover stories" to be used, when necessary to help a child tell the truth in a way that does not compromise his ability to keep some of his history confidential from other children or from teachers.

Adopting a Whale (Highway, Park)

Some elementary or middle school teachers may attempt to increase community involvement through programs to adopt a zoo animal (or street, park, etc.). Such an assignment can be problematic for young, concrete thinkers who believe that adoption involves only signing up and paying money annually. "Do their parents have to pay more money every year to keep them? And if their parents do not pay the money, will they be thrown out?"[3] An exercise to increase the children's responsibility for their environment is a great idea, but it should not be tied to adoption by using that language.

Using the Most Appropriate Language

Finally, teachers need help learning appropriate language and terminology associated with adoption. As part of the larger community, teachers have sometimes developed attitudes and beliefs about adoption that are inaccurate and even potentially harmful to children who live in adoptive families. Teachers and guidance counselors need to learn from adoptive parents what terminology to use in talking with children about adoption and foster care. Appropriate language should be used in discussing adoption with a single child who expresses feelings about adoption, with two or three children who have had a conflict involving name-calling at recess, or with the entire class in thinking about ways families are formed. Parents should use the information presented in Chapter Seven to help educators understand appropriate language to use in discussing adoption with children and teens.

CREATING PROFESSIONAL AWARENESS: DO'S AND DON'TS FOR EDUCATORS

The following list presents some do's and don'ts for educators as they seek to improve their sensitivity to the issues of adopted children.

Do	Don't
Ensure that books about adoption and foster care are available for all children in the classroom and in the school library. Check with a local adoptive parent association or agency for recommendations.	Assume that all children in your classrooms are living in two-parent, biological families. Children living with both biological parents are now a minority, and nontraditional families are becoming the norm.
Learn and use appropriate adoption language.	Talk about "real" parents, siblings, etc., in reference to birth family members.
Consider the potential impact of any assignments made on all children who live in nontraditional families. Think about ways to minimize any potential negative consequences for those children who have multiple families and attachments.	Insist that assignments related to family issues be done in a prescribed, rigid manner with little or no room for flexibility or creativity. Publicly display family-related assignments for the entire class to view and question.
Talk with adoptive parents and guidance counselors about the need for a support group series for children who live in nontraditional families. Explore resources such as post-adoption service providers, the North American Council for Adoptable Children, and the National Adoption Clearinghouse for potential curricula for such groups.	Expect that education can be a "one size fits all" experience. Refuse to address or "benevolently" ignore the special needs brought to school by children.
Talk with parents about potential anniversary reactions, anxieties, and fears related to a particular child's adoption.	Stereotype adopted or foster children as "problem children." Refuse to see children as individuals who have experienced trauma.
Learn about the developmental awareness of adoption typical of children in your classrooms to understand common questions and concerns of children in your particular age range.	Create expectations that children who have experienced trauma and separation will be developmentally unaffected by their histories.

Do	Don't
Assure that other children in the classroom become more aware of and sensitive to issues related to adoption.	Ignore comments or conflicts of children related to family or adoption issues. Neglect to teach *and model* values of understanding and respect for feelings of others, diversity in families, and the worthiness of all persons.
Be alert for signs that the child is experiencing grief or depression. Report concerns to adoptive parents for intervention and support.	Assume that misbehavior is an indication that a child is a "bad" kid whose problem behavior can be resolved by additional punishment.

HELPING NONADOPTED CHILDREN BECOME MORE AWARE

Even children born into adoptive families who grow up as siblings to adopted children have difficulty understanding the feelings and behaviors of their adopted brothers and sisters. It is not surprising, then, that children who have had little experience with adoption would have many misconceptions and would lack empathy.

Adopted youth have suffered from schoolyard taunts, name-calling (Cabbage-Patch Kid, bastard, etc.), and comments about being unwanted, unworthy, and without "real" parents. Transracially adopted children may also suffer from acts of discrimination from both majority and minority groups because their family is so different. As a result of the insensitivity of their peers, many adopted children feel embarrassed or shamed about their status as an adopted person, "go underground," and want to share very little about their adoptions outside the family.

Matt, age sixteen, was a biracial young man attending high school. He had been adopted at birth by two Caucasian parents. For years, Matt had tried to hide from his friends the fact that he was adopted. He did not invite friends to his home, and he repeatedly found excuses to keep both parents from attending conferences, sporting events, or other special events at school. Matt believed that his friends would not suspect that he was adopted if they did not see that both of his parents were white. Matt was ashamed of being adopted because, when in elementary school, other children had told him that his "real" mother did not want him. Some of his schoolmates had lorded over him the fact that they were wanted and kept by their real mothers, taunting Matt that there was something wrong with him because his own mother did not want him. Matt had never shared these experiences with his adoptive parents, not wanting to hurt their feelings because they were not his "real" parents. He suffered quietly with feelings of being unlovable and unworthy. He tried to hide his adoption as he grew older and more sophisticated in his relationships with peers. He tried to blend in with the other children who understood little or nothing about his history. His feelings of shame about his lack of worth were expressed through a fear of failure (and therefore a fear of trying to be successful in spite of considerable natural gifts of intellect, art and creativity, and sports) and a fear of close relationships/friendships with others.

Children do not like to feel different from their peers, and they do not tolerate differences in others well. Children must be taught to have sensitivity and respect for others. Such teaching can occur most effectively through modeling, use of proper adoption language, access to resources and learning about adoption, and perhaps special bulletin boards with information about adoption (famous adopted people and characters: Moses, Superman, Dave Thomas, former President Gerald Ford, Olympic diver Greg Louganis), or class discussion about various ways families are formed.

Teachers should remember that, while only 1–2 percent of the general population is adopted (this figure does not include stepparent adoption), approximately one in four persons is in some way touched by adoption. That is, they themselves or at least one person in their family is a member of the adoption triad (adoptive parent, adopted person, birth parent). At least 1 million children in the United States are adopted,[4] and many researchers believe that the number is much higher, perhaps 2.5 to 5 million children.[5] It is estimated that 2–4 percent of all American families have adopted.[6] Further, at the end of 1995, there were 483,000 children in the United States living in foster care. This represents a 72 percent increase over the number of children in foster care in 1986.[7] Adoption and foster care touch many more lives than has been widely perceived, and learning about nontraditional families can benefit all children within the school system.

THE ROLE OF GUIDANCE COUNSELORS

Guidance counselors, as professionals who address the emotional needs of children that can interfere with learning, should become educated about the issues that are faced by adopted and foster children and about resources available within the community to address the needs of those children. It has been widely estimated that 33–40 percent of adopted children have attention deficit disorder (ADD) or attention deficit hyperactivity disorder (ADHD). It is likely that a disproportionate number of children not raised by their birth families is affected with these and other neurological problems, largely due to substance abuse in utero, child maltreatment, multiple moves, genetics, institutionalization, and lack of stimulation. However, it is also likely that adopted and foster children are sometimes mistakenly diagnosed as having ADD,

ADHD, or other learning disorders because they are *preoccupied* with the emotional work of resolving loss, identity development, anger, lack of trust, and so on. Such preoccupation gets in the way of learning because it funnels the child's available energy and attention away from the cognitive domain, the learning domain, of human development. Instead of placing angry, frightened, insecure children in time-out, we need to place them with counselors, therapists, and/or support groups that address their issues and allow them to concentrate and engage in learning.

Guidance counselors should provide the school system's leadership in learning about the dynamics of growing up adopted. They must understand completely the impact of child maltreatment and separation from the birth family on child development. And they must find or create programs to assist adopted children and youth in addressing anxiety, anger, and confusion. Guidance counselors can consult with post-adoption service providers, adoption agencies, adoptive parent support groups, the North American Council for Adoptable Children (651–644-3036), or adoption-related web sites on the Internet to learn about resources for adopted children.

Additional resources of particular interest for schools and adoptive parents include the following:

- *Adoption and the Schools Project, Volume 1: A Manual for Parents, and Volume 2: A Guide for Educators.* Available from FAIR (Families Adopting in Response), P.O. Box 51436, Palo Alto, CA 94303. (Price is $25.00 for each manual and $5.00 for shipping).
- "Adoption and School Issues," National Adoption Information Clearinghouse, http://www.calib.com/naic/factsheet/school.html
- Adoptive Families Bookstore (800–372–3300).
- *Moses, Jesus, Superman, and Me,* a twenty to thirty-minute presentation designed for children in kindergarten through fifth grade. Contact Patricia Irwin Johnston, Perspectives Press, P.O. Box 90318, Indianapolis, IN 46290–0318 (317–872-3055).
- "Adoption Education: A Multicultural/Family Curriculum," a curriculum guide for children in grades K-3 written for teachers, support groups, adoptive parents, and adoption professionals. Available through the Illinois Committee for Adoption, 721 N. LaSalle St., Chicago, IL 60610 (312–655–7596). (Price is $110.00; includes shipping)
- *The Adopted Child in the Classroom,* audiocassette, ninety minutes. A detailed discussion of the needs of the adopted child in the classroom. Order from Adopted Child, P.O. Box 9362, Moscow, ID 83843 (208–882-1794). (Price is $11.00)
- Making Sense of Adoption at School, a training curriculum with a discussion of adoption issues at school: positive adoption language, classroom assignments, promoting adoption sensitivity, and a videotape of children talking

about adoption. Order from Cindy Fleischer and Lisa Maynard, P.O. Box 178, Pittsford, NY 14534 (716–924–5295 or 716–586-9586).

SUMMARY

The school system has a tremendous impact on children. To assure that the impact on adopted children is one that helps them learn and ultimately mature into productive adults, the school system must become more aggressive in learning about and meeting the needs of this growing segment of the population.

- Parents must consider their own child and school setting in making a decision about sharing adoption history with the school, considering carefully the ramifications and "hidden messages" of sharing and not sharing.
- Parents may decide to educate the educators individually, through group presentations to teachers and guidance counselors and/or students.
- Parents must seek ways to involve their own child in decision making about the design of any educational presentation (either individual or group). The child's particular history should never be shared in a public forum.
- Parents should be alert to the impact of school assignments or interactions with peers at school on their child's understanding of adoption and his feelings about himself, his birth family and/or culture, and adoption in general.

QUESTIONS

1. Do you feel you should share your child's adoption history with the school? Why or why not?
2. What critical incidents regarding adoption has your child dealt with at school? How did your child respond? How did you respond?
3. How do you intend to prevent future critical incidents at school?
4. What resources do you need to educate teachers and guidance counselors in your child's school?
5. Are you interested in forming a support group for adopted children in your child's school? What would be the necessary steps to implement such a plan?

NOTES

1. L. Freidman-Kessler, "The Measurement of Teachers' Attitudes Toward Adopted Children," Ph.D. dissertation. Fielding Institute, Santa Barbara, California, 1987, as quoted in National Adoption Clearinghouse website: www.calib. com/naic/factsheet/school.html.

2. Patricia Irwin Johnston, "Teaching about Adoption," *Adoptive Families Magazine*, May/June 1999, 56–57.

3. "Adoption and School Issues," National Adoption Information Clearinghouse website: www.calib.com/naic/factsheet/school.html. Updated 1999.

4. Stolley, 1993, as quoted by Evan B. Donaldson Adoption Institute, www.adoptioninstitute.org. Updated May 1999.

5. Hollinger, 1998, as quoted by Evan B. Donaldson Adoption Institute.

6. Moorman and Hernandez, 1998, as quoted by Evan B. Donaldson Adoption Institute.

7. Evan B. Donaldson Adoption Institute, www.adoptioninstitute.org. Updated May 1999.

Epilogue

As this book about adoption communication draws to a close, we would like to emphasize the following principles to guide adoptive families in helping children understand their histories:

First, the needs of adopted children are to be held paramount in all decisions regarding adoption history. For too many years, adults of the adoption triad have been "protected" at the expense of the children involved. The priority must now be shifted to adopted persons. The needs of adopted children for compassion, empathy, understanding, and positive self-esteem and identity must supersede the needs of adults who wish to deny, withhold, or distort information because they find it painful, embarrassing, or shameful.

Second, honesty is essential to integrity. Truly, it is better to light a candle than to curse the darkness. An unwavering principle of honesty should guide all parents in their communications with adopted and foster children.

Finally, love for your children and hope for their future as well-adjusted, secure individuals should be the final principle underlying communication about adoption. Adoptive parents hardly need assistance with this final, but most critical, ingredient for positive communication.

We hope the information and tools provided in these pages will be helpful as you share your children's history in a way that helps them grow up understanding themselves, while at the same time living these principles.

Bibliography

Anderson, R. *Second Choices: Growing Up Adopted.* Chesterfield, Mo.: Badger Press, 1993.

Anthony, Beth. "A Place for Mike." *Guideposts Magazine,* July 1999.

Babb, Anne, and Rita Laws. *Adopting and Advocating for the Special Needs Child.* Westport, Conn.: Bergin and Garvey, 1997.

Benson, Peter L., Anu R. Sharma, and Eugene Roehlkepartain. *Growing Up Adopted: A Portrait of Adolescents and Their Families.* Minneapolis: Search Institute, 1994.

Brindo, Beth. Personal interview, Bellefaire Jewish Children's Bureau, July 23, 1999 by Betsy Keefer, Cleveland, Ohio.

Brodzinsky, David, and Marshall Schechter. *The Psychology of Adoption.* New York: Oxford University Press, 1990.

Brohl, Kathryn. *Working with Traumatized Children.* Washington, D.C.: CWLA Press, 1996.

Bruke, Kay. Personal interview, June 16, 1994 by Jayne Schooler, Dayton, Ohio.

Burley, Nancy, D. Goodman, B. Keefer, C. Reber, and J. Schooler. *Openness in Adoption.* A training curriculum developed for the Ohio Child Welfare Training Program by the Institute for Human Services, Columbus, Ohio, 1999.

Carp, Walter. *Family Matters: Secrecy and Disclosure in the History of Adoption.* Cambridge, Mass.: Harvard University Press, 1998.

Child Welfare League of America. *Standards of Adoption Practice.* Washington, D.C.: CWLA, 1932.

———. *Standards of Adoption Practice.* Washington, D.C.: CWLA, 1959.

Clark, Deborah. *Teen Talk.* www.parentingteens.com/commun.html. Updated 1999.

Cox, Susan. "Search and Reunion in International Search," 1998. Available through Holt International Children's Services, P.O. Box 2880 (1195 City View), Eugene, Oregon 97402.

Cross, William. *Boys No More*. Beverly Hills: Glencoe Press, 1971.

Evan B. Donaldson Adoption Institute. www.adoptioninstitute.org. Updated May 1999.

Fahlberg, Vera. *A Child's Journey Through Placement*. Indianapolis: Perspectives Press, 1991.

Freidman-Kessler, L. "The Measurement of Teachers' Attitudes Toward Adopted Children." Ph.D. dissertation, Fielding Institute, Santa Barbara, California, 1987.

Freundlich, Madelyn, and Lisa Peterson. *Wrongful Adoption: Law, Policy and Practice*. Washington, D.C.: Child Welfare League of America; New York: The Evan B. Donaldson Adoption Institute, 1998.

Ginott, Haim. *Between Parent and Teenager*. New York: Macmillan, 1969.

Goodman, Denise. "Seven Reasons Why Children Need a Lifebook." 1995. A training curriculum for the Ohio Child Welfare Training Program, Columbus, Ohio.

Goodman, Denise, and Dan Houston. "Cultural Issues in Permanency Planning," Tier II Adoption Assessor Curriculum, Ohio Child Welfare Training Program, 1998.

Gravel, K., and S. Fischer. *Where Are My Birth Parents? A Guide for Teenage Adoptees*. New York: Walker and Co., 1993.

Gritter, James. *The Spirit of Open Adoption*. Washington, D.C.: CWLA Press, 1998.

Grotevant, H., and R. McRoy. *Openness in Adoption: Exploring Family Connections*. Thousand Oaks, Calif.: Sage Publications, 1998.

Groza, Victor. Personal interview, 1998 by Jayne Schooler, Cleveland, Ohio.

Hall, Beth. "Grief." In *A Collection of the Best Articles on Talking with Kids About Adoption: Best of PACT Press*. San Francisco: PACT Press, 1998.

Hechtman, L. "Families of Children with Attention Deficit Hyperactivity Disorder: A Review." *Canadian Journal of Psychiatry* 41 (August 1996): 350–60.

Hochman, G., and A. Huston. *Providing Background Information to Adoptive Parents*. Washington, D.C.: National Adoption Information Clearinghouse, 1998.

Keck, Greg. "Affirming the Hurt Adoptee's Reality." *Jewel among Jewell Adoption News*, Spring 1999.

———. Personal interview, May 12, 1999 by Jayne Schooler, Cleveland, Ohio.

"Keeping the Family Tree Intact Through Kinship Care." Washington, D.C.: National Adoption Information Clearinghouse, 1999.

Kirk, H. D. *Looking Back, Looking Forward: An Adoptive Father's Sociological Testament*. Indianapolis: Perspectives Press, 1995.

Kohstaat, B., and A. M. Johnson. "Some Suggestions for Practice in Infant Adoptions." *Social Casework* 35 (1954): 91–99.

Komar, Miriam. *Communicating with the Adopted Child*. New York: Walker Publishing, 1991.

Lifton, Betty Jean. *Journey of the Adopted Self: A Quest for Wholeness*. New York: Basic Books, 1993.

Maguire Pavao, Joyce. *Searching for a Past*, July 1994.

Mask, Michael, Julie Mask, Jeanne Hensley, and Steven Craig. *Family Secrets*. Nashville: Thomas Nelson, 1995.

McRoy, R. G., H. D. Grotevant, and L. A. Zucher. *Openness in Adoption: New Practices, New Issues*. New York: Praeger, 1988.

Melina, Lois, and Sharon Roszia. *The Open Adoption Experience*. New York: HarperCollins, 1993.

Nast, Jane. Phone interview, August 7, 1999 by Jayne Schooler, Dayton, Ohio.

Nigg, J. T., J. M. Wanson, and S. P. Hinshaw. "Covert Visual Spatial Attention in Boys with ADHD: Lateral Effects, Mehylphenidate Response and Results for Parents." *Neuropsychologia* 35 (February 1997): 165–76.

Paddock, Dee. *Affirmations for Conscious Living as Adoptive Families*. Highlands Ranch, Colo.: Families with a Difference, 1998. www.adopting.org.

Reza, Frances. "Are You an Approachable Parent?" *Parenting Today's Teen*. www.parentingteens.com/commun5.html. May 25, 1999.

Rhodes, J. Lynn. *Dysfunctional Behavior in Adopted Children*. 1993.

Roszia, Sharon Kaplan, and Deborah Silverstein. "The Seven Core Issues of Adoption." Workshop presented at the American Adoption Congress, 1988.

Rycus, Judith, and Ronald Hughes. *Field Guide to Child Welfare*. Washington, D.C.: CWLA Press; Columbus, Ohio: Institute for Human Services, 1998.

Schooler, Jayne. *Searching for a Past*. Colorado Springs: Pinon Press, 1995.

———. *The Whole Life Adoption Book*. Colorado Springs: Pinon Press, 1993.

Schooler, Jayne, and Betsy Keefer. *Mystery History: Helping Adopted Children Understand the Past*. A training curriculum for foster and adopted parents. Columbus, Ohio: Institute for Human Services, 1998.

Schooler, Jayne, Betsy Keefer, and Maureen Hefferan. *Gathering and Documenting Background Information: Preventing Wrongful Adoption*. Adoption assessor training curriculum. Columbus, Ohio: Institute for Human Services and Ohio Child Welfare Training Program, 1999.

Severson, Randolph. "Talking to Your Adopted Adolescent about Adoption." In *A Collection of the Best Articles on Talking with Kids About Adoption: Best of PACT Press*. San Francisco: PACT Press, 1998.

———. *To Bless Him Unaware: The Adopted Child Conceived by Rape*. Dallas: House of Tomorrow, 1992.

Singerland, W. *Child-Placing in Families: A Manual for Students and Social Workers*. New York: Russell Sage Foundation, 1919.

Smede, Lewis B. *Shame and Grace: Healing the Shame We Don't Deserve*. San Francisco: Harper and Row, 1993.

Steinberg, Gail, and Beth Hall. *An Insider's Guide to Transracial Adoption*. San Francisco: PACT Press, 1998.

Thornton, Jesse. "Permanency Planning for Children in Kinship Foster Homes." *Child Welfare* (September-October 1991).

van Gulden, Holly. "Talking with Children about Difficult Birth History." In *A Collection of the Best Articles on Talking with Kids About Adoption: Best of PACT Press*. San Francisco: PACT Press, 1998.

Watkins, Mary, and Susan Fisher. *Talking with Young Children about Adoption*. New Haven, Conn.: Yale University Press, 1993.

Webster, Harriet. *Family Secrets: How Telling and Not Telling Affects Our Children, Our Relationships and Our Lives*. Reading, Mass.: Addison-Wesley, 1991.

Weinrob, M., and B. C. Murphy. "The Birth Mother: A Feminist Perspective for the Helping Professional." *Woman and Therapy* 7, no. 1 (1988).

Index

Abandonment, 30–31, 35, 49–50, 64–65, 99–100
Abortion, 138
Adolescents, 193; adjustment success of, 181–82; adoptee perceptions and, 61–65; adoption communication and, 188–90; anger and, personalization of, 191–92; catastrophizing/labeling and, 186; commitment to, 192–93; communication strategies and, 183–91; conciseness and, 186; conflict resolution and, 184; control/decision-making and, 191; development tasks of, 195–96; dysfunctional behavior and, 182; fantasies and, 190; honoring roots and, 190; identity formation and, 27–28, 61 62, 181, 195, 196, 199; identity needs and, 192; independence and, 185; minimization of pain and, 187; overreacting and, 186–87, 189–90; positive focus and, 185; privacy and, 185–86; rules and, 191; stress vulnerability and, 182–83; support groups and, 190; timing and, 187; transition/loss stress and, 192;

transracial adoptions and, 150. *See also* Opening closed adoption in adolescence
Adopt-a-Child, 138
Adopted Child, 156
The Adopted Child in the Classroom, 220
Adoptee perceptions, 69; abandonment and, 64–65; anger and, 61, 62; anniversary reactions and, 66–67; birthday and, 66; denial and, 59; depression and, 65; early adolescence and, 61–63; emancipation from adoptive family and, 68–69; fairness and, 59; films/television and, 68; grieving and, 59, 61, 65; holidays and, 67 identity formation and, 61, 62; infancy and, 54–55; intimacy and, 64–65; language and, 53–54; late adolescence and, 63–65; loss experience and, 67; loss of parent and, 67–68; loving two sets of parents and, 60; Mother's Day and, 66; moving and, 68; preschool (age three to seven) and, 55–58; romantic relationships and, 64–65; school age (eight to twelve) and, 58–61;

About the Authors

BETSY KEEFER, is a Training Consultant for the Institute for Human Services in Columbus, Ohio, where she has been instrumental in the development of adoption training curriculum for professionals used nationwide. She has almost thirty years of experience in child welfare, adoption placement, post adoption services, and training.

JAYNE E. SCHOOLER, an affiliate trainer with the Institute for Human Services and Program Manager for the National Foster Parent Association, has over twenty years of experience in child welfare, first as a foster parent, then as adoptive parent, adoptive professional and educator. She is the author of *The Whole Life Adoption Book* (1993) and *Searching for a Past* (1995).